C000181449

The Channel Islands War

1940–1945

PETER KING

ROBERT HALE · LONDON

© *Peter King 1991*
First published in Great Britain 1991

ISBN 0 7090 4512 3

Robert Hale Limited
Clerkenwell House
Clerkenwell Green
London EC1R 0HT

The right of Peter King to be identified as author of this work has been asserted by him in accordance with the Copyright, Designs and Patents Act 1988.

Photoset in North Wales by
Derek Doyle & Associates, Mold, Clwyd.
Printed in Great Britain by
St Edmundsbury Press, Bury St Edmunds, Suffolk.
and bound by WBC Bookbinders Ltd, Bridgend, Glamorgan.

Contents

Part 6 Hitler's New Order in the Channel Islands

To
Cecil Horace Beeby
and
Peter Frank Wells
formerly
Headmaster, and Second
Master of
The Skinners' School
Tunbridge Wells

Illustrations

Plates

Between pages 30 and 31

Between pages 78 and 79

Between pages 126 and 127

Figures

Maps

PICTURE CREDITS

From *Festung Guernsey* by permission of the Royal Court of Guernsey: 1, 4, 15. Bundesarchiv: 2, 5, 8, 10–11. After the Battle Publications: 3, 6, 12–14. The Alderney Society: 7, 9, 16. Peter Arnold: 17–18. Carel Toms: 19–21. The Imperial War Museum: 22

Acknowledgements

I should particularly like to thank the following for offering me helpful advice and information: Martin Gilbert for a point concerning Churchill and the Islands, Michael Ginns, Secretary of the Channel Islands Occupation Society, Colin Partridge, Molly Bihet, Frank Stroobant, and Peter Arnold. Also, the Imperial War Museum's Department of Manuscripts, particularly their assistant keeper, Philip Reed; my colleagues Joan Peters and James Gowans for help with the German involved in preparing the text, and Sally Mathieson who typed the script superbly in three months.

Every effort has been made to trace the owners of copyright. The author and publishers would be glad to hear of any inadvertent errors or omissions and will publish any missing acknowledgements in any future edition.

Thanks are due to the following for permission to reproduce copyright material:

Mrs Cruickshank for permission to quote from her husband's work *The German Occupation of the Channel Islands* (OUP, 1979).

Michael Ginns, Secretary of the Channel Islands Occupation Society for permission to quote from articles concerning Jersey in the *Channel Islands Occupation Review* by himself, Margaret Ginns, John Bouchère and Richard Mayne.

Norman Longmate for permission to quote from *How We Lived Then* (Hutchinson, 1971; Arrow Books, 1981) and *If Britain Had Fallen* (BBC and Hutchinson, 1972; Arrow Books, 1975).

Harper Collins for permission to quote from Solomon H. Steckoll's *The Alderney Death Camp* (Granada, 1982).

A.M. Heath on behalf of Alan and Mary Wood, for permission to quote from their book *Islands in Danger* (Evans Brothers, 1955).

Octopus Publishing Group for permission to quote from Sibyl Hathaway's *Dame of Sark, An Autobiography* (Heinemann, 1961).

Phillimore and Co. Ltd., Chichester, for permission to quote from the following works: H.R.S. Pocock, *The Memoirs of Lord Coutanche* (Phillimore, 1975); T.X.S. Pantcheff, *Alderney: Fortress Island* (Phillimore, 1981); and (ed. and trans.) K. Nowlan, *The Von Aufsess Occupation Diary* (Phillimore, 1985).

Frank Stroobant for permission to quote from his book *One Man's War* (Guernsey Press, 1967) and the gift of one of his works.

Molly Bihet for her interest and permission to quote from her memoirs *A Child's War* (Guernsey Press, 1985).

Leslie Sinel for permission to quote from his work *The German Occupation of Jersey: A Complete Diary of Events, June 1940–June 1945* (*Jersey Evening Post*, 1945).

For the provision of illustrations and help with them, I should particularly like to thank the following:

Peter Arnold for lending me two of his own pictures, and for his efforts in tracing and having reproduced pictures from the Alderney Museum library.

Mr W.G. Ramsey for the prompt despatch of photographs from After the Battle Publications.

Dr Hofmann and Herr Raillard of the Bundesarchiv, and Colin Partridge for providing me with reference numbers for some of these pictures.

The Royal Court of Guernsey and the Bailiff's secretary, Mr A. Richings, for permission to use pictures from *Festung Guernsey*, a collection of pictures by a German photographer, and the photographic department of the Imperial War Museum – especially Mr D. Parry – for help in locating and reproducing these pictures.

It is only fair to add that the opinions expressed throughout the book are my own. I hold no one else responsible for them.

Lastly, a word about the dedication to my former headmaster and head of history. Both of them fought in the war described in this book, and will find plenty of evidence for the justice of the cause for which they fought. To a boy still at school in the 1950s they were the epitome of the values fought for in that war. Half a century later those values appear, like so much in the Channel Islands story, very much part of far away and long ago, but a time which turned out to be, in spite of failures, the finest hour in more ways than one.

(Pittard) Names in Brackets. People who helped British Military and escapers.

⟶ British Military actions.

- - -> Escapers' routes (approximate). Number who escaped in brackets eg September 1942 (4).

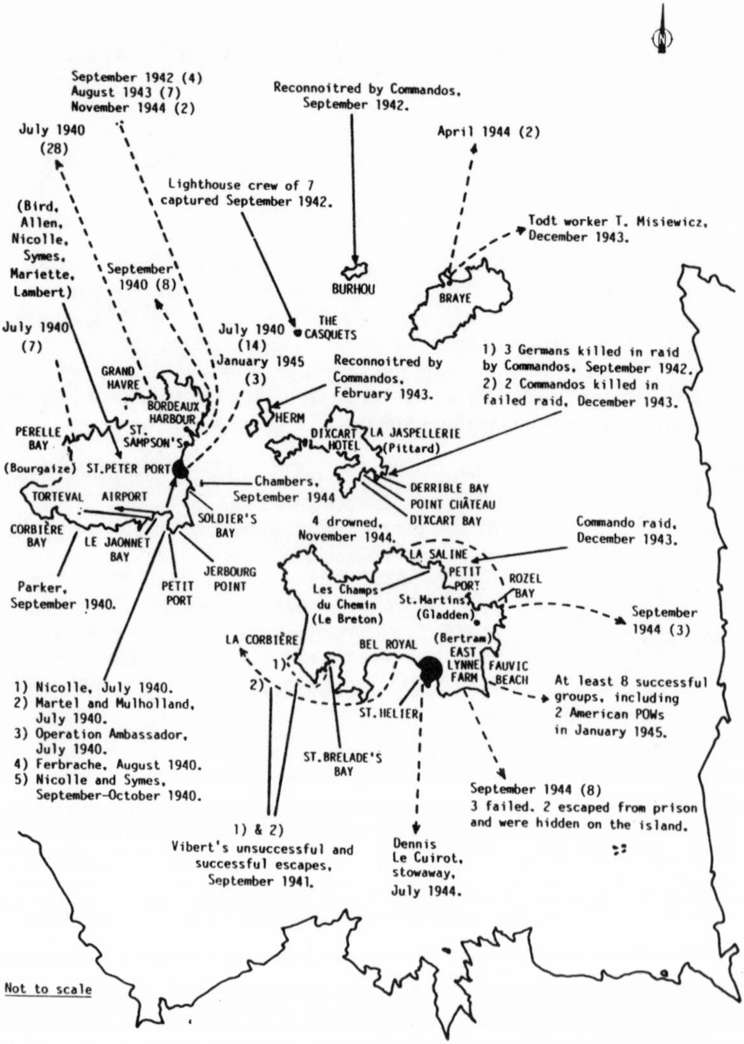

September 1942 (4)
August 1943 (7)
November 1944 (2)

Reconnoitred by Commandos, September 1942.

July 1940 (28)

April 1944 (2)

Lighthouse crew of 7 captured September 1942.

(Bird, Allen, Nicolle, Symes, Mariette, Lambert)

Todt worker T. Misiewicz, December 1943.

September 1940 (8)

BURHOU

BRAYE

THE CASQUETS

July 1940 (7)

July 1940 (14)
January 1945 (3)

Reconnoitred by Commandos, February 1943.

1) 3 Germans killed in raid by Commandos, September 1942.
2) 2 Commandos killed in failed raid, December 1943.

GRAND HAVRE

BORDEAUX HARBOUR

HERM

PERELLE BAY

ST. SAMPSON'S

DIXCART HOTEL

LA JASPELLERIE (Pittard)

(Bourgaize)

ST.PETER PORT

Chambers, September 1944

DERRIBLE BAY

POINT CHÂTEAU

DIXCART BAY

TORTEVAL

AIRPORT

SOLDIER'S BAY

CORBIÈRE BAY

LE JAONNET BAY

4 drowned, November 1944.

Commando raid, December 1943.

LA SALINE

JERBOURG POINT

PETIT PORT

PETIT PORT

ROZEL BAY

Parker, September 1940.

Les Champs du Chemin (Le Breton)

St.Martins (Gladden)

September 1944 (3)

LA CORBIÈRE

BEL ROYAL

(Bertram) EAST LYNNE FARM

FAUVIC BEACH

1) Nicolle, July 1940.
2) Martel and Mulholland, July 1940.
3) Operation Ambassador, July 1940.
4) Ferbrache, August 1940.
5) Nicolle and Symes, September-October 1940.

At least 8 successful groups, including 2 American POWs in January 1945.

ST.HELIER

ST.BRELADE'S BAY

September 1944 (8)
3 failed. 2 escaped from prison and were hidden on the island.

1) & 2)
Vibert's unsuccessful and successful escapes, September 1941.

Dennis Le Cuirot, stowaway, July 1944.

Not to scale

BRITISH MILITARY ACTIONS AND ISLAND RESISTANCE

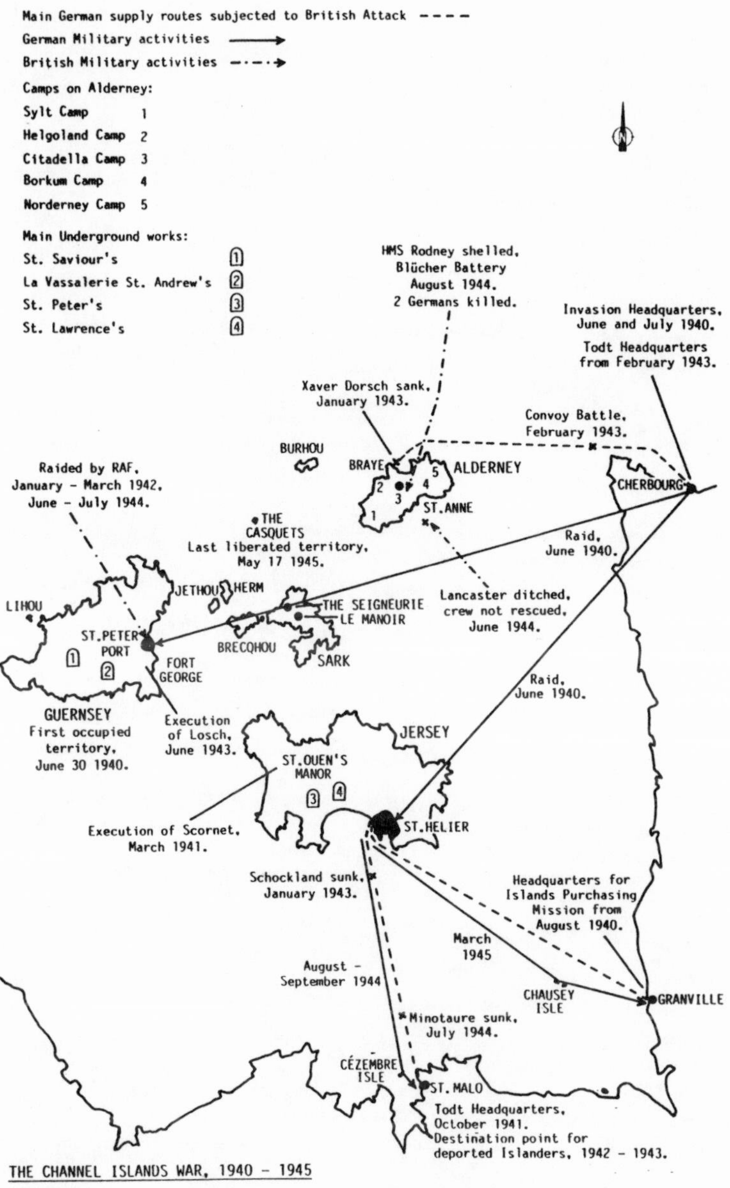

Main German supply routes subjected to British Attack - - - -
German Military activities →
British Military activities -·-·→
Camps on Alderney:
Sylt Camp 1
Helgoland Camp 2
Citadella Camp 3
Borkum Camp 4
Norderney Camp 5
Main Underground works:
St. Saviour's 1
La Vassalerie St. Andrew's 2
St. Peter's 3
St. Lawrence's 4
N
HMS Rodney shelled, Blücher Battery August 1944. 2 Germans killed.
Invasion Headquarters, June and July 1940.
Todt Headquarters from February 1943.
Xaver Dorsch sank, January 1943.
Convoy Battle, February 1943.
BURHOU
BRAYE
ALDERNEY
1
2
3
4
5
ST. ANNE
CHERBOURG
Raided by RAF, January - March 1942, June - July 1944.
THE CASQUETS
Last liberated territory, May 17 1945.
Raid, June 1940.
LIHOU
JETHOU
HERM
THE SEIGNEURIE
LE MANOIR
Lancaster ditched, crew not rescued, June 1944.
ST.PETER PORT
BRECQHOU
SARK
FORT GEORGE
Raid, June 1940.
GUERNSEY
First occupied territory, June 30 1940.
Execution of Losch, June 1943.
JERSEY
ST.OUEN'S MANOR
3
4
ST.HELIER
Execution of Scornet, March 1941.
Schockland sunk, January 1943.
Headquarters for Islands Purchasing Mission from August 1940.
March 1945
August - September 1944
CHAUSEY ISLE
GRANVILLE
Minotaure sunk, July 1944.
CÉZEMBRE ISLE
ST. MALO
Todt Headquarters, October 1941.
Destination point for deported Islanders, 1942 - 1943.

THE CHANNEL ISLANDS WAR, 1940 - 1945

Not to scale

Preface

In May 1945, Herbert Morrison, the home secretary, reported to the cabinet on his recent visit to the Channel Islands a week after they had been liberated from five years of German occupation. 'Nobody', said Morrison, 'who has not lived under the Nazis can fully realize what this means'. It is important in studying such a situation as an enemy occupation, with its undertones of hatred and treachery, anger and guilt, not to fall into the role of an armchair critic doling out blame on all and sundry for acting as they did, or for failing to take actions which seem obvious to us with the benefit of hindsight. What each of us might have done under Nazi rule is unknown because mainland Britain did not have the same experience. If Hitler had landed, brave people and cowards might have been found in all kinds of surprising places.

Evidence is part of the historian's craft and, when it is lacking, although reasoned inferences can be drawn it is important to realize that without specific evidence one cannot be absolutely sure. There is hardly a part of this book where this does not apply. There was no Royal Commission in 1945. The official history was only commissioned in 1970, and mention of the Islands in standard works on collaboration, resistance, and Hitler's New Order is noticeably lacking. The official history drew attention to gaps in the records of the Military government or *Kommandantur*, and of Organization Todt that ran most of the camps. SS records are noticeably reticent about their camp, Sylt, on Alderney, and the German authorities are still cagey about disclosing details of SS trials.

Island records too, are sparse, particularly the police files. Unlike the rest of occupied Europe, the Island governments made no effort in the 1940s to collect information about either collaboration or resistance. There is even a lack of memorials to escapers, Jews, resisters, or those who lost their lives. Herbert Morrison told the cabinet that atrocities would be investigated, but many of the statements taken then have vanished for 'lack of space', and even official reports have disappeared. An investigation into possible collaboration was carried out, but in November 1946, the next home secretary, Chuter Ede, said there would be no prosecutions. Only twelve cases had even been considered. The records of evidence taken in this matter remain closed until 2045. In spite of investigations by Major Pantcheff and others no one was tried for war crimes. Eight guards were later punished for killing two Alderney Todt prisoners in transit at Sollstedt. From this lack of official response it would seem that the Islands, uniquely in Fortress Europe, experienced neither the evil of Nazi cruelty nor the shame of collaboration.

The last time a general history of the Islands was written, and it was a good one, was by Alan and Mary Wood in 1955. The long-delayed official history by Charles Cruickshank came out in 1975. Although it had valuable material from German and British government records, and sheds much light on the official reasons for certain events, it has little to say about the issues of collaboration and resistance, surely central to any occupation history? It makes no attempt to assess in numerical terms the crimes and suffering of the times, and mentions very few of the well-authenticated cases of cruelty and death. Islanders who died in Europe are almost completely ignored, for example. It is essentially an administrative history which makes no use of detailed diaries of events deposited in the Imperial War Museum which confirm the picture presented by other well-known contemporary sources.

This is surprising because the occupation has become part of Channel Islands' life. What the Germans left behind has become a major tourist attraction with numerous museums containing items like informers' letters. Many an occupation tale is told in the bars of St Helier and St Peter Port, and there has been a continuous stream of diaries, articles and books. Some of this material is unhistorical, containing factual errors such as confusing the *Feldpolizei* with the Gestapo and statements which are extreme or unproven. Nevertheless, this contemporary information, by and large presents a different picture from the one put forward by the Island governments, the British government, or in the official history.

For the first time this book brings together the official story and the evidence accumulated over the years of what happened to ordinary Islanders. In particular I have used articles from the *Channel Islands Occupation Review (CIOR)*, previously neglected in histories of the time. As a continuous commentary on events I have selected one contemporary record from each of the Islands which internal evidence suggests is largely accurate, and not written in a hysterical state of mind. For Sark I have relied on Julia Tremayne's little-used letters, for Guernsey on Mrs Cortvriend's account based on a diary and published in 1947, and for Jersey on the well-known detailed account by Leslie Sinel published in 1945. In 1985 the diary of Baron von Aufsess, a Jersey official of the *Kommandantur* was published providing an invaluable check from the other side, and this confirms in many ways the grim picture of occupation given in this book. Although I do not agree with some of the allegations, facts, or surmises in Solomon Steckoll's book on Alderney, it contains important documents which, although fragmentary, substantiate the darker side of occupation life.

What has emerged is, I hope, a new picture of total war in the Islands. They were part of Hitler's New Order. They were a massively fortified and heavily garrisoned fortress. They contained a large population of Todt workers and POWs. They were in the Channel war zone seeing air and sea warfare in all five years of occupation. The people experienced every misery of their compatriots in mainland Britain with the Germans living next door. Thousands went through the war divided from their families by evacuation and deportation, and had no leave-time meetings with their serving relatives. The treatment of the concentration camp inmates, the Todt workers, and certain categories of foreigners, like Russian POWs or French escapers, meant that few Islanders avoided contact with brutality and degradation. Most of the Islanders, except for a privileged few, suffered degrees of deprivation in every essential of civilized living for far longer than is often realized, and remained in bondage and suffering in spite of limited measures to help them taken from December 1944. Some Islanders may be annoyed by what I have written. I have tried to stay clear of Island history buffs and form conclusions based on general resistance and wartime history: to judge the Islands in the light of what we know of German methods and resistance history today. It is often not a pretty story.

But Islanders must accept both sides of the story. The book also reveals how ordinary people suffered emphasizing that wartime and occupation hazards went together, and affected particular families in several, not just one, respect. The book describes the resistance that took place. It gives details of brave acts of defiance that led to imprisonment and death. There were Islanders who helped the British military, Island escapers, and Todt workers. There were many more escapers than is often realized, some of whom took out valuable information. The record of the courageous and patriotic, by the standards of those times, is made plain.

There is, however, the other side. As German brutality and Island sacrifice is revealed, the argument that it was a moderate occupation, and therefore did not justify official resistance, wears increasingly thin. It begins to look like a justification for mistakes in policy by the British government and the Island governments. The conduct of the Island governments which Cruickshank called passive co-operation looks increasingly like collaboration of various kinds. Collaboration by black-marketeers, Jerry bags, informers, and those who worked with the Germans is along the lines familiar enough in Denmark or Norway of the time. The Island governments opposed resistance and while, occasionally protesting and helping with individual acts of generosity, carried out German orders concerning the Jews deportation and other matters to the letter. In all this there emerged two occupations: one for ordinary Islanders and one for the privileged classes.

Peter King
Hurstpierpoint
1990

A Selected Chronology of Events in the Channel Isles 1940–1945

1940

12 June	Imperial staff presented a paper to the cabinet on the Channel Isles. First French refugees arrived in Alderney
15	Decision to carry out demilitarization of the Islands made
16 – 20	Military evacuation carried out
17 – 19	Channel Islands' small boats help in evacuation of St Malo
19	Islands informed of decision to demilitarize, Germans not told until 30 June, and to evacuate on an *ad hoc* basis
21	Victor Carey, bailiff of Guernsey, and Alexander Coutanche, bailiff of Jersey, sworn in as acting governors. Guernsey Controlling Committee set up
21 – 3	Haphazard civilian evacuation: 30,000 go, and 60,000 stay
23	All but 20 of Alderney's 1,442 inhabitants leave
24	Jersey Superior Council set up
28	Air raid on St Peter Port, Guernsey, and St Helier, Jersey kills 44 people
30	Operational conference for invasion of Channel Isles meets in Paris. Operation *Grüne Pfeile* started by Luftwaffe. Occupation of Guernsey
1 July	Jersey occupied. Arrival of Albrecht Lanz and Erich Gussek, the first German commanders
1 – 2	First escapers from the main islands, to be followed by *c.*80 from Jersey, and *c.*80 from Guernsey
2	Token occupation of Alderney
3	Sark occupied
9 – 28	Philip Martel and Desmond Mulholland land in Guernsey, give themselves up, and are sent to France
13 – 14	The first 'commando' raid on Alderney fails
1 Aug	Ambrose Sherwill broadcasts on Radio Bremen
9	FK 515 military government established under General Friedrich Schumacher with HQ at Victoria College, St Saviour's in Jersey

16	Purchasing mission established at Granville by Raymond Falla
4 Sept. – 21 Oct.	Hubert Nicolle and James Symes hide on Guernsey. On their surrender three officials are deprived of office, wireless sets confiscated, and a heavy fine of £3,000 is imposed
27 Sept	First anti-Semitic Laws introduced (others on 31 May 1941 and 26 June 1942). The arrival of the first military commander, Colonel Graf Rudolf von Schmettow
2 Nov	Fifteen Guernsey Islanders imprisoned in Cherche Midi, Paris where Louis Symes committed suicide (Dec 22)

1941

17 Mar	Execution of François Scornet at St Ouen's Manor, Jersey
21	Carey denounces sabotage as 'stupid and criminal'
24	Bread rationing starts
30	Arrival of 319 Division. The garrison eventually rose to a maximum of 36,960 early in 1943
May – Aug	Work party of 15 Sarkees go to maintain St Anne breakwater
15 June	Hitler orders the fortification of the Islands
June	*Geheime Feldpolizei* 131 (troops), and 312 (civilians) established in the Islands with HQ at Silvertide, St Helier, Jersey, and the Albion Hotel, St Peter Port, Guernsey
8 July	Carey issues a poster offering £25 reward to informers for chalking up V-Victory signs. Kathleen Le Norman and Mrs Kinniard imprisoned at Caen for this offence Major Carl Hoffmann becomes Commandant of Alderney
Aug.	Milk rationing starts
13 Oct.	Mrs Winifred Green sent to Caen for using insulting words
18	Major Friedrich Knackfuss replaces Schumacher in charge of FK515
20	Hitler's Fortification Directive. Major-General Erich Müller becomes Commander until September 1943 with his HQ at Hotel Metropole, St Helier and later at La Corbinerie, the Oberlands in Guernsey
Nov.	Visit of Dr Fritz Todt whose organization based at St Malo, and later Cherbourg, begins a fortification programme. Some 16,000 OT workers came to the Islands.
Dec.	Fuel rationing introduced.

1942

Jan.	Raids on St Peter Port by RAF sink ships and kill harbour workers. Dr Wilhelm Casper succeeded by Baron von Aufsess as Chief of Administration in Jersey. Four camps (Helgoland, Norderney, Borkum and Sylt) start on Alderney
Feb.	The first of three German brothels opens. Lieutenant-Colonel Zuske, appointed Commandant of Alderney
Mar.	Eighteen Guernsey policemen involved in black market activities arrested
6 Apr.	Start of the teaching of German in primary schools
21	Auguste Spitz and Theresia Steiner, Austrian Jews, deported
2 May	Three boys fail to escape from Jersey with military secrets. One drowned, two imprisoned. One, Maurice Gould, later died at Wittlich Camp. Start of *Guernsey Underground News Service* (*GUNS*) with a circulation of about three hundred
June	Sherwill returns as Attorney-General in Guernsey. *Bulletin of British Patriots* published in Jersey. Ten hostages taken. Herbert and George Gallichan sentenced to Wolfenbüttel and Dijon for producing the bulletin
26 June	Surrender of all wirelesses.
7 July	The extended Jersey railways reopen for quarry purposes
8 Aug.	Casquets lighthouse raided and seven Germans captured
15 Sept.	Deportation order issued by Knackfuss on orders from Berlin
16, 18, 29	1,186 deported from Jersey: 26, 27, 834 from Guernsey and Sark. Suicide of Major John Skelton to avoid deportation
19	Escape of two fishermen and two girls from St Sampson's in Guernsey
Sept.	Edward and Nan Ross imprisoned for feeding Todt workers
Oct.	Order issued forbidding Germans to fraternize with Island women
3 – 4 Oct.	Operation *Basalt* in Sark. Two Germans killed and one captured. Lieutenant Herdt court-martialled
12	Trial by court-martial of 14 boys involved in riot at the time of the deportations
Nov.	Lancaster crashes on Aeroplane Field, Sark. Three crew captured. This was one of *c*.30 Allied aircraft which crashed on the Islands or nearby.

1943

Jan.	The *Xaver Dorsch* went aground at Braye, and the *Schockland* sank off Jersey
6	Stanley Green, who had provided photography for resisters, and cut telephone wires, was sentenced for having a wireless and sent to Fresnes and Buchenwald
18	German made compulsory at all educational institutions
12, 13, 25, Feb.	Second deportation order. Suicides at Grouville and Beaumont. 87 deported from Jersey, and 114 from Guernsey and Sark; no news of them for six weeks.
23 Feb.	Sylt becomes a concentration camp with 1,100 prisoners
Mar.	Captain Maximilian List becomes Sylt's camp commandant
3 Mar.	Illegal conscription of Island labour begins and, in spite of protests, continues until 24 August
30 Apr.	Illegal reduction in bread ration which continues in spite of protests until 1 August
6 June	Franzeph Losch, a Todt worker, executed at Fort George for possessing a wireless transmitter
13	Two Guernsey fishermen killed and two injured when their boat hits a mine
22	Mrs Louisa Gould and Harold le Druillenec sentenced for hiding a Todt worker. Le Druillenec ended at Belsen, and Mrs Gould died at Ravensbrück in February 1945
2 Aug.	Complete ban on fishing
14	Four men and three women escape to Dartmouth from St Sampson's
Sept.	Von Schmettow resumes command of the military, and moves his HQ to Guernsey. Colonel Siegfried Heine replaces him in Jersey
23 – 24 Oct.	Convoy battle west of the Islands. Loss by the British of HMS *Charybdis* and HMS *Limbourne* with 504 killed
Nov.	Lieutenant-Colonel Schwalm becomes Alderney Commandant
17	*Charybdis* Day when 41 of the naval dead in the convoy battle were buried, and large numbers of the public attended
26 Dec.	Mrs Tremayne's house, Grand Dixcart on Sark, subjected to house search after raid on Sark. Two Frenchmen killed.
27 – 8	Failure of last raid on Jersey and death of Captain Ayton

1944

3 Mar.	The Channel Islands declared fortresses. Knackfuss replaced by Heider. Lieutenant Braun becomes commandant of Sylt camp
6 Apr.	*GUNS* trial. Legg, Duquemin, and Falla imprisoned in Frankfurt and Naumberg. Machon and Gillingham died in prison
8	Two Guernsey men become the only civilian escapers from Alderney
5 May	Schwalm's order to hand Sylt inmates over to the SS if there was an invasion
19 May	FK515 becomes PKI with a reduced status
May – Aug.	Air war over the Islands with attacks on forts, ports, and shipping: 22 raids sink 12 ships and damage 13
17 June	Hitler declares the Islands must be defended 'to the last'
24	Alderney bombed. About 200 civilians evacuated to Guernsey
27	Capture of Cherbourg, Granville (30 July), and St Malo (17 Aug.), cuts the Islands off from supplies
July	Removal of camp inmates to St Malo and later Buchenwald. Some escape in Belgium. OT workers evacuated
7	Sinking of *Minotaure* by the British with the loss of 250 lives including French Jews
27	Lancaster shot down south-west of Alderney. Captain Massmann, the harbour commandant refuses to allow the rescue vessel to put out. Arrival of German casualties for underground hospitals at La Vassalerie in Guernsey and St Lawrence in Jersey
8 Aug.	HMS *Rodney* shelled *Blücher* battery in Alderney killing two Germans
25	Mr Jehan of St Saviour's killed and his son wounded trying to drive off German marauders
1 Sept.	Violation of food regulations made subject to the death penalty
9	End of the gas supply in Jersey
18	Keitel's OKW Directive for 'the complete stopping of rations' if necessary on the Islands
19	Germany informed the Swiss that civilian supplies 'are exhausted'
Sept. – Dec.	66 people try to escape from Jersey and 44 of them succeed
Sept.	Vice-Admiral Friedrich Hüffmeier replaces von Helldorf as Chief of Staff
7 Oct.	Deputy E. Le Quesne sentenced for having a wireless, and then released after only a fortnight

11	Douglas Le Marchand shot while trying to escape
25	Admiral Krancke placed in charge of Island administration
3 Nov.	Frederick Noyon and William Enticott escape with information on the food shortage
5	Germans permit the bailiffs to appeal to the Red Cross
7	Britain agrees to Red Cross relief provided Germans maintain the basic rations (Germany accepted this 23 Nov.)
11	Four drown off Jersey trying to escape when Germans refuse to rescue them
2 Dec.	Mmes, Malherbe and Schwab sentenced to death for anti-German propaganda
21	End of the gas supply in Guernsey
27 – 30 Dec.	First visit of the Red Cross ship *Vega* with 750 tons of food, and medical supplies. Other visits: 7 – 11 Feb., 6 – 9 Mar., 5 – 8 Apr. and 3 – 7 May)

1945

8 Jan.	Two American airmen become the only successful evaders on the Islands
13	Telephone service ends. Three milkless days start. The first cases of malnutrition in the German forces reported
16	Order banning the cutting of all timber
23	Escape of the le Page brothers and Xavier Golivet with naval information
25	Electricity supply ceased
17 Feb.	Bread ration ends (until 12 Mar.)
22	Five escape from Jersey with military information
28	Hüffmeier replaces von Schmettow, and naval captains von Kleve and Reich put in charge of Jersey and Guernsey. Major General Rudolf Wulf placed in command of 319 division
7 Mar.	Explosion at the Palace Hotel, Bagatele kills nine Germans
8 – 9	German raid on Granville releases 55 POWs and captures 30 men
18	Attempt to kill Major General Wulf fails
25	Hüffmeier's picture palace speech saying there would be no surrender
23	All communal kitchens, cafés, and ovens closed
28	Von Helldorf banished to Herm Island
8 May	Operation *Nestegg* liberation fleet arrived off the Islands

9	German surrender. 27,000 POWs captured. Jersey, Guernsey and Sark liberated. Brigadier Alfred Snow sets up military government
13	German POWs start to leave
14–15	Visit of Herbert Morrison, the home secretary
16	Alderney liberated
7 June	Visit of King George VI
25	Evacuees begin to return from Britain
Aug.	2,190 deportees return after being screened at Stanmore. German POWs clear 117,000 mines from the Islands
25	New lieutenant governors arrived, and the government of the Islands restored
12 Dec.	The War Honours List largely ignores escapers, prisoners, and resisters
15	Start of the return of 685 people to Alderney

Part 1

The Sound and Fury of Battle

1

War Comes to the Islands, June and July 1940

In the spring of 1940 life in the Channel Islands, like that in mainland Britain, had been little changed by real war. People wanting to visit the Islands for Easter were assured by the home secretary that there were no travel restrictions, but sadly not every visitor who accepted his assurance that all was well was able to return. Mr and Mrs Dunkley of Ramsgate who went to see relatives were trapped on the Islands, and the whole family were deported to Laufen early in 1943. However, the Islands were still seen that spring as a safe haven from the expected mass-bombing of Britain. Some evacuees were sent there from Southampton, and Sark offered to take 15 children. The Peace Pledge Union urged men who did not want to be called up to take agricultural work on the Islands and over a hundred arrived in Jersey. Trapped by the German invasion some of them worked for Organization Todt when it was established on the Islands. One of them, Derek Leister, grandson of a German baker from Camden Town, found his way from Jersey to a girlfriend and flat in a suburb of Berlin and membership of John Amery's British Free Corps.

No one had any reason to suppose the Islands would be invaded, and preparation for war was piecemeal and slow. An Air Raid Precautions organization was set up under Major William Crawford-Morrison, but no shelters were constructed. There was a National Savings Campaign, and a Special Aid Society to provide comforts for soldiers at the front. The ancient defence forces of the Islands – the Royal Guernsey Militia and the Jersey Insular Defence Corps – were embodied, and a few measures of self-defence, like the construction of a machine-gun post to protect the Guernsey telephone exchange and the blocking of roads with obstacles, were carried out in early summer. The last regular army unit had just left the Islands although there were fortifications like Fort George south of St Peter Port. About a thousand assorted military personnel were still there including naval ratings, the Royal Army Service Corps, and an army technical school for boys. These were joined in the period before demilitarization by Royal Engineers, small anti-aircraft units, and briefly, two squadrons of Hurricanes. The last units were only despatched to the Islands on 14 June, and it seems clear that until then at least it was proposed to retain and even defend them. A machine-gun training school equipped with fuel dumps and a military hospital was set up on Alderney.

But successive defeats in Norway and Belgium, and the collapse of France; produced a change of heart at the War Office. On 15 June the Imperial General Staff recommended to the cabinet that complete demilitarization take place, and agreement was given the same day in spite of grumbling from Churchill. Britain needed all the troops she could get, and had no resources to fling across the Channel to defend the Islands. It was a sensible decision. The next day, the administrator in charge of Alderney, Judge Frederick French, was told that military evacuation had to take place within six hours – although official notification was not given to the bailiffs in Guernsey and Jersey until two days later. Within four days, military evacuation was completed at such speed that only on Alderney was there time to destroy facilities. The Royal Engineers who came to Jersey for this purpose were rebuffed by the bailiff, Alexander Coutanche, and as a result recently completed cables to France stayed intact. The limited civil defence and fortification measures were put into reverse, and the Island militias joined those of military age leaving the Islands. Lastly, on 21 June the two lieutenant-governors, who were also military commanders of Jersey and Guernsey, withdrew delegating their functions to the bailiffs.

There followed an administrative comedy of errors that turned to tragedy. Because the evacuation of troops from France was still going on, followed by that of Island civilians, it was decided by the Home Office that the press release prepared for 22 June to say the Islands were demilitarized should be delayed, and the War Office agreed saying the Germans probably knew anyway through intelligence sources. On 24 June a message from King George VI was received by the bailiffs, but as this referred to the withdrawal of the armed forces the Home Office stressed that care should be taken not to publish the message. In Guernsey the bailiff, Victor Carey, read it out two days later on a loudspeaker from the window of the *Guernsey Evening Press* in South Street, and few therefore knew the message had come. Four days after the civilian evacuation was completed, the BBC was allowed to mention the demilitarization on 28 June, but it was only on the day that the Germans started their occupation that the Foreign Office officially informed Germany about demilitarization.

Near as they were to France the Islands were not left long in doubt about events there. As early as 9 June clouds of smoke could be seen rising from French harbours, and soon fishing boats, with crucifixes nailed to the masts and pathetic bundles of possessions in their bottoms, arrived with the first refugees. Six boat loads reached St Peter Port and also brought over nearly a hundred French naval ratings. On Sunday 16 June Coutanche received a telegram from London which asked the Islands to help evacuate the remaining personnel from St Malo. Potato boats and small craft were commandeered that evening and put under the command of the yacht club commodore, William Le Masurier. A destroyer arrived in St Helier to take a native pilot on board for the trip to St Malo. Soon afterwards the first of 17 boats put out for France as a British task force complete with NAAFI canteen arrived to cope with any rescued troops. The Island boats brought off the demolition party, wounded troops, civilians and a party of Belgian nuns, although the main bulk of the troops from St Malo were carried straight across the Channel.

By now alarm created by demilitarization and refugees, and the obvious collapse of France, was causing the bailiffs desperate concern because there was still no word from London about the fate of the Islanders. On 16 June the Home Office asked that Island representatives be sent to discussions, and it was decided that a Jersey jurat, Edgar Dorey, should represent both Islands. He flew to London next day to meet Alexander Maxwell and Charles Markbreiter, the officials responsible for the Channel Isles. It was agreed demilitarization should be announced, together with evacuation of certain groups of civilians. But when Dorey flew back to Guernsey and then on to Jersey on 19 June it was by no means clear who should be evacuated. Unlike Gibraltar, where the whole population was to be taken off, confusion marked events in the Channel Islands. Categories specified were vague and evacuation was to be voluntary, throwing the burden of decision on to individuals torn between accusations of cowardice, fear of the unknown, and fear of staying. In spite of experience gleaned in Britain no advice was given by the Home Office, although the Treasury insisted that the Islands foot the bill for any shipping involved.

It was the appearance of official notices on 19 June stating that 'those desirous of being evacuated must register their names and addresses with the Constable of their parish at the Parish Douzaine Room as soon as possible and at latest by 8 p.m. today' which really brought war to the Islands. The notice referred to schoolchildren, their teachers and helpers, mothers with children under school age, expectant mothers, and men of military age between 20 and 33. To these categories were soon added unmarried women and widows, women with children up to 17 years of age and 'other persons than the above'. It was not clear if everyone was intended to leave, or if shipping would be available.

Evacuation began in confusion and near panic, but ended successfully four days later. By that time about 11,000 had left Jersey, and about twice that number, Guernsey. All but 20 of Alderney's population had left, and all but 15 of Sark's had stayed. So in total about 30,000 left, and some 60,000 remained. Those were days of fearful partings and administrative chaos. The first to go were the children. All over the Islands anxious and white-faced parents gathered in schoolrooms to hear details of evacuation. Mrs Cortvriend in Guernsey recalled she had last sat in the schoolroom to watch a Nativity play in 1939. She wrote: 'Our own children were rather pale and subdued at the last breakfast time we spent together, and kept saying "But what about you, Mummy? You and Daddy will come afterwards won't you?" ' Three weeks after the evacuation, the schoolroom became a billet for German troops.

On 20 June, shiploads of children pulled away from the Islands, although it was a ten-and-a-half hour wait for some on Guernsey. The crossing in slow boats was pleasant enough for some, but others found it less pleasing. 'We are all taking it in turns to rush to the side of the boat and be violently sick,' said Daphne Martel.

The *Tonbridge* arrived at Weymouth to find there was no pilot, and had to wait 30 hours before docking with only one nursing sister on board. Mothers fainted or became hysterical, but eventually at midnight food was brought on board, and the children bedded down for the night in cattle stalls. A child of eleven who was already ill died during the evacuation, and a woman gave birth crossing the Channel. Parents left behind had to wait until March 1941 before Red Cross letter forms arrived assuring them of their children's safety or otherwise in the blitz then taking place in British cities.

People registered at constables' offices in the towns, and in the countryside at the Douzaine rooms. In St Helier crowds surrounded the town hall, besieged the shipping offices, and offered motor cars in exchange for seats on the last flights out. Banks found themselves transacting so much business they had to restrict withdrawals to £25 each, and two couriers came in with £30,000 to steady the banks' reserves against possible panic. But after strong statements from Edgar Dorey on his return, and by Alexander Coutanche, things had calmed down by the evening of 20 June. In Guernsey, Victor Carey and Ambrose Sherwill handled matters less effectively first saying all could go, then saying shipping would not be available for all, and trying to urge restraint following signs of panic. Ralph Durand described how, 'Some farmers killed cattle that in the months to come could ill be spared. Some people before abandoning their homes turned their pet animals out of doors to fend for themselves; some with still less humanity left fowls and rabbits shut up without food or water. Some houses were left open, beds unmade and the remains of a hurried morning meal on the table.'

After the departure of the evacuees the Island governments passed a law vesting control of all goods and property left behind in the hands of the state, but it was not long before houses were broken into, robbed or occupied as billets by the Germans, and Todt workers. In Alderney some of the early looting was done by Islanders from Guernsey sent to carry out salvage work, and a number were imprisoned. One man returned to Guernsey with 77 carpets, 76 curtains, 13 clocks, and quantities of food and cigarettes.

Many of the craft involved in evacuation were cargo boats, and maintained speeds of no more than seven knots. As a result the Channel passage to Weymouth often took many hours. Then came lengthy train journeys to the north of England (most of the early evacuees went to Lancashire or Cheshire), and the problems of settling into a new country. Men of military age entered the armed services: the Jersey men, for example, joined the Hampshire Regiment in a body. A Channel Islands Refugee Committee was formed with C.T. Le Quesne and M.E. Weatherall as the most prominent members, and funds were raised to help the Islanders settle in.

Once the bustle and excitement was over an uneasy calm descended on the Islands broken only by German reconnaissance planes. The banks opened again on June 25th, and from the packing sheds growers worked to load boats with agricultural produce. The newly appointed Controlling Commission met to organize the collection of petrol and perishable food, and to make financial arrangements for abandoned businesses. Mrs Cortvriend commented on the oddness of not hearing children's voices. In Jersey R.C.F. Maugham found himself at a neighbour's deserted farm, its door swinging in the wind, and wondered who would milk the full-uddered cattle left in the field.

The total population of the third most important Island, Alderney, was 1,432. Nearest to France, remote Alderney had quickly felt the effect of war with the coming and going of the machine-gun school, and the French refugees. Judge Frederick French, an ex-Indian army major, had only recently been appointed. Lacking a telephone system and unable to use wireless because of the security danger, French felt isolated and ill-advised, and had to glean information from Guernsey where Carey and Sherwill's confusing messages did not help him much. French became convinced that lack of vital food supplies and cash reserves in the banks meant they would have to evacuate the Island particularly since the regular supply ship had not arrived. On Friday 21 June a Trinity House ship, which was taking off lighthouse crews throughout the Islands, stopped at Braye Harbour, and French was able to send out messages to the Admiralty asking for evacuation ships, and to Sherwill complaining that no ships had yet called.

Next day French who had been stopped in his car by angry people demanding action sent a Town Crier round the Island to summon a meeting on the playing field behind the Grand Hotel, known as the Butes. He stood on a lorry to address his fellow Islanders, and gave a grim picture. Food, he said, was running out, and the Germans were approaching. He ended by asking them what they wanted to do.

Discussion then took place, and the people cried out that they wished to leave. Meanwhile Sherwill had telephoned the Ministry of Shipping on Alderney's behalf. Early on Sunday morning, six small cargo boats sailed into Braye Harbour, and Judge French ordered the church bells of St Anne to be rung. Carrying no more than two suitcases each the Alderney Islanders boarded the vessels, including French himself who left his yacht behind, and by midday the little flotilla was away into the Channel leaving about 20 people behind. Most of these left a few days later when a boat came to take off cows and horses which were shipped to St Peter Port only to be attacked in the German raid a day later. Apart from Frank Oselton, a farmer, and George Pope, and his family, who became lighthouse pilot to the Casquets lighthouse, Alderney was deserted.

In Sark, the most medieval of the Islands, still largely controlled by Sibyl Hathaway, exactly the opposite happened. On the same Sunday that the people of Alderney were leaving William Carré, the Island seneschal, summoned most of the 470 Sarkees to a meeting at St Peter's Church. Hathaway said that she, her husband, and one of her daughters would remain, and strongly urged them to do likewise. Carré asked for the names of those wishing to leave. Major Breen, a former press attaché in Berlin, said that he was definitely going in his yacht, and offered passage to others. Fourteen English residents accepted. The German air attack on the Islands passed over Sark frightening the inhabitants, including Mrs Tremayne's daughter Norah who was out shopping, and had to get into a ditch. No word came from Guernsey, and Mrs Tremayne waited fearfully for the coming of the Germans.

At three o'clock on Thursday 20 June a wireless signal was sent from Naval High Command in Berlin to Admiral Karlgeorg Schuster, Commander in France, stating that the capture of the British Channel Islands was urgent. It was followed the same day by a directive from Admiral Schniewind, the cautious-minded Director of Naval Operations to the Flag Officer Commanding, Northern France, Admiral Eugen Lindau. The British Imperial General Staff had declared the Islands to have no strategic importance when discussing demilitarization. But the Naval Directive received by Admiral Lindau claimed that the Islands constituted a forward enemy observation post on the flank of German operations. Although no decision had then been made about invading Britain, the Islands would be valuable to the Germans if it was possible to deny their communication, air and naval facilities to the British. Possession of the Islands effectively sealed off a wide part of the West Coast of France from naval attack, and with guns mounted on the Islands controlled the gap between Alderney and Cherbourg. The Islands also provided a useful base for Channel operations in the ceaseless convoy battles between German E-Boats and the Royal Navy. The Islands could provide repair and supply facilities. Even if German forces in the Islands were to be out of all proportion to their strategic value they were nevertheless useful enough, and their possession later helped the Germans to inflict losses on British forces.

For Hitler the Islands possessed another importance because they were the only British territory directly occupied by Germans. Chattering to his cronies before lunch on 22 July 1942 Hitler said '... with the fortifications we have constructed and the permanent garrison of a whole division, we have ensured against the possibility of the Islands ever falling into the hands of the British. *After the war* they can be handed over to Robert Ley for, with their wonderful climate, they constitute a marvellous health resort for the Strength Through Joy organisation.'

Every propaganda ploy was used to present the occupation as a model to the outside world because the example of good relations on the Islands would lull the British into false belief in German moderation, and make good copy for Goebbels. By January 1941 the first propaganda film was being made. In the early days of the occupation when a kid-gloves policy was being deliberately operated even members of the Island governments were caught up in German propaganda, and Ambrose Sherwill was to give a notorious broadcast over Radio Bremen praising German behaviour. Under the stress of German power there were others willing to do Goebbels' work. Pearl Vardon, a Jersey schoolmistress, was sentenced to nine months in prison after the War for broadcasting from the Concordia Bureau in Berlin from February 1944. John Lingsham, who was deported in 1943, was approached at Laufen Camp, and agreed to monitor news broadcasts for the Germans. He was sentenced to five years in prison after the war. Another camp inmate, Denis Cleary, was deliberately sent back by the Germans from Dorsten to give a favourable account of deportation camp conditions in local papers.

Capture of the Islands might seem at first an easy matter. Britain was under siege, defeated, and short of every kind of war material, while a German army of a hundred divisions, and a Luftwaffe with 3,200 serviceable machines had rolled to the French coast in a matter of weeks. But the Kriegsmarine was naturally cautious about amphibious attack in the Channel where Britain could still concentrate overwhelming naval forces, and worried about what faced them on landing particularly since the Islands' small harbours prevented the use of large craft. Reconnaissance flights over the Islands began on 18 June, and were combined with an earlier outdated appreciation by a German spy to give an intelligence overview that there were manned fortifications in port areas. So certain was the Kriegsmarine of this that even when Reuters reported on 29 June that the Islands had been demilitarized Schuster discounted the report. The reason was that the existence of old fortifications, the movement of evacuation, potato, and other cargo boats, and the presence of farmers' lorries at the ports convinced the Germans there was some military activity. It was this uncertain situation that led to a reconnaissance in force to test possible defences.

The invasion plan, Operation Grüne Pfeile was conceived as mainly a naval affair with strong Luftwaffe support from Luftflotte 3. The plan involved the landing of six battalions from 216 Division accompanied by naval assault troops and two companies of engineers. They would carry only light weapons, and take with them a small amount of captured French artillery. The Kriegsmarine was almost absurdly cautious interrogating French fishermen about currents and tides, and stressing the need to be prepared for minefields. Landing craft of the right size were in short supply, and therefore the occupation would take two days, Alderney and Guernsey being taken on the first, and Jersey on the second day. The Luftwaffe was required to provide air cover from dawn on invasion days, Stuka dive bombers to accompany the small unarmed ships, heavy fighter protection at Cherbourg where the forces assembled, and softening up attacks on the preceding days. The day after the reconnaissance in force on 28 June Schuster attended a staff meeting in Berlin, and next day an operational conference in Paris. In spite of the welcome news from the raid, and of demilitarization the Germans hesitated. Orders were given for a further raid on 1 July, and an operational conference was summoned to meet at Deauville at six o'clock that day to consider if attack should start.

Six Heinkels came in from the east over Sark on 28 June where roofs were sprayed with bullets, and began to drop about 180 bombs on Jersey and Guernsey accompanied by considerable cannon fire and machine-gunning. In St Helier the main casualties occurred in the La Roque area, and ten planes passed over Gréve d'Azette and Fort Regent machine-gunning and bombing the port before sweeping towards Beaumont and St Aubin and then turning again across the open sea. In Guernsey the evening sun was setting over St Peter Port, and many people who had been listening to a talk by Sherwill went to watch the busy harbour scene from White Rock. The mail boat and the boat from Alderney loaded with cattle and horses were in together with boats being loaded with baskets of tomatoes from a line of lorries and horse-drawn vans on the quayside. Sherwill was just ringing up the Home Office at 6.45 p.m. as the planes attacked, and he held the instrument so that Markbreiter at the other end could hear the noise. Between two and three hundred people were in the harbour area, most of whom were saved by sheltering on a concrete platform under the jetty or in sheds where they covered themselves with sacks of flour. Others were less fortunate. The lorry drivers were a sitting target. 'Some tried to shelter under their vehicles only to be crushed as the fires started and the vans and trucks collapsed. The blood of the wounded and the dying mingled with the juice of the tomatoes, and when I came on the scene just as the last Hun plane faded into the distance the sight was one I shall never forget; the flames, the bodies, the cries of the dying and injured, and the straggling line of people emerging from their shelter under the pier jetty', wrote an eyewitness. The main damage occurred from St Julian Avenue to Salerie Corner, and in the countryside bombs fell at St Saviour's, and Vazon. The only reply was some desultory fire from anti-aircraft guns on the *Isle of Sark* steamer, and the Germans had long gone when six RAF Ansons appeared.

Limited civil defence forces did what they could. Members of St John's Ambulance Brigade, the police, special constables, the Auxiliary Fire Service, and the ARP hurried to the scene. Among the dead were an ambulance driver, Joseph Way, a policeman, Clifford Bougourd, and out at sea, Harold Hobbs, son of the Guernsey lifeboat skipper, killed as the Heinkels straffed boats. The youngest of the 44 victims was 14 and the oldest 71.

But the lack of response had convinced the Luftwaffe that the Kriegsmarine were being over cautious, and Schuster and Lindau's plans were short circuited. Soon after midday on Sunday 30 June Captain Liebe-Pieteritz and three other Dornier pilots were on reconnaissance over Guernsey when he decided to land at the airport. He entered the airport building finding no one and leaving his pistol behind. According to German sources the Dorniers engaged Blenheims in a dogfight shooting down two of them. Between six and seven that evening four or six transport planes with a small contingent of Luftwaffe soldiers landed under Liebe-Pieteritz's command. Sherwill rang up Markbreiter to say the Germans had arrived, and despatched Inspector William Sculpher, Chief of Guernsey Police, to the airfield with a document stating the Island was demilitarized. The soldiers and Sculpher then drove to the Royal Hotel, and Sherwill was sent for by a policeman and a German officer.

Sherwill picked up Carey, the bailiff, and together they went to the hotel where they found about six Germans, the harbour-master, and a Swiss hotel owner to act as possible interpreter although some of the Germans spoke English. Instructions were issued, and it was agreed to produce special editions of the *Guernsey Evening Press*, and the *Star* containing them. The meeting broke up, and apart from the smashing of wireless apparatus at the harbour nothing else happened that night. Frank Falla of the *Star* went in to work on the special edition: 'I got out my bike and started on my way, but I'd not gone very far along the coast road when my worst fears were confirmed. I stopped and stood staring along the road ahead of me. I found I was gazing at the first member of Hitler's army I had ever seen in real life: the green uniform, queer-shaped helmet, the jackboots, the gas mask in a tin, and the rifle at the ready.'

Lindau was now stung into action, and prepared to take Guernsey next morning only to find himself delayed by fog. At last in the evening Junkers transport planes with naval assault troops, a company of infantry, and a light anti-aircraft unit occupied the Island.

That day Guernsey people read in their papers a statement by Carey that the public were to offer no resistance, and to obey the orders printed in the paper. These orders included a curfew, no use of private motor vehicles, the handing in of all weapons, a ban on the sale of petrol, the advancing of clocks and watches to Central European Time, the banning of all boat movements, the closure of the aerodrome to the public, and a demand that all British military personnel report to the authorities. On Tuesday 2 July Major Albrecht Lanz, the first commandant of Guernsey, and his English-speaking chief of staff, Major-Doctor Maass, arrived, and had a meeting with Island officials after which a second list of German orders was issued.

In Jersey the first indication of the coming German invasion was the dropping of several copies of a demand early on the morning of 1 July. Because no one in government circles could read German, a Jesuit was sent for to translate the document which ordered the Island to display white crosses on various places, and stated that if this was not done 'a heavy bombardment will take place'. But once again the Luftwaffe could not resist taking swifter action. This time it was Lieutenant Richard Kern who landed at the airport to be met by the airport controller. Kern asked why white flags were not displayed, and it was pointed out that the bailiff had to get agreement before acting, but that they intended to surrender. Coutanche held a meeting in Royal Square, and there was considerable discontent in the crowd when he said they must surrender. 'We've got men, we've got our fists' called out someone. But there was no alternative. The white flags were put up, and Coutanche accompanied by Duret Aubin, the attorney general, went to the airport. By this time, a small number of planes under the command of Staff Captain Obernitz had arrived, and it was to Kern and Obernitz that actual surrender was made. As in Guernsey some Germans entered the car with the bailiff and the attorney general, and they drove to St Helier town hall which became their headquarters. A meeting was arranged for ten o'clock next morning.

At the meeting Coutanche, Duret Aubin, Edgar Dorey, and the bailiff's secretary, Ralph Mollet met the German commandant, Captain Erich Gussek. A more detailed set of occupation orders was presented and agreed. These laid down the relationship between the Germans and the existing government. They ended with an ominous little clause saying, that the privileges granted to the civilian population were dependent on their good behaviour, and that military necessity might require the orders now in force to be made more stringent.

On 2 July two small planes under the command of Sergeant-Major Schmidt landed on Alderney to find it practically deserted. It was decided that all that was needed there for the moment was a small detachment of 80 harbour defence troops under the command of Captain Koch.

The old Guernsey lifeboat brought Lanz and Maass to Sark on 3 July with a small contingent of ten men and a sergeant who were billeted in the Bel Air Hotel. When the Germans entered the Seigneurie, they gave the Nazi salute to Sibyl Hathaway and her husband, after they had walked up from the harbour with the seneschal. They began by presenting a copy of the conditions, but matters relaxed when Sibyl Hathaway spoke in German. Lunch was served, and thereafter 'I was treated with great courtesy by the senior officers, and I, in turn, extended to them the hospitality of the Seigneurie'.

These first few days were halcyon ones. The German commandants were all civilized men on the surface even if they served the Nazi régime. The first orders were not oppressive, and the first German soldiers were young healthy men more interested in good food, buying up goods in the shops, and getting down to the beaches than in any brutal occupation tactics. The occupation orders contained an important reassurance which said that 'The German Commandant has taken over the military powers of the Islands of Guernsey and Jersey. The population is hereby required to retain calmness, order and discipline. If this is assured, the life and property of the population will be respected and guaranteed.'

Both sides thought occupation might not last long. The Germans thought England would fall. The Islanders believed they would be rescued in some way. Julia Tremayne was disappointed when Churchill's broadcast urging the French to resist made no mention of the Channel Islands, but as late as December she was writing 'we long for the British Navy to come and put the fear of God in their hearts, and I pray it won't be far off'. For a few months the Islanders could get used to Germans passing Boots the Chemist and Barclays Bank, marching along the lanes singing, and even to meeting them at dances or football matches. As the Germans anticipated this was not what people expected. They had achieved a bloodless conquest, and had established themselves without a shadow of opposition, apart from a few incidents as when James Colgan struck a German soldier in a St Helier café for which offence he received a month in prison.

2

Inside the Channel War Zone for Five Years

Not long after D-Day when the government on Jersey plucked up a little courage to complain about food and other shortages the Military commandant von Schmettow replied, 'People in the Islands do not know what war is, nor what war means. They can have no idea of what every German town, the whole of France, London and the South of England are experiencing daily in the way of sacrifices and sufferings.' Morrison, the home secretary, made the same point when he told his cabinet colleagues that the Islanders had 'lost touch with events in the outside world' and 'had no comprehension of conditions in this country, including the bombing and war time privations'.

Churchill was naturally furious when he heard about the seizure of the Channel Islands, and minuted General Ismay demanding that 'plans should be studied to land secretly by night on the Islands and kill or capture the invaders'. The prime minister thought this would be a useful task for the newly forming commandos. As a result his large scale attacks on one or more of the Channel Islands were considered in 1941 and 1942. In February 1941 Operation Attaboy was put forward involving the landing of 5,000 troops on Alderney. Sir Roger Keyes, Director of Combined Operations, was asked to make plans, and Churchill was prepared to accept heavy casualties. Keyes and the Joint Planning Staff put forward numerous objections saying fighter cover would be menaced by the Luftwaffe in France, and that though capturing Alderney or another Island was feasible, it would bring no strategic gain, and a long-term maintenance problem. Churchill argued for even a day's occupation, but the plan was abandoned.

1942 saw the development of a second major operation called at first Operation Blazing. Consideration was given to capturing all three main Islands although it was stressed that either Guernsey or Jersey would require up to 8,000 troops with large scale air and naval support. Vice-Admiral Lord Louis Mountbatten had just taken over as Chief of Combined Operations and supported Blazing because he knew Churchill liked offensive actions of this kind. He argued that Island captures would provide facilities for attacking German shipping while at the same time helping the Navy with a Channel base, extending air cover of France, and providing a useful starting-point for raids on the French coast by Commando forces. Mountbatten proposed an invasion of Alderney with 5,000 troops landing from up to 23 ships protected by six destroyers, and covering air attack designed particularly to eliminate Fort Albert overlooking Braye. But once this plan was put forward the chiefs of both Fighter and Bomber Command, and the newly appointed head of the Airborne Division all objected, and Churchill and Mountbatten abandoned the plan on 11 May.

In spite of disaster at Dieppe that summer, the plan was resurrected before the end of the year as Operation Constellation. Three separate plans for the Islands were drawn up, and a serious effort was made to collect information under the code-name Concubine. All three plans involved large forces. That for Alderney required the dropping of nearly 5,000 tons of bombs while that for Jersey involved air attack, infantry and commando landings on the coast, and parachute drops from 190 aircraft of the Airborne Division on the race-course, airfield and at St Peter's Mill. The climax of the operation was to be a three-pronged advance on St Helier with a tank column coming from the north, and other forces from east and west and it is clear evacuation of remaining civilians was to be considered suggesting widespread devastation. Fortunately these plans were stillborn, and after D-Day, massive German fortifications, and the fate of French coastal towns subject to air attack, were convincing arguments against attempting any such invasion.

But in June and July 1940 when the Islands fell Churchill was involved in the creation of the commandos based on striking companies recently employed in Norway. He told General Ismay on 4 June that 'we should immediately set to work to organize raiding forces', and two days later came his vital minute ordering the planning of such forces. The director of military operations prepared blueprints, and on 5 July the first commando brigade (Number 3) was formed at Plymouth under Major John Durnford-Slater. It was unclear if their main purpose was to harry the enemy tying down his forces, and encouraging resistance, or whether they were intelligence gathering units. Naturally the organization was at its flimsiest in the early months, but the Channel Isles provided an obvious testing ground, particularly since military men with knowledge of the Islands were available in the services. From July to September 1940 a series of small operations were carried out along the south Guernsey coast which while providing some military information were hamstrung by lack of resources, ended in failure, and presented the Island government of Carey and Sherwill with a serious crisis. Every raid faced some Islanders with the problem of aiding the invaders, and therefore raised the collaboration-resistance issue for the first time.

Twenty-year-old Hubert Nicolle serving in the Hampshire Regiment was the first man sent to Guernsey. His expedition was so amateur that he had to buy his canoe at Gamages before travelling down to Plymouth to set off for the Island in a submarine on 5 July. It was impossible for the submarine to come close inshore, and Nicolle and Sub-Lieutenant Leitch had to row two miles to Le Jaonnet Bay. Leitch landed him and Nicolle made his way inland meeting two old friends. The second of these, Thomas Mansell, agreed to obtain information about the airport for him and donning dark glasses Nicolle then borrowed a bicycle and cycled home. His Uncle Frank Nicolle was assistant harbour-master, and he was able to provide naval information. From a local grocer given the task of supplying the garrison Nicolle obtained details of German ration strength. On 9 July, three days after his arrival, Nicolle made for the bay where a dinghy appeared which landed two men and then took him back to the submarine.

The two men arriving were second lieutenants Philip Martel and Desmond Mulholland, both Guernsey men who had been asked to make a reconnaissance and guide in a raiding party on the night of 12 July. But after hiding out for two days and returning to the beach the two men found nothing happening, unaware that the attack had been postponed for 48 hours. Martel had visited his sister, Mrs Michael, but he was unwilling to return to her house so the two men set off to hide on the Island in a barn near Vazon and in a house that belonged to Colonel and Mrs Cantan, son-in-law, and daughter of Sibyl Hathaway. The Dame claimed in her memoirs to have taken them supplies under the pretext of visiting her property. The two men went to Sark to try and get a boat, but German restrictions on fishing boats made this impossible, and a boat they stole at Perelle Bay in Guernsey broke up on the rocks. They were cut off and in great danger.

Operation Ambassador took place on the night of 14–15 July. It was meant to be a three-pronged attack. One part, would land at Point de la Moye and make for the airport to destroy planes and fuel. A second one would land at Le Jaonnet to intercept relieving troops going to the airport, and a third party would land at Petit Port to immobilize a machine-gun post there. Unfortunately there was a shortage of proper landing-craft, and in tough sea conditions everything went wrong. The airport group failed to land, as did the Le Jaonnet group misled by a faulty compass. The group who landed at Petit Port found no machine-gun post, and when it came to taking them off this proved impossible. Their boat was smashed after five attempts, and as the Germans were now alerted they had to be left behind although there was a reserve plan to return on the night of 17/18 July. Four soldiers, McGoldrick, Drain, Ross and Dumper, therefore had to stay hidden. They found a garden shed at the home of Doctor and Mrs Sullivan, a retired couple where they hid for two days, but unknown to them the relief force had been cancelled in order to cut losses. The men found refuge with Walter and Ada Bourgaize, at their general shop at Torteval even though German troops were billeted nearby. After one or two nights at the store, and failure to obtain a boat, they realized they would have to leave. Corporal Dumper left all his personal possessions behind, which caused the Bourgaizes considerable worry because they included a service revolver which had to be buried in a tin under the coal tip. The four soldiers were arrested walking along the road to the airport, and sent to Lamsdorf Stalag for the duration of the war.

Martel and Mulholland had still to be rescued. Another Guernseyman, Stanley Ferbrache, volunteered to go to the Island and bring them back.

He landed on 3 August at Le Jaonnet from a motor torpedo boat and then called on his uncle, Albert Callighan. That night he went to the bungalow where Mulholland's mother, Mrs Le Masurier lived, but she told him he was too late. The two men had surrendered the previous week. Ferbrache had to content himself with collecting information and even walked round the airport perimeter. He was taken off on the night of 6 August. In spite of these failures it was still thought valuable to establish contact with the local population, and Hubert Nicolle was sent back with another Hampshire Regiment Guernseyman, James Symes. They landed at Petit Port on 4 September, and went first to Nicolle's uncle, Frank. The two men were to remain at large for five weeks, and precipitate severe German reaction.

But Churchill was still determined on attack, and Operation Tomato was in preparation to land forces of up to 500 men who would immobilize Guernsey and Jersey aerodromes as well as landing on Sark and Alderney. Captain John Parker, an Islander whose father still lived there, was chosen to obtain intelligence, and discover the fate of the four missing men. Unfortunately, his landing at La Corbière was in the wrong place. He fell into a ditch, startling a German sentry, and was promptly arrested. He and his father were interrogated, and Parker was then sent to the Cherche Midi in Paris, and later to a POW camp. Keyes probably wrote with some relief to Churchill that, 'I understand from my conversation with you today that in present circumstances you do not wish me to proceed further with the project against the Channel Islands.'

Parker's capture on 30 September a week later brought to an end the first attempt to bring war to the Islands.

Martel and Mulholland surrendered to the Germans on 28 July and Nicolle and Symes on 21 October, as a result of a policy adopted by Ambrose Sherwill on behalf of the Island government. As early as 18 July Sherwill had drafted a complaint to the home office about the dispatch of missions saying Carey, he, and 'many prominent people' objected to them although it is noteworthy that all the ordinary Islanders who met the troops gave them assistance. This was not, however, the policy of the ruling group who were thoroughly alarmed on two grounds: such events would damage good relations with the Germans or precipitate action against the population as a whole, and secondly, their own relatives and government positions were at stake. Nicolle's uncle was harbour-master, and his father, Emile, was secretary to the Control Commission. Carey's secretary, Louis Guillemette found out his brother was to have been used in a raid, and Sherwill naturally feared his serving son, John, might be involved. In Jersey, Coutanche had a serving son who might be involved, and the Le Masuriers knew of an attempt to land Robert on Jersey. In Sark, Sibyl Hathaway knew Martel and Mulholland had visited her daughter Amice's house. As a result of the four agents' presence, Sherwill, both Nicolles, and H.E. Marquand, the States Supervisor, were to lose their posts.

These factors would undoubtedly have weighed with Sherwill as much as the safety of the Islanders as a whole, and it led him to take action which in other European countries would have been seen as collaboration. When in desperation Martel and Mulholland arrived at Havelet House willing to surrender Sherwill backed their decision, although a further effort was made to rescue them a week later. Sherwill rang up Doctor Maass after providing them with uniforms, and the two men surrendered. They were interrogated and then sent to POW camp for the rest of the war. Mrs Michael and Mrs Le Masurier were confined under house arrest at St-Lô until January 1941.

Nicolle and Symes presented a more serious challenge to the Germans as the weeks passed, and gradually involved an increasing number of Islanders in their fate. Hubert Nicolle stayed with his uncle, and met his girlfriend, Jessie Mariette, while James Symes went to stay with his girlfriend Mary Bird's parents. Her father, Wilfred Bird, was working at Elizabeth College, and the two evaders spent three nights in the college cricket pavilion and had meals with William Allen, the groundsman, who lived in a cottage nearby. The two men made four escape attempts which failed, and a ban on the use of fishing boats resulting from some successful Island escapes blocked any chance of getting away. The arrival of the first Island Military Commander, von Schmettow, and his subordinate in Guernsey, Major Bandelow, meant pressure was stepped up because the Germans had no way of knowing how many British troops were still at large. On 11 October Bandelow wrote to Sherwill saying he knew soldiers were present, and stressing that harbouring such people was a serious crime. He said that he would arrange a date by which time all those at large must surrender: 'Those reporting up to that date will be treated as prisoners of war; also no measures will be taken against their relatives who had assisted in hiding them. Those members of the British forces who may be found after this time limit must expect to be treated as agents of an enemy power.'

Sherwill's reply, which even he later described as 'a bit too smarmy', stressed his appreciation of this gesture, condemned escapers and any assistance to military activity against the regime, and ended, 'It gives me ground for confidence that at a period when the nations to which we respectively belong are locked in combat ... it is possible – though only in the Channel Islands – for a German officer and a British official to enter into friendly correspondence ...'

Von Schmettow and his officers were anxious to give a good impression, and to assert some degree of independence from Paris where General Schreiber, head of the military government organization, was calling for severe action. After some argument it was agreed to issue a statement on the lines proposed by Bandelow. The men in hiding were to report to St Peter Port police station by six in the evening on Monday 21 October, and a few minutes before this time Nicolle and Symes appeared.

The two men were taken to Fort George and interrogated by Captain Schröder of the Feldpolizei. Their role as spies was appreciated, and after a court martial they were sentenced to death. A further order was issued stating that anyone harbouring British subjects who had returned to the Islands and who did not report this by 5 November would be shot. On 2 November William Allen, Mary Bird and her parents, Thomas Mansell, Jessie Mariette and her parents, Mr and Mrs Frank Nicolle, Mr and Mrs

Emile Nicolle, Mr and Mrs Louis Symes, and Sherwill were all arrested. They were questioned, and then removed to the Cherche Midi Prison in Paris. Von Schmettow and Schumacher were angry that their word as officers that neither course of action would be taken had been overruled, and after considerable argument Symes and Nicolle were let off a second trial demanded in Paris by Schreiber and sent to be POWs.

But the German promise not to punish anyone was broken. A collective punishment was imposed on the Island including a fine of £3,000 and the confiscation of wireless sets until a few days before Christmas. The captives remained in solitary for 50 days until they were released on 30 December from Cherche Midi Prison. They were only allowed out 'to empty their sanitary buckets in a cesspool in the yard. Soon Captain Nicolle was denied this privilege after he was caught giving part of his bread ration to an RAF prisoner in the cell opposite him. Hubert Nicolle had a bullet flattened on the wall beside his head when he had climbed on a chair and table to have a look out.' Only at Christmas time were they let out together, and forced to sing Christmas carols, but by then tragedy had struck. Depressed by solitary confinement, Louis Symes was found kneeling in his cell, his eyes fixed on an open Bible, and his wrist arteries severed. He had committed suicide three days before Christmas.

There were no more raids on the Islands for exactly two years, and when they started again they were carried out by the Small Scale Raiding Force commanded by Major Gustavas March-Phillipps. On the night of 23 September 1942 a party of 12 men led by March-Phillipps and Captain Geoffrey Appleyard sailed from Portland to capture the German crew of seven manning the Casquets lighthouse. Lying off Alderney it had not been well fortified, and the raid was a complete success except for an injury to Appleyard. Hitler demanded details and his first reaction was an OKW (German High Command) order withdrawing exposed lighthouse crews. However, it was obvious lighthouses were needed, and later a new garrison of 33 men was installed together with barbed wire and mines.

Appleyard commanded Operation Basalt, the first raid on Sark, carried out on the foggy night of Saturday and Sunday 3 and 4 October. His party consisted of seven men from the SSRF including the distinguished Lieutenant Anders Lassen, and five from Number 12 Commando. They landed at Point Chateau on Dixcart Bay, and ascended the Hogs Back to level country avoiding a German patrol. After a time they entered an isolated house called La Jaspellerie and met Frances Pittard. Mrs Pittard, the wife of a doctor who had recently died, was a friend of Mrs Tremayne. She gave the troops a map and told them there were Germans billeted a few hundred yards away in the Dixcart Hotel.

Although they only had four hours the commandos decided to raid the hotel. In the annex they found five members of an engineer detachment, and bundled them half-dressed out of bed. They were shoved outside, their hands secured by soldiers' toggles, and their trousers unbuttoned to stop them escaping. Although neither Appleyard's nor the German official report mention it, access to the annex had been gained after Lassen knifed the guard who was probably Peter Oswald buried with other raid victims at Fort George. Had they known it, the commandos were also benefiting for once from German incompetence. The orderly corporal had been informed of suspicious noises, but had not informed the Island commandant, Lieutenant Herdt. Appleyard wanted an officer from the main hotel, but the prisoners began to make a noise, and a running fight broke out. One escaped naked and unharmed, and so did another although he was wounded. Two Germans – Esslinger and Bleyer – were killed, and one, Lance-Corporal Weinrich remained a prisoner. Lights came on in the hotel, and the party set out for the shore where the MTB (motor torpedo boat) was waiting as they were late, and Germans were in pursuit followed by an armed customs boat. The party got away with a few minutes to spare.

The repercussions of this raid were considerable. General Müller was furious and his situation report made it clear that both Herdt, who was relieved of command and replaced by Lieutenant Knauf, and the orderly officer were to be court-martialled. 'Contrary to my orders', said Müller, Herdt 'had billeted an engineer detatchment carelessly in Dixcart House, without protection, and away from the Company Reserve'. On Sark it was decided to remove troops from Stocks Hotel and various houses and concentrate them round Le Manoir farm in the centre of the Island. The thatch was torn off the farm roof and replaced with corrugated iron, and the church windows were bricked up as they overlooked the new quarters. It was then necessary to reinforce the garrison, and three small tanks were brought over to the Island. An army report stressed the need to block all landing grounds, and to increase the existing 939 mines by a further 1,400. Eventually there were 4,000 mines on the beaches, strung on wires across the bays and parts of the harbour, and down some cliffs on ropes. This led to tragic consequences for the innocent, like Nanette Carré, killed by a mine playing near her home in October 1944. She was just four years old.

After the attack German soldiers with fixed bayonets raided houses, and a series of measures designed as punishments were enforced. The curfew was reduced to even shorter hours, fishing was banned, and houses along parts of the shoreline were deliberately destroyed. Throughout the Island guards were doubled and armed. Then the Feldpolizei arrived and for weeks the Islanders went in fear of what might happen to them. Mrs Tremayne commented that 'We used to read about the "Gestapo" in Germany taking people off in the middle of their dinner and putting them into concentration camps, but to enter your house and march you off at a moment's notice, without any explanation, is a ghastly thing to do. No one knows whose turn it will be next.'

A number of people like Issac Carré and George Hammon, were taken to Guernsey for questioning, and the two owners of the Dixcart Hotel, Miss Duckett and Miss Page, who claimed to have slept through it all, were closely questioned. Mrs Pittard who had met the British force was arrested and sent to Guernsey Prison for eleven weeks.

The raid once again received Hitler's personal attention, and he was apparently infuriated by the suggestion that the dead men had been unable to defend themselves because they had been previously bound by some grey cord. Or it may have been because of the raid's success. One eyewitness has said that a Polish evader who was among Todt workers on the Island known as 'Armand' or 'Roman' Zwadaski was also rescued at a prearranged rendezvous. The raid certainly resulted in the release to the outside world of details of recent deportations from the Islands when the British government published photostats of German orders. The Führer ordered the shackling of some Dieppe prisoners as a reprisal and the Canadians retaliated by shackling German prisoners. Following other commando and SOE successes the raid may have been the last straw leading to the issue of the infamous Commando Extermination Order (*Kommandobefehl*) in October. 'Their captured orders divulge', Hitler said, 'that they are directed not only to shackle prisoners, but also to kill defenceless prisoners on the spot'. All commandos in or out of uniform were to be 'exterminated to the last man', and if they surrendered 'all quarter is to be denied on principle'. Individuals were to be handed over to the SD for treatment, and this order was to be followed by many horrific massacres large and small. Hitler overruled a proposal that women and children who had been deported from the Islands might return, and further deportations early in 1943, including Mrs Pittard, Miss Duckett and Miss Page were largely a punishment for this raid.

The last raids on the Islands code-named Hardtack were designed as part of the run-up to D-Day to obtain prisoners and military information, but by this time German anti-raid measures had been properly established. The two raids on Sark and Jersey were planned for 25-6 December, but the Sark raid led by Lieutenant A.J. McGonigal landed at a point where the cliffs proved unscaleable, and had to return two nights later. The Germans were alerted, and on Boxing Day Mrs Tremayne who had enjoyed Christmas with a gift of candles from Mrs Hathaway and a piece of chocolate sent from the vicar now in a deportation camp, had retired to bed when, 'In the early hours of the night, about two or three, we were awakened by a thunderous knock at the door which kept on until we had the courage to leap out of bed in the dark, and throw open the window to ask who was there. Four Germans stood there, fully armed, and the officer said "Open the door at once" – they had come to search the house at that time of night.' Mrs Tremayne and her daughter Norah had to follow the Germans through the house by the light of a torch as they searched turning out cupboards and chests, Mrs Tremayne had her heart in her mouth that they would find her diary. Afterwards they sat having hot drinks in the kitchen unable to sleep. When the raiders returned therefore she wrote, 'I cannot see myself what good the landing here does', as 'the last one brought us nothing but misery'. The raid also brought misery to the commandos because their second attempt stumbled into a mine-field, and four out of five were wounded. Two Frenchmen, Corporal Bellamy and Private Dignac, were killed. 'Two graves were dug in our little churchyard and they were thrown in at dawn one morning, with not one prayer said over them, poor dears. A wooden cross was erected, their names put on and Mrs Hathaway sent two wreaths of camellia,' said Mrs Tremayne.

The other 1943 Christmas night raid on Jersey was led by Captain Philip Ayton, and landed at Petit Port on the north-east coast. There were nine in the party. Passing through the ruins of Egypt Farm destroyed by the

Germans they came to La Geonnière where Miss Le Feuvre refused to open to them, later claiming she thought they were Germans trying to speak English. They moved on to Le Champ du Chemin, owned by John and Hedley Le Breton, where they received a better welcome and information about which strong points were occupied. In spite of some resentment the two farmers stressed there was no resistance, and that their greatest fear was of Russian Todt workers foraging for food. On the way back Ayton was injured by a mine, and died on their return to Dartmouth that evening. He was just 22 years old.

Other raids contemplated, but not carried out, might well have led to further loss of life: one was for blowing up shipping in St Peter Port, and another for capturing the whole German garrison on Sark. The balance sheet for the raids is hard to draw. Brave men sacrificed their lives, and brave Islanders put their lives at risk to help them. Something at least was done to harrass the Germans and make the Islanders feel they were not completely neglected. Information was obtained. A few Germans were captured or killed. But several were captured and killed in the ranks of the commandos, and in the case of the two serious raids: Ambassador and Basalt, Islanders on Guernsey and Sark suffered a good deal through imprisonment or deportation, damage to property, fines, curfew, fishing restrictions, and the frightening presence of the Feldpolizei which they mistook for the Gestapo. Had the raids got worse there can be little doubt that the German response would have escalated, and so the taste of war the raids brought to the Islands was received with mixed feelings.

Morrison's remark about the Island's being isolated from the war was wide of the mark in other ways. It did not take account of the closeness of the Island to occupied France. Knowledge of events there was constantly in the minds of Islanders, not least because many of them passed through a variety of French prisons and camps like Caen, Dijon, Cherche Midi, and Compiègne. For administrative purposes the Islands were part of the Department of La Manche, and links with Granville, St Malo, and Cherbourg increased during the occupation. Ultimately the Island authorities were answerable to the military government of General Stülpnagel in Paris who visited the Islands on occasion. After cable-cutting had taken place his order was published stating that, 'any person involved in such an act, as a perpetrator, participant, or instigator will upon conviction by court martial without power of appeal be condemned to suffer the death penalty'. The order also said that if further acts occurred, 'the entire population will have to suffer the consequences of the reprisals which will follow'. Cases like that of Louis Berrier of Ernes in France, shot for sending a pigeon with a message to England were displayed, and had their effect. 'The walls', said Mrs Tremayne, 'are all posted with notices about what we are not to do, and it all ends with death penalties'; she had noticed the Berrier poster.

The treatment of the French on the Islands, including their workers and women, was a constant reminder to Islanders of what might happen to them. According to one writer, some 50 French escapers reached the Islands, but got no further, many being returned to their deaths; although the French consul on Guernsey, M.L.V. Lambert, did help escapers sheltering them in a shed and on rare occasions getting boats for them. In December 1940 a party of 16 young men led by 21-year-old François Scornet escaped from Ploujean near Finisterre. They landed at Vazon Bay in Guernsey, thinking they had reached England, only to be captured and sent to Jersey. Early in February, Scornet was tried as their leader in the committee room of the Old Court, and he was executed on 17 March 1941 at St Ouen Manor. His companions were returned to France where some of them later died in prison, although one managed to escape to join the resistance. Sibyl Hathaway had been among the first to turn in military escapers when a few days after the occupation two Frenchmen and a Pole arrived in a dinghy, and were brought to the Seigneurie. The Frenchmen said they wished to join the Free French, but although people were escaping from Guernsey that day, Hathaway said there was no alternative to surrender because the fishing boats had been impounded. They were, she said in her memoirs, 'bitterly disappointed and I did my best to comfort them'.

Because the Islands were in a war zone, Islanders experienced dangers from crashed planes of both sides, and witnessed the death or capture of many Allied airmen. One list of such crashes also includes 26 German planes. A good many of these were the result of airport collisions due to the large number of transport planes involved in air-lifting supplies and personnel. A Messerschmitt collided with an anti-aircraft position at Guernsey airport killing three gunners in August 1940, and on other occasions German anti-aircraft guns opened up on their own planes. A Junkers 88 crashed near Eden Chapel in Jersey in April 1944 as a result of such an action, and four crew were killed. In other cases planes came down as a result of air war over the Islands which was intense during the Battle of Britain, at the time of convoy battles, and in the period of the D-Day invasion. Although only three German air crew were buried on the Islands the number of deaths was higher; perhaps as many as 25.

Naturally it was Allied air-crew that Island attention focused on most. On 3 June 1943 the body of Sergeant Dennis Butlin was picked up at La Pulente, and soon afterwards that of Sergeant Abraham Holden at Samares. They were buried at Mont-a-l'Abbe Cemetery on 6 June, and at their burial on Jersey hundreds lined the route and two lorry loads of wreaths followed the cortège. Information about air war over the Islands is notoriously incomplete, but there were 23 confirmed Allied air losses, and there were others like Squadron Leader Gonay, a Belgian, killed when his plane crashed on a farm at St Ouen in June 1944. Mrs Cortvriend said that, 'the mere sight of a British or Allied plane was a thrill and a signal for rejoicing to most of us'. On Sark a Lancaster bomber managed to land in what is now known as 'Aeroplane Field'.

Whenever possible, Islanders did their best to treat Allied air-crew with kindness, although that was as far as they dared to go in view of German warnings. In Guernsey when the first plane, an Anson, crashed and four crew came ashore in a dinghy at Portinfer, they were looked after by Reginald Blatchford of the St John Ambulance Brigade before they were handed over to the police. Pilot Officer Robert Stirling whose Hurricane came down near Lihou Island, managed to walk in darkness along the causeway to Guernsey in April 1941. The 23-year-old Scotsman also managed to avoid a German cycle patrol, and sheltered at Mr and Mrs T. Brouard's house at L'Erée overnight.

At the time of the Nicolle-Symes affair, Schumacher's order had made it clear that anyone who sheltered British subjects 'particularly members of the British armed forces, shall be shot', and this order was reissued on a number of occasions. In August 1941, for example, the *Guernsey Evening Press* contained this order over Carey's name: 'Attention is called to the fact that under the Order relative to protection against acts of sabotage, dated October 10th 1940, any person who hides or shelters escaped prisoners of war shall be punished with death. The same applies for the hiding or sheltering of members of enemy forces, for instance, crews of landing aircraft, parachutists etc. Anyone lending assistance to such persons in their escape is also liable to the death sentence.' Mrs Tremayne saw this notice. 'Just fancy', she wrote, 'it might easily be one of our own and someone we know'. No accurate figures are available for Allied air losses in the Channel Islands, but the list includes ten deaths, sadly not all as a result of enemy action. The pilot of a Spitfire that crashed to the south of Guernsey in May 1944 was killed when his parachute failed to open. Usually crews that came down over land or ditched in the sea were rescued and the list also includes at least 20 rescued crew members. The Germans co-operated in such rescues, although there is one unexplained incident that took place off Alderney. In January 1944 four crew members were saved from a Lancaster that ditched to the west of the Island, but at some time late in June that year another Lancaster crashed west of Essex Castle. Captain Massmann, harbour commandant at Braye since 1943, did not order out any boats, and two of his staff later stated 'all of us were surprised that nothing was done for their rescue'. After the war Massmann was brought to London with a view to prosecution, but none took place.

Although most air-crew and naval personnel were sent to stalags in Germany, there was a POW camp at Mount Bingham in Jersey, and it was from this camp that the only successful escape and evasion took place by two Americans, Captain Edward Clark, and Lieutenant George Haas. They escaped on 8 January 1945, and a German order soon appeared stating, 'They will attempt to obtain shelter and help from the English civilian population. It is expressly announced that anyone who takes in or extends help in any way to Captain Clark or Lieutenant Haas will be punished by death'. After four days Clark and Haas reached East Lynne Farm on Grouville Bay owned by Wilfred Bertram, one of the Islanders who actively helped escapers. The Americans got away from the bay on 19 January, and Bertram was later awarded the United States Medal of Freedom.

The victims, both people and planes, of air war are a reminder that the Islands were in a war zone. Air war over the Islands had the regrettable dimension that the RAF were bound to sink supply ships, and vessels containing Todt workers and POWs, and even to inflict losses on the Islanders. Raids had to be faced by a population whose powers of resistance were already sapped by occupation conditions, and there were only rudimentary civil defence precautions and ever decreasing medical facilities. According to one writer there were at least 22 raids in the Channel Isles resulting in 93 deaths and 250 injuries – many of these Todt port workers caught at their jobs or on transports to and from France. Attacks on air facilities in 1940, on the ports in 1942, and on ports and military installations in 1944 were the worst raids, but, as in Britain, there was a constant menace from planes. Even in the most peaceful year, Mrs Tremayne referred in May and June 1943 to serious fighting that 'has been going on all this week around the Islands and live shells from the Guernsey guns have been whistling over Sark, breaking glass and scattering over the roofs of houses. Our huge bombers have been flying over, very low, and they have sunk a minesweeper off Sark and lots of ships in Jersey harbour'.

The first raids that Mrs Tremayne noticed were three consecutive night attacks on Guernsey Airport in August 1940 which she described as 'perfect Bedlam'. During the night of 23 August she experienced the fall of the first bomb in Sark. 'The noise was so heavy, and the suspense and worry until we could hear at daylight what had happened, were intense. It is a mercy no fire was started, or it could never have been put out, as there is no water and no appliances of any sort. It fell near the Manoir [the Old Vicarage], all Mrs Cook's block had the glass shattered and holes cut in the roofs everywhere.' In July 1941, when the airport was the target again, German guns shook her house with their reverberations. The bombing, she wrote, 'is almost hourly now, night and day', and she found it 'very alarming at times'. On 3 September Julia and her daughter Norah stood on Gouliot top and watched an air attack by many planes on barges moving towards Guernsey, and later on the airport. 1942 opened with more severe raids on Guernsey now mainly directed at the harbour and sufficiently large for the glow of the fires to light up Sark eight miles away. The raids went on for several nights, two ships were sunk, and Polish Todt workers killed. Damage was done in St Peter Port itself.

1944 was the worst year for raids, and as early as April Mrs Tremayne heard the noise of guns and bombs. Mrs Cortvriend on Guernsey noticed an attack on 27 May by USAAF Thunderbolts aimed at the barracks and Fort George. One person was killed and several injured by shrapnel from German anti-aircraft defences. A bomb exploding near her house fractured their water-pipes. From then on 'scarcely a day passed without large formations of planes flying overhead'. Mrs Tremayne heard that the raid on Fort George killed a number of Germans at a football match. On 15 June she recorded 'another hellish night', and her comments continued with little intermission for the next three months. Mrs Cortvriend and Mrs Tremayne described the destruction in St Peter Port which was the main target in their islands. Windows of the town church, St Peter's, the main shops, and many houses were blown in, and people cut by flying glass. At night, said Mrs Cortvriend, 'from our bedroom we were able to witness brilliant flare and tracer bullet displays, while the beams of numerous searchlights swept the skies. The boom of our naval guns could often be heard … large fires were distinguished on the French coast, and heavy explosions shook our house throughout the days and nights.' There could be little doubt the Islands were often in the front line of their own particular blitz.

One day in February 1942, Norah Tremayne was looking out to sea when she saw three ships go by: they were the *Scharnhorst, Gneisenau*, and *Prinz Eugen* escaping from Brest and returning to Germany, a vivid reminder of the naval war that also affected the Channel Islands. Once, on 12 August 1944, HMS *Rodney* bombarded Alderney to try and destroy *Blücher* Battery, which severely damaged a gun and killed two Germans. The usual naval target was enemy shipping: E-boats and submarines, supply ships, and troop transports. German naval personnel were buried on the Islands, and many more British sailors are remembered still on Charybdis Day, 17 November, which commemorates the worst British loss of the war in the Channel during Operation Tunnel on the night of the 23/24 October 1943. The intention was to attack a convoy of 12 German ships, but six destroyers led by the light cruiser HMS *Charybdis* encountered an escort of E-boats, and the cruiser sustained direct hits sinking almost at once with the loss of 462 lives. HMS *Limbourne* was hit with the loss of 42 lives, and subsequently had to be sunk. Bodies from the disaster were washed up on the Islands, including a stoker on Sark, and on the shores of France. When the burials of some of these took place large crowds of Islanders attended, and the turn-out so worried the Germans that such demonstrations at funerals were banned.

It has been stated there were six or seven major convoy battles in the area, some of these taking place in February and September 1943, and August 1944. In February 1943, two destroyers sank two transports and possibly two mine-sweepers on the Alderney–Cherbourg route, and German losses included the Harbour Commandant, Parsenow. Battles at sea in dark and fog were bound to lead to exaggerated accounts. In August 1944 Mrs Tremayne said, after a convoy battle which it was too misty to see, that several boats were lost and 'the sea must be full of dead bodies'.

The size of the garrison meant that at least 500 Germans a week were moving in both directions, and sometimes they were caught by the Royal Navy, or met with accident in treacherous waters. In January 1943 the *Schockland* sank off the south coast of Jersey after hitting a rock. Most of the Germans together with 15 prostitutes from German brothels were below decks and had to negotiate a single ladder before climbing through an 18-inch square hatch. As a result perhaps half the complement of 250 perished. They were buried at St Brelade's churchyard which became the main German burial ground on Jersey with over 200 graves. On 4 July 1944 the *Minotaure*, carrying Sylt prisoners and Todt workers from Alderney, sank with two other ships not far from St Malo. About 250 were drowned including a number of French Jews. By the end of the war the graveyards of the Channel Islands contained at least 560 German dead although most Luftwaffe casualties were taken off the Islands. The cemeteries also contained a substantial number of British dead from air and sea battles, and victims of accidents caused by the war, like deaths from mines. War had by no means passed the Islands by as Morrison and von Schmettow had suggested.

3

Inselwahn: Hitler's Channel Fortress, and its Garrison

By far the most obvious effect of the German occupation was the presence of the garrison, and by far the most long-lasting impression made by it was the construction of massive fortifications which still exist. 'The Island echoes', wrote one observer 'with the coarse singing of the troops on the march'. Wherever Island people went there were troops, marines, engineers, anti-aircraft forces, and a host of organizations necessary to run a modern army. They swarmed into holiday hotels using them as billets and offices, and their fortifications soon impinged on every stretch of coast destroying houses and farms, denying access to roads and beaches, and ruining agricultural land. Soldiers in their everyday lives, and carrying out mock battles and training were oppressive in themselves. 'I am so weary of this occupation and the sight of the Germans', wrote one woman who had had Germans standing in her house just staring at her, or invading her garden.

'The mental torture', wrote Mrs Tremayne, 'from this German occupation is becoming indescribable'. Some, like the teacher on Sark, broke down under the strain, and it will always be impossible to say how many lives were shortened by the experience of occupation, or how many suicides resulted from mental pressure. According to Doctor Lewis there were three in Jersey shortly after Occupation, and there were at least three caused by the threat of deportation in 1942–3.

At first the Islands were held by small forces on the main Islands and token contingents in Alderney and Sark. As late as June 1941 there were only 13,000 military personnel on the Islands, but then two decisions were taken that altered the position. On 15 June a major strengthening of the garrison was ordered, and on 20 October an order to fortify the Islands was given which led to a massive increase in troops, and to the presence of the Organization Todt and its slave workers, as well as other organizations like the Reichsarbeitsdienst (RAD). By the end of 1941 there were 15,000 Wehrmacht, 5,000 Luftwaffe, and 1,000 Kriegsmarine forces on the Island. The Luftwaffe men were 'flak' or anti-aircraft and maintenance and repair crews, and the Kriegsmarine defended the harbours. Two companies of engineers, the 14 on Jersey, and the 19 on Guernsey and Alderney accounted for 1,400 troops while supply forces accounted for

3,500. There was constant movement of forces to and from the Islands, but on paper at least the garrison reached a strength of 37,600 in April 1942 equal in size to the evacuated population and giving a ratio of one German for every two inhabitants.

The bulk of the new forces ordered in was Infantry Division 319 from the Seventh Army which replaced Division 216. Amounting to some 21,000 troops they were commanded independently from October 1941 to September 1943 by Major-General Erich Müller, and from February 1945 by Major-General Rudolf Wulf. At other times the troops were under the orders of the Islands' military commandant from October 1940 to February 1945, Colonel Graf Rudolf von Schmettow. The only exception were Alderney troops who until December 1941 were under naval command from Cherbourg. Throughout the occupation the troops varied in quality with a steady tendency to decline. At first, life, wrote a Guernsey baker in March 1941, had been tolerable enough, 'owing to the general courtesy and inoffensiveness of the German officers and soldiers'.

But as German chances of occupying Britain, and then of leaving the Islands, declined and war turned against the Reich, troops began to change, particularly those who had seen service in Russia, and could not unlive their new brutality. Russian war also brought to the islands companies of Russian troops fighting for the Germans (ROA). A new relationship based on fear and suppressed hatred resulted as a typical incident involving Russian troops will show. Bonamy Martel agreed to help night-watch at a friend's farm. He had with him a member of the Feldpolizei, and the two men hid under hay in a stable for the night. In the early hours of the morning, the farm was approached by two Luftwaffe men who ran off when they were challenged. After an hour two ROA soldiers appeared. The security policeman was shot dead, and one of the Russians ran off. The murderer produced a knife and stabbed Martel, and a grim fight began in the barn. The Russian tried to finish Martel off with the gun, but he broke his aim with some lead-piping. The two Russians were captured, and the murderer was executed.

Alderney had 3,000 and Sark nearly 300 military encamped on them by 1944. After D-Day the Islands lost most of their Todt workers, except on a maintenance basis, but more naval troops arrived, and in August 1944 evacuated forces from St Malo including 600 wounded who soon filled the military hospitals. A few escapers also reached the Islands, five from Granville in December, and in March 1945 35 German POWs were rescued from Granville by force. At the time of the German surrender in May 1945, 2,832 in Alderney, 275 in Sark, and about 24,000 troops in the main Islands surrendered. By then they were a demoralized and starving force, and many were hospital cases. 'When we were first occupied', wrote Molly Finigan, 'and for a good while afterwards it seemed the Germans were always marching in groups and singing in the streets of the town. Now all was quiet, no more shouting, no more singing their familiar song I.E.I.O.' By the winter of 1944 the once proud occupiers, 'go about unshaven and dirty, badly clad and some in rags, seeking roots or potatoes to eat' wrote Mrs Tremayne. The last six months brought home to the Germans the conditions many Islanders had lived with for years.

But in the early years it had been very different. The newly arrived forces represented the summit of years of training in the Hitler Youth, *Land Jahr*, and armed forces. When William Shirer saw the first British prisoners after Dunkirk he contrasted their physical condition with poor teeth, thin chests, and rounded shoulders after years on the dole with that of the Germans who really looked like a master race.

Two groups found it particularly hard to ignore so handsome and stirring a body of men: the women and children. In Jersey Chapman noticed within a short time of Occupation that more and more girls were seen with Germans. 'They dined openly with them in restaurants, swam with them, entertained them, and attended their concerts.'

In April 1941 Mrs Tremayne noticed 'some of the Sark girls are walking out with German soldiers, silly little asses, I feel I would like to shake them', while Frank Falla, who had to visit the *Kommandantur* as a reporter for the *Star* saw 'What upset me considerably at first – the sight of the local lovelies, Guernsey, Irish and Austrian, disporting themselves in plush chairs and settees with Wehrmacht and Luftwaffe officers and no doubt later sharing their beds.'

To an older woman like Mrs Tremayne the behaviour of the Germans was shocking. Her early tolerance soon gave way to suppressed hatred describing them as 'swine' and 'sweating bulls'. To her they were: 'A foul, fat, ugly, bullet-headed lot, capable of doing any dirty deed. They drink all day and night. They do no drill of any kind, just strut along the lanes armed to the teeth, with their behinds bursting out of their breeches with such good living.' She disliked their bathing and sunbathing habits. She noticed them 'wearing nothing more than a loin cloth, their bodies are a mahogany colour'. On one occasion soldiers opened her garden gate on a Sunday afternoon and came down the path in their trunks, although they ran off when her dog appeared.

But some things that she disliked appealed to younger women, and some Island women were to become collaborators in bed. Fraternization was sometimes a genuine relationship. Phyllis Barker on Sark who knew German was often called in to interpret for the German medical staff, and later married Werner Rang, a medical orderly. Sergeant Hesse, a billeting officer in Guernsey, returned after the war to marry his girlfriend, and open a restaurant. But most relationships were casual. Mrs Tremayne noticed women whose husbands were away had soldiers in their houses in the evening, and she thought the way the young girls played up to Germans 'really too disgusting for words'. These good relations did not disappear in spite of brutality, the decline in living standards, or even as a result of the general war. As late as August 1944, Germans were able to swim from a public beach, and afterwards played their wireless. They switched on English dance-band tunes, and were soon surrounded by mothers and children while the Battle of Normandy could be heard in the distance. Such relationships could always lead to trouble. Molly Finigan found she got on well with soldiers as a young girl of thirteen. One day, however, she and her sister took a pram and shovel to a sawmill at Piette to collect wood shavings and sawdust for fuel, and, 'a young German soldier came over to me and offered a large loaf. He could not speak any

English and started jabbering in German. I must have looked surprised, not knowing what he was on about until she heard the word "bett" on the end of his jabber, with him pointing up the stairs.'

Schoolchildren were particularly vulnerable to the German presence. Gifts of food and sweets were handed out, and children were taken for rides in cars and military vehicles. Even officers indulged in this fraternization. But the closest link was forged by the introduction of German into schools. Begun voluntarily in 1941, this was made compulsory in primary schools in April 1942, and throughout all educational institutions in January 1943. The Island education authority on Guernsey objected, pointing out that children already learned French, but their letter of complaint was forwarded without support by Carey, and the Germans had their way. In Sark, Hathaway did her best to support the policy. She appealed for help with books, and said she was prepared to have the children in the Seigneurie for their German lessons when there were difficulties over heating at the school. Although the schoolmistress, Miss Howard, could not teach the subject, a local German speaker obliged instead. The language created a bond between the children and the German soldiers, and its teaching was a way of influencing them. Molly Finigan described how a German officer visited her intermediate school in St Peter Port, to check progress and question the children. At Molly's school, two Germans attended her prize-giving and the children had to learn a German song for the occasion. Although an internal minute on compulsory German had suggested people would not like it this did not prove to be the case. By July 1943 one observer heard 'quite little kids talking it in the shops and lanes'.

Five years is a long time in a child's life, living under conditions of censorship and propaganda. The children learnt German marching songs. Boys were soon practising and playing at soldiers, doing the German drills, the goosestep, and marching four abreast, bowing from the waist, heel-clicking, and glorying in it!

Most realized that it was pointless to blame the children, but such behaviour was evidence of the extent to which fraternization by adults gave the Germans the opportunity to influence the young. Older boys were invited to drink with the Germans particularly on occasions like Hitler's birthday. In April 1944 a witness saw boys who had been drinking brandy with the Germans rolling home drunk and 'heiling' Hitler as they went. A few of those indoctrinated in this way proved to be informers when other youths discussed escape or resistance; for example, in November 1944 the Jersey Physical Culture Club was closed after discussion of escape had taken place because someone had informed on them.

From the beginning, fostering good relations was part of official policy. At the highest level officials were chosen to present the acceptable face of fascism, and consolidate good relations with the Island ruling class. But the policy applied to ordinary Islanders, backed by the Führer himself. He drew a distinction between British subjects living on the Islands, and the 'native' Islanders whom he curiously saw as 'French' and therefore opposed to being members of the British Empire. He believed they could be won over to support the Reich, 'if our occupation troops play their cards properly'.

The Operation Hardtack report in December 1943 included the sentence: 'the population generally is not hostile to the Germans'. The voices of those like Sherwill and Carey who praised the Germans saying 'the conduct of the German soldiers is exemplary', and 'the German authorities, both military and civil, have treated us with humanity and consideration' were never balanced by open criticism because this was an offence; and the Germans took full advantage of this to pretend their occupation had been a very model of civilized occupations. Von Schmettow told Carey in 1944, when the population was deprived of every basic necessity of life, that the Germans had 'made every effort to prevent every hardship that could be avoided', and von Aufsess, chief of administration, confided to his diary the view that up to December 1944, 'our conduct of affairs in these Islands has been reasonably fair and decent'. When, in 1945, Morrison and the British and Island governments all agreed with this view it must have seemed remarkable to those who had lived through five very different years.

There were individual decent soldiers, and kind-hearted administrators, but *bonhomie* was policy and propaganda, not evidence of a genuine desire to behave liberally. Early in January 1941 the Germans were busy with their first propaganda film. On Sark they asked a local couple if they would walk past Stocks Hotel, their headquarters, driving cows, and saluting as they passed. They were told the film was being made 'because the Sark people have given no trouble and had been very kind'. The couple declined. At social events cameras were present to record them for military magazines, or films. A series of dances with the troops was organized and the censored local press had to report them as successes. There were sporting events, including a Luftwaffe–Jersey match during the Battle of Britain won by Jersey 5–1.

Gradually for many Islanders the truth about military occupation emerged: that it brought no joy to anyone, neither civilians, nor, after June 1944, the soldiers themselves. The soldiers' mood could quickly change from outward friendliness as Molly Finigan found. Sometimes she stayed behind after school to forage for potatoes that had fallen off farmers' lorries, and the troops usually ignored her. One day a German seeing she had a basketful of potatoes chased her down Truchot Street shouting at her, and although she was a girl of only thirteen or fourteen gave her a hard kick with his army boot. Strict laws forbade criticism of the German forces, or remarks suggesting they deserved to be dealt with by British forces. A waitress who put down four meals and said, 'four dinners for four gangsters', received a month in prison.

One well-known case was the imprisonment of Mrs Winifred Green, who worked as a waitress at the Royal Hotel. Also working there was a pro-German woman who constantly taunted Mrs Green so she could inform on her. Matters reached a crisis during staff lunch one day. Mrs Green was asked if she wanted any rice pudding. You can have it, said the woman, if you say 'Heil Hitler' first. Mrs Green's reply: 'To Hell with Hitler for a rice pudding – and one made of skim milk too!', led to her appearance before a military court on 13 October 1941 when she received a sentence of six months. After two weeks in the Island gaol, and several days in

Granville Prison, she was sent to Caen to serve her sentence.

Other incidents were more violent. In October 1941 a hairdresser had been sent over to Sark where a German soldier set on him calling him a bloody Swiss, hit him in the jaw and almost kicked him out of an hotel. Not content with that he followed him along the lane shooting with his revolver. Sentences gradually increased so that a local boxer who struck a German ended up on the Continent for the rest of the war. Frank Mallett, owner of an engineering and joiner's business at St Sampson's had an argument with a German interfering with his lathe, and when he pushed the German back the soldier fell over. Mallett was sentenced to pay a fine of 5,000 marks, and to six months in prison.

Mrs Tremayne heard of a man put in prison for saying, 'I wish a few Spitfires would come and settle them', and a particularly tragic case of this kind was that of John Ingrouille. A 15-year-old boy of limited intelligence, he worked as a cook, and made silly remarks, including one that he could find 500 lads to fight the German soldiers. He was informed against by a mother and her daughter and sentenced in December 1940. He was left in Caen Prison for 18 months, and then moved to Germany. His parents begged for the case to be retried. It was, in Germany, and the sentence then increased. Ingrouille remained in prison to the end of the war, by which time his health was undermined, and he died at Brussels on 13 June 1945 on the way home. This was one reality of German occupation: informers, a savage sentence, and death.

Islanders had little means of redress against soldiers, particularly when poor people were unaccompanied in the courts by Island lawyers as was often the case. On 25 August 1944, Mr Jehan of St Saviour's in Guernsey disturbed a soldier digging up his potatoes. He and his son gave chase. The German killed Mr Jehan and wounded his son. No action was taken, and von Aufsess simply saw the event as the 'first intimation of the coming battle for food'. In the one case of rape by a soldier, however, the Germans acted fairly. A drunken soldier raped an elderly woman in Guernsey. The Germans provided a translator and allowed the woman to give evidence from a separate room during the court martial. He was sentenced to death, and almost certainly shot in France.

In the mean time, co-operation by the Island authorities, and the vast majority of Islanders, and the lack of serious sabotage or resistance made life for German soldiers in the Islands preferable to that anywhere else in Europe. When they arrived the Germans were described as 'living like fighting cocks'. The rate of exchange was fixed at five occupation marks to the pound. So eager were they to buy anything in sight that they purchased rationed goods and food stocks in spite of prohibitions. Described as leeches and locusts the soldiers rushed to buy cigarettes, wine, toiletries, jewellery, and clothes. Mrs Cortvriend described them in women's clothes shops where, 'There was a continental absence of prudishness among the shoppers who showed no diffidence in presenting their wives most intimate garments, much the worse for wear, to match for size, and a stalwart grey-clad soldier holding a dainty piece of feminine lingerie against his own body to judge of its measurement was a customary sight and afforded much amusement to shop assistants.'

A German soldier manhandling a 50 mm PAK anti-tank gun into position somewhere on Guernsey

A German sentry at the Forest Hotel in Guernsey. A squadron of Hurricanes had been based there for a short while in the spring of 1941 – hence the notice

East Lynne Farm, Fauvic Beach on Grouville Bay, Jersey. The home of Wilfred Bertram and his relatives, they were responsible for helping at least eight groups of escapers, including two American POWs

A small German patrol boat of the kind used to accompany fishing vessels or help stop escapers, in St Peter Port harbour

Searchlight and machine-gun at Château à l'Etoc on Alderney of the kind used to prevent escapes from beaches

Chouet Tower on Guernsey. This was one of seven *marinepeilestande* designed as communication and observation posts in case of possible invasion

So many clothes and so much footwear was bought that this helped to create serious shortages for Islanders who were forced to make wooden shoes, or clothes from curtains and blankets before the end of the occupation. In ordinary shops Germans demanded to be served first, and this was made law in March 1944. Special shops were set up for the soldiers to buy imported goods from France, and this naturally added to the bitterness of Islanders gradually deprived of almost every basic domestic item.

There was good living for the troops, except in Alderney, as far as accommodation and administrative offices were concerned because they moved into empty hotels, and took the best (unmined) beaches for themselves. From September 1941 they had priority in all places of entertainment, and to the local cinemas and theatres were added soldatenheims or military clubs. In St Helier the officers' club was at Fort D'Auvergne, while NCOs and other ranks had theirs at the Mayfair Hotel. One for all ranks was situated at St Brelade's Bay Hotel. In Alderney, where accommodation was limited, the Connaught was taken over by the commandant, and the soldatenheim was located in a former Roman Catholic school. In Sark the Germans burnt down their first hotel, the Bel Air, and moved to the Dixcart and Stocks until the commando raid forced them inland to the Manoir. The Germans commandeered bicycles, motor cycles and cars and used them with reckless abandon, driving on the wrong side of the road. Orders against this had little effect, and although the rule of the road was changed to the right in 1941 serious accidents continued.

Brothels for the troops were established in 1942, with the exception of Alderney where only the Organization Todt had one, and the soldiers had to make do with groups of imported French women. Guernsey had two brothels at St Martin's for the officers, and in Saumarez Street for NCOs and the ranks. In Jersey there was only one at the Victor Hugo Hotel at Grève d'Azette. The Todt brothels were at George Street in St Peter Port, while in Jersey their first one was loyally demolished for the fortifications, and was re-located at the Norman House Hotel.

By and large the discipline of the German army was good. Returning from church in July 1942, Mrs Tremayne saw an open air court martial taking place on the lawn of Le Manoir where three soldiers were being tried. A crowd of onlookers leaned on the wall watching while the officer roared and bellowed at the accused in whose eyes, 'I have never seen such terror or fear'. But in the case of three offences: dangerous driving, drinking, and theft, the courts for all their severity did not prevent the crimes; and after June 1944 theft turned to scavenging for food on a massive scale involving considerable violence. The Germans had to admit failure to check it in spite of death sentences. Although Julia Tremayne paid tribute to German efforts to curb drunkenness at Christmas-time in 1942 it was not really curbed. In July next year she complained troops got drunk at the Vieux Clos, smashed all the furniture, and then drove round the Island on a further binge.

Above all, the military authorities failed to curb looting which broke army regulations, the German occupation terms, and the Hague

Convention. Down to the summer of 1944 it was mainly concerned with theft of property; afterwards with stealing food. All too often looting was accompanied with senseless destruction which added to that caused by billeting and building fortifications. As early as August 1940, unit commanders were alerted to this problem, but from the first many Germans acted as if they were in a conquered territory. One of Mrs Cortvriend's friends had troops billeted in his house, and was invited to attend a party there by the officer. When he turned up, he found all their most valuable possessions in use even down to his clothes which were hanging up to dry on the linen line. He lost some of these possessions when the unit moved, and others lost not only moveables, but fittings like baths, mantelpieces, and basins. These war crimes went unpunished, and inflicted additional misery on thousands of Islanders, particularly on evacuees who returned to find their property destroyed or looted. Order followed order, but in 1943 reported incidents of looting were running at over 330 a month.

After June 1941, Island service had an added attraction for the troops; it was not the Russian front. As early as August that year troops assembled at St Peter Port for Russia resisted orders. Some committed suicide; others were shot, and the officers involved were forced to march from the harbour to Vazon and back in bare feet. The remainder were herded on board. Just opposite the Finigan's house was the depot for troops leaving the Island. 'Many a time we have seen these young soldiers hiding in our gardens among the bushes trying to evade the count when they were all lined up in the street. We knew of German soldiers trying to injure themselves to prevent their going on active service. They would deliberately fall over our garden wall into the road below and we did hear that two had died through their head injuries.' Nevertheless some German troops were discontented even with life on the Islands, and occupied their time with drunkenness, sexual licence, and violence. As years passed, the 319th Division felt bored and isolated, and the quality of the troops declined. Mrs Tremayne heard of troops threatening suicide, and several did kill themselves. In May 1944 she heard of 'great restlessness among the German troops'. Once D-Day and fighting in France cut off the Islands there were no more imports from France, no more leave, fraternization was forbidden amidst increasing privations. Desertions occurred, and in one case a Jersey girl was sentenced to death for hiding a deserter. Before the final year of occupation, however, good relations usually prevailed apart from occasional outbursts of anger or bitterness on Islanders' part, and lapses of discipline among the Germans often due to drink. Soldiers were sent on leave to the Island because of the relaxing atmosphere.

The consequences of this relatively friendly situation were serious. The Germans were able to recruit workers, and even forced labour from among civilians, and this benefited the German war effort. Massive German fortifications went unsabotaged, and the Germans were able to shelter and repair planes and ships engaged in the Channel battle, capture Allied personnel, and maintain valuable communications uninterrupted.

The Channel Island guns protected a sweep of the French coastline from direct attack. It may be true that a terrible fate would have awaited the Islanders if they had carried out sabotage, but this terror did not deter people elsewhere in Europe. Mrs Cortvriend pointed out that all Germans, however civilized or pleasant, were cogs in the same war machine, good relations were maintained to help protect the garrison in its war work, and the right balance of force and friendliness secured this protection admirably.

Hitler's *inselwahn* or Island madness about the Channel Islands created the most powerful fortress in Western Europe, the construction and maintenance of which added to the horrors of occupation. By early 1944 one-twelfth of the resources in terms of fortifications and hardware for the whole Atlantic Wall was concentrated on the Islands where 1,623 concrete defences of one sort or another had been built. The Wall could have been ten per cent stronger along its whole length including the Normandy beaches had this material and the efforts of 16,000 Todt workers involved been directed elsewhere. According to Rommel's chief of staff, General Hans Speidel, the Island coastline of 92 miles boasted the same number of heavy batteries and only one less strongpoint than the 620 miles of coastline from Dieppe to St Nazaire. When the garrison surrendered it was not only troops who were captured, but a 1,000 guns, and 50,000 tons of ammunition. Successive commanders in the West opposed this policy, and after D-Day Rommel begged that the forces be withdrawn. Instead they were subjected to a long-range siege, and their absence from the battlefield was among many factors helping defeat the Germans in France. For this error Hitler was almost entirely to blame because of his Island obsession.

Hitler's motivation was confused, contradictory and strategically wrong, but Keitel and Jodl at OKW offered no objection, and the Army High Command (OKH), and Army Group D in the West had perforce to accept. The problems involved were very great – and the allocation of resources therefore correspondingly large. Weather presented a serious hazard as the sinking of two ships in the January gales of 1943 showed. Bringing armaments detached from the Maginot Line to the Islands was bound to expose shipping to Allied air attack. Quarries were opened on the Islands and this in turn necessitated the construction of railway systems to move the material due to the poor roads. 'Difficult terrain', said a report in September 1941, 'will necessitate the employment of considerable construction forces'. Islanders were to be conscripted for several months in 1943, while others helped in paid employment in quarries and power stations, or in transport.

The decision to strengthen the garrison over a fourteen-month period was taken on 15 June 1941 following a report by Keitel, which stated 'the infantry defence of the Channel Islands is insufficient'. Ten days later there was a Führer conference to consider the Islands. Hitler was convinced, 'that raids against the Channel Islands were most likely with the aim of regaining possession of the Islands, and by engaging German forces to prove the willingness of the British to aid Russia. Bold action by the enemy must be expected.'

His thinking on what this action might involve was highly confused. At one point he spoke of small raids on moonless nights in periods of bad weather; at another of larger raids when tide and weather conditions were favourable. Even allowing for full scale attack his preparations were excessive, and a mixture of other reasons was put forward. The British could raid German submarine bases from the Islands if they captured them and, once there, the Islands would become another Malta for them. Strong German control would protect a large part of the French coast, and provide a forward base for Channel communications. In fact, the strategic arguments were all weak; the real reason for the excessive fortification was that as an OKW document said on 10 June 1941, 'consideration must be taken that after the conclusion of peace the Channel Islands will remain German territory and must be unassailable'.

Through the summer months and early autumn of 1941 reinforcement went ahead and 319 Division settled in. Mrs Tremayne noticed large guns and small French tanks arriving on Sark, as well as stocks of timber to build huts for the troops. The garrison there rose to 300. On 5 October, General Schmundt, Hitler's adjutant, came to the Islands and von Schmettow told him he lacked almost every basic requirement for completing their defences. On 8 October and ten days later two OKW meetings considered the Channel Islands and reinforcement and fortification policies were linked together. On 20 October the directive for *eine unangriefbare Festung* in the Islands was issued. Organization Todt, based at St Malo, and, from February 1943 on Cherbourg was ordered to carry out the work, and Dr Fritz Todt himself visited the Islands in November 1942 to organize Operations Jakob (Jersey), Gustav (Guernsey), and Adolf (Alderney). At the meeting, Hitler had demanded not only heavier artillery of every kind but up to 250 strong points. Detailed maps with line illustrations were prepared for each Island (those for Guernsey still survive), and on one occasion the man in charge of them was dismissed for not updating them. Von Schmettow was delighted with the increased importance of his command, and as a Christmas present he sent the Führer a specially commissioned account of the Islands which Schmundt had the pleasure of reading in part to Hitler on Christmas Eve 1941. There was a chorus of opposition from OKH and Army Group D saying the Islands would only duplicate existing defences on the mainland, and offer a hostage to fortune since German prestige would require they should not be surrendered. Hitler simply pressed ahead.

Year by year the fortifications proceeded and were still being built when D-Day slowed them down with the departure of most Todt workers in July 1944. By January 1944, 484,000 cubic metres of concrete fortifications adorned the Islands. In February, the three Islands were declared fortresses and three fortress governors appointed; von Schmettow, Heine, and Schwalm. Next month the Feldkommandantur or civilian military organization was reduced in status to prepare the way for fortress life. There is little doubt that von Schmettow thought the policy mistaken, and more fervent Nazis in the Kriegsmarine began a campaign against him. This was led by Vice-Admiral Friedrich Hüffmeier who, Dönitz told Hitler in November 1944, believed the Islands could hold out to the end of

1945 provided the civilian population was sacrificed. When he eventually became fortress commander in February 1945 Hüffmeier's first order of the day stated, 'I have only one aim: to hold out until final victory', and Mrs Tremayne heard he had said his men would eat grass before he surrendered.

The fortifications constructed were almost bewildering in their number and complexity. Because of the threat of air attack, underground works played an important part involving massive movement of earth and concrete tunnelling. On the main Islands, sixteen tunnels were planned, although only three were fully completed with air-conditioning, central heating, hot and cold water, power, drainage and emergency escape shafts. In Jersey, one at St Lawrence involving the removal of 14,000 tons of earth and absorbed 4,000 tons of concrete. Nine workers were killed by a rock fall and left unburied behind it. On Guernsey there were two tunnels. One by St Sampson's Church was used for munitions; the other at La Vassalerie with one-and-a-half miles of tunnel was used as a hospital. There were 900 medical corps and nurses on the Islands, and the hospitals were able to treat hundreds of wounded from St Malo. During the building of this tunnel, 22 workers were killed, and buried later at Les Vauxbelets.

On Alderney, apart from an escape tunnel for the commandant of Sylt concentration camp, and a few other small tunnels, the main ones were east of the upper Braye Road leading out of St Anne. On Sark, 'the whole Island is burrowed and tunnelled'. A tunnel linking Stocks Hotel with the headquarters at Le Manoir was still being completed and furnished in August 1944.

Inland there were field fortifications, but the main defences were naturally built on the coast or near to it as a second line of resistance. Older military buildings were frequently utilized. On Alderney, Fort Albert; on Guernsey, Castle Cornet and Fort George; and on Jersey, Elizabeth Castle and Fort Henry were among the medieval and Victorian castles that echoed to German commands. Fort George was used for court martials, interrogation, and military or Todt executions while Elizabeth Castle was the Todt punishment laager. Old martello towers and mills were utilized or pulled down if they interrupted the artillery's range. Where there were no such towers, communications required them, and seven *marinepeilstande* unique to the Islands were built like those at Chouet in Guernsey or Les Landes in Jersey.

There was a network of smaller works including fortified posts, machine-gun nests, and machine-gun turrets. Along beaches and bays were the usual barbed-wire, mined stakes, and searchlights, and where beaches provided easy access for landing-craft or vehicles, anti-tank walls six metres high and two metres thick were built. 'Huge concrete walls', said Sinel, 'disfigure many of our lovely bays', although they later proved so durable as to become part of Island sea defences. Above all, there was intensive mining of the Islands. By the end there were no less than 177,925 mines distributed in 305 locations. 'If half the mines they have laid go off, this little Island will go up in smoke', wrote Julia Tremayne.

The only victims of the mines, apart from British commandos in 1943, were accidental ones. On Sark, the Commandant, Major Johann Hinkel was killed by a mine in March 1943 and only a few months later two German soldiers were killed by suspended mines while looking for gulls eggs on the cliffs. Those who suffered most were fishermen whose lives were made a misery by restrictions, and military war games, as well as by the deadly mines. In June 1943, 'Four poor Guernsey fishermen were caught in a minefield last week. Two were killed outright, and the other two, who were good swimmers, were saved, but their boat was blown to bits.'

Mounted in the fortifications was a formidable array of anti-aircraft and other artillery. In Jersey alone there were 15 heavy batteries, containing 59 guns, and 137 anti-aircraft positions including 37 with the renowned 88mm 'flak' guns. Practices were frequent, with shells roaring over the Islands, and many gun positions brought disruption and misery to families that lived near them. Molly Finigan wrote that, 'Although our curfew hours were 9 p.m. or sometimes 10 p.m. – some early mornings Germans would knock on our doors and tell us to get out and leave the house – usually this order came at approximately 4 or 5 a.m. "*Achtung, achtung*", would be the cry. All along the top of Les Cotils were several gun emplacements with very big guns and we would all have to leave the house while the practicising of these great guns was carried out. All doors and windows had to be left open and off we had to go.'

Besides the daily misery inflicted there was a more permanent result – the systematic damage to historical sites, property, and attractive views. Mrs Cortvriend summarized the effect of the fortifications on the environment as, 'Famous beauty spots became vistas of incredible ugliness covered with huge excavations, massive concrete blockhouses and gun emplacements. Houses, cottages, gardens, trees, or anything that was in the way were ruthlessly swept aside before the encroaching tide of steel and concrete.

Part 2

Ruled by the Third Reich

4

The German Rulers and their Organizations

Hitler's new Order in Europe, of which the Channel Islands formed a tiny fragment, was not based on any rational theory of government or long considered plan for European unity. He knew how to force conquered territories to pay the cost of their own occupation. Up to March 1944, the Channel Islands paid over two million marks in occupation costs although later the Germans bore the brunt of the fortification costs. Hitler's government knew, too, how to imprison, enslave, execute and torture the virtually endless enemies of an Aryan-dominated Europe. 'Shoot everyone who gives you a black look', he once remarked, and his personal responsibility for such decrees as the Final Solution, hostage-taking, and commando extermination is well known. All Führer orders increased and never decreased suffering. Gradually the powers of the Gestapo and SS prevailed until much of Europe, in Michel's famous phrase, 'became a prison until such time as it became a graveyard'.

But in day to day administration Hitler's empire was an administrative jungle. Rival individuals and organizations jockeyed for power, and systems created for one purpose were soon overturned by some new Führer order, or Reich authority responsible only to himself. Each Western country had a different regime. The Channel Isles were in the war zone, and could not have a civilian government, or even the presence and help of Switzerland, the British protecting power during the war. The Islands therefore had a military government, and eventually became four fortresses with a resident civilian population.

Those who arrived in charge of the occupying forces in June 1940 were temporary commanders, and their rule lasted eleven weeks. Major Albrecht Lanz on Guernsey and Captain Erich Gussek on Jersey were, however, responsible for issuing on 2 and 8 July the ordinances regulating the German government, stating the Germans had 'taken over the military power of the Islands', leaving the existing civilian government and law courts intact, but subject to veto by the commandant. Sark was to be automatically included in any Guernsey orders, while Alderney had no government until February 1941, and no formal commander until July that year. The ease with which the Germans accomplished their task, and their belief that they were going on to the mainland before long, meant

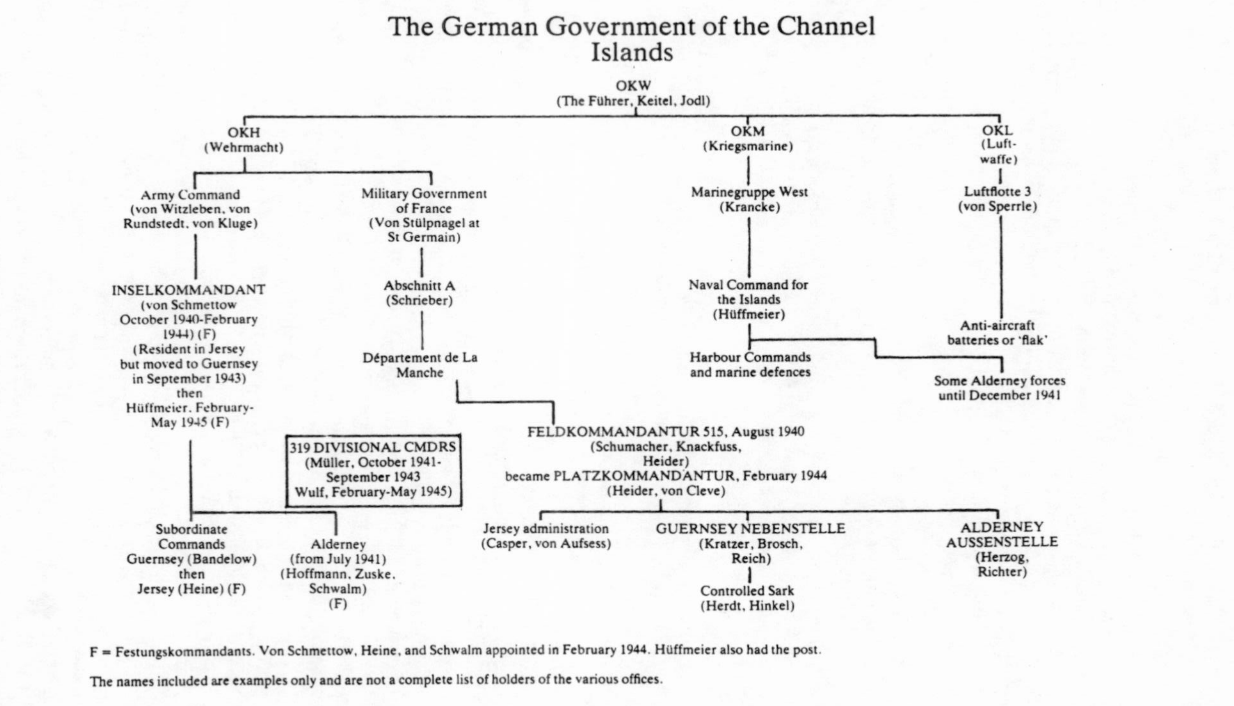
The German Government of the Channel Islands
OKW (The Führer, Keitel, Jodl)
OKH (Wehrmacht)
OKM (Kriegsmarine)
OKL (Luftwaffe)
Army Command (von Witzleben, von Rundstedt, von Kluge)
Military Government of France (Von Stülpnagel at St Germain)
Marinegruppe West (Krancke)
Luftflotte 3 (von Sperrle)
INSELKOMMANDANT (von Schmettow October 1940-February 1944) (F) (Resident in Jersey but moved to Guernsey in September 1943) then Hüffmeier, February-May 1945 (F)
Abschnitt A (Schrieber)
Naval Command for the Islands (Hüffmeier)
Anti-aircraft batteries or 'flak'
Département de La Manche
Harbour Commands and marine defences
Some Alderney forces until December 1941
FELDKOMMANDANTUR 515, August 1940 (Schumacher, Knackfuss, Heider) became PLATZKOMMANDANTUR, February 1944 (Heider, von Cleve)
319 DIVISIONAL CMDRS (Müller, October 1941-September 1943 Wulf, February-May 1945)
Subordinate Commands Guernsey (Bandelow) then Jersey (Heine) (F)
Alderney (from July 1941) (Hoffmann, Zuske, Schwalm) (F)
Jersey administration (Casper, von Aufsess)
GUERNSEY NEBENSTELLE (Kratzer, Brosch, Reich)
ALDERNEY AUSSENSTELLE (Herzog, Richter)
Controlled Sark (Herdt, Hinkel)
F = Festungskommandants. Von Schmettow, Heine, and Schwalm appointed in February 1944. Hüffmeier also had the post.
The names included are examples only and are not a complete list of holders of the various offices.

that the early months of occupation as far as the administrators on the Islands were concerned were a period of surprisingly good relations. Ambrose Sherwill, in his Radio Bremen broadcast on 8 August 1940, said 'The Lieutenant-Governor and Bailiff, Mr Victor Carey, and every other Island official has been, and is being treated, with every consideration and with the greatest courtesy by the German military authorities ...'

Speaking to the states later he said 'May this occupation be a model to the world – on one hand tolerance on the part of the military authority and courtesy and correctness on the part of the occupying forces, and on the other, dignity and courtesy and exemplary behaviour on the part of the civilian population; perfect obedience to law and order, conformity – the strictest conformity – with blackout regulations and with orders and regulations issued by the German commandant and the civil authorities.'

The Germans stated that if good relations continued, 'the life and property of the population will be respected and guaranteed'. They broke their side of the bargain, but the Island governments kept theirs.

On 9 August 1940 the military government of the Channel Islands was established. It consisted of two parts: a military organization for civilian affairs, and an occupation garrison under military command. The administration came under the military government of France run from St Germain by Otto and, from January 1942, Heinrich-Karl von Stülpnagel. The Islands were part of District A, Département de La Manche, headed by General Schreiber, and were run by Feldkommandantur 515, formed in Munich, which had seen service in Luxemburg, before transferring to the Channel Islands. Their headquarters were in Victoria College House on Jersey while day-to-day business on the Island was handled from offices in the town hall in York Street, St Helier. On Guernsey their headquarters were at Grange Lodge Hotel, and their St Peter Port office was in the Islands Hotel (now the Savoy). Although there were arguments about jurisdiction, and an external enquiry, the structure remained unchanged until 19 May 1944 when the administration's status was reduced to that of Platzkommandantur (PKI), and the final appeal in the courts was transferred to the military.

The first Feldkommandant was Major Friedrich Schumacher, an elderly, portly man, who was in the Islands for a year before he was replaced in October 1941 by Major Friedrich Knackfuss. He left in February 1944, and was replaced by Major I.V. Heider who became Platzkommandant and remained in that position until February 1945 when a shake-up took place in the personnel of the occupation government. The branch or *nebenstelle* in Guernsey was run by Major Kratzer, and two Sonderführer (a title with no precise equivalent in English) were responsible for Alderney and an outpost at Granville handling economic and shipping matters. Alderney was brought into the administrative structure in 1941, with the appointment of SF Heinz Herzog who established his headquarters in Lloyd's Bank in Victoria Street, St Anne.

There is general agreement that in spite of harsh orders and violations of the Hague Convention which FK515 administrators were required to issue, their conduct of affairs was often intelligent and sympathetic. The

Feldkommandants could act severely. Schumacher ordered sixty Guernsey Islanders to patrol telephone wires at night for a fortnight after there had been a minor case of sabotage. Knackfuss arrested ten Jersey citizens as possible hostages when a seditious news sheet was produced. But in France there would have been shootings. Schumacher and the Military Commander had early shown in the case of Nicolle and Symes they wished to handle matters their way in the Islands and using the excuse that they had given their words as officers they overruled St Germain and prevented the execution of the two men. Knackfuss strongly objected to the deportation orders in 1942, but he could not defy a direct Führer order. Heider regarded by von Aufsess as a moderate was deprived of his post when extreme policies prevailed in February 1945.

Courteous relations between senior officers and the Islands' upper class were the rule. On Sark after receiving Lanz courteously, Hathaway continued to receive German officers from various Islands, and was allowed guests like Countess Blücher and Countess Radziwill. On Guernsey, Prince Fürst von Oettingen was a member of the Kommandantur and Hathaway dealt with him on important matters. He was 'charming' to both her and her American husband, Robert. They had mutual friends and 'talked as friends do, and it seemed incredible that we were enemies'. When Sibyl's son, Lionel, died in a German raid on Liverpool von Schmettow conveyed his sympathies; she did likewise two years later when his son was killed. This relationship was to help the Germans, and encourage collaboration. It smelt of a privileged existence at one level in society for those fraternizing with German administrators. After the war, the Hathaways and other members of the ruling class visited their wartime colleagues in Bavaria.

The occupation garrison which formed the military aspect of German government soon received its inselkommandant, Major Graf Rudolf von Schmettow, who arrived in Jersey on 27 September 1940. Von Schmettow, a dignified, courtly, tall Prussian of the old school, was ideally suited for the post, and he was a skilful commander for the first four years of the occupation. He was under the command of Army Group D in the West successively headed by von Witzleben, von Rundstedt, Kluge and Model. He was a nephew of von Rundstedt's who visited him on the Islands. He was accompanied by his Chief of Staff, similarly courteous and tall, and sporting a monocle, Count von Helldorf. Although von Schmettow was to remain inselkommandant officially until February 1945 his power was effectively reduced in September the previous year when von Helldorf was replaced as his chief of staff by a fanatical Nazi. Thereafter von Schmettow became increasingly harsh in his rule. At first his headquarters were on Jersey at St Monaco in St Saviours, and from April 1941 at the Hotel Metropole. He lived in the former Government House waited on by the same servants that had served the British lieutenant-governor. A subordinate command was created on Guernsey under Major Bandelow. In September 1943, von Schmettow transferred his headquarters to Guernsey, and it became necessary to make a subordinate command in Jersey instead. This was occupied by a Nazi,

Major Siegfried Heine who later joined the headquarters staff of Vice-Admiral Hüffmeier, the last commandant, and devoted adherent of Hitler.

In Alderney, a separate command was created in July 1941 under Captain Carl Hoffmann, but it was not until the end of the year that all troops on the Island came fully under the Island Commander's authority. By then there had been several changes in command although Hoffmann remained as an adviser, and was promoted before being transferred to Jersey. Early in 1942, Lieutenant-Colonel Zuske became the Island commander, and he was succeeded in November 1943 by Lieutenant-Colonel Schwalm, who remained in charge until the surrender. When the Islands were made a fortress in February 1944, von Schmettow, Heine, and Schwalm became the respective festungskommandants of Guernsey, Jersey and Alderney. Sark had its own succession of Island commanders, but they were usually majors or captains, under the control of Guernsey.

Similar good relations existed with this military hierarchy as far as the Islands' rulers were concerned. Alexander Coutanche, who von Aufsess described as the 'wily' Bailiff of Jersey, illustrated his privileged position, and the closeness of relations between occupied and occupier at his social level in one passage of autobiography. 'One morning I looked out of my bedroom window and saw a German strolling about on my lawn, which was very precious to me. He was taking measurements, fairly obviously for digging a trench. I dressed and went down, and in the faltering German which I had acquired by this time, asked him what was going on. "Oh", he said, "we're digging trenches all round here, it's inside the military zone, and we have decided to put a trench across this grass." ' Coutanche rang the butler at Government House where von Schmettow lived, and complained, and within a short time an officer arrived to order the trench to be dug elsewhere.

This incident shows Coutanche's earlier statement in his memoirs that he agreed with von Schmettow that there must be no social contact of any kind between them was untrue. Like Hathaway, Coutanche was willing to mix on social terms with the occupiers. Von Aufsess' diary is revealing because he was keen to show how well he and other Germans had got on with the Islanders or rather the well-off Islanders. In December 1944, for example, von Aufsess asked Coutanche, Carey and his sister-in-law to lunch at the Royal Hotel, when Coutanche had gone over to Guernsey to receive the first Red Cross food ship to arrive in the Islands. Von Aufsess described it as 'an excellent meal', while Julia Tremayne was lamenting in her diary a few days later, 'how the Germans can let us starve and their own troops as well, beats me'. When von Aufsess had tea with the Coutanches in January 1945 he found the atmosphere 'pleasantly informal and stimulating'.

There can be no doubt that such pleasantness on the Germans' part was part of an agreed policy, and even someone like von Aufsess, who was a genuinely civilized man, was a cog in the machine of the Reich. He saw 'our personal contacts over the years' as being valuable in the task of administering the Islands because, 'such a strong bond of personal liking and understanding [was formed] that all questions that might have led to difficulties were quickly cleared up.' He spoke of the velvet glove which had 'served them well', and saw his task as building golden bridges in plenty.

This policy was not only administratively valuable, but enabled the Germans to enjoy life. Von Schmettow lived in Government House, and Schumacher and his successors at Linden Court, waited on by the former servants. Von Aufsess who lived at White Lodge commented when he moved to Linden Court that he had spent three years 'happy time' in his former house. The officers had their own soldatenheims and special clubs. As late as April 1945 when an Island official called to see him at Langford House, von Aufsess could write that sitting on the smooth lawn, 'with the wisteria, tulips and fruit trees in blossom all around it was difficult to imagine the war,' and this at a time when Islanders were tearing down trees in the main streets for firewood, and there were no fruit or vegetables for them.

Although German officers enjoyed almost halcyon conditions in their private lives and relations with the Island rulers this was only the background to the serious business of day-to-day military occupation, particularly after the decisions in 1941 to reinforce the garrison, and build the fortifications. There was plenty of hard work involved in carrying out these orders, and many practices and war games were necessary to test the defences. The arrival in June 1941 of 319 Division to replace 216 Division troops, was followed in October by the arrival of their divisional commander, Major-General Erich Müller, who outranked von Schmettow and, while he was in the Islands until September 1943, became the inselkommandant in his own right. To avoid any clash with von Schmettow, it was decided to establish divisional headquarters near the signals headquarters in Guernsey although this brought a heavier burden of troops to the poorer of the two main Islands. The command complex was based on a house called La Corbinerie off the Oberlands Road where command bunkers were built for the infantry and artillery commanders with drawbridges and camouflage defences, barracks and hospital facilities. Müller was a short, bucolic looking bachelor of irascible temper. Because he was primarily a field commander, Müller had little to do with administration, and made little impression before he left for the Russian front. Von Schmettow then regained full command and shifted his headquarters to the bunkers on Guernsey.

Alderney was the most heavily fortified of the Islands, and took slightly longer to bring into the command structure. Elements of 89 Division on the Island remained under the command of Cherbourg until December 1941. In July that year, Captain Carl Hoffmann arrived to take command, although he did not retain office for long because it was decided the Island should be under the command of a lieutenant-colonel. However, he remained at headquarters to give advice. In 1945 Hoffmann was interrogated at the London Cage, and then interned. According to some sources he was offered for trial to the Russians on the dubious grounds that all Alderney prisoners had been Russians, and it was therefore their responsibility to act on crimes against their nationals. It was said, and has been repeated, since that Hoffmann was publicly executed at Kiev in late

1945, although Solomon Steckoll who looked at over three thousand 'Carl Hoffmanns' in German records has argued that he was released from a British POW camp in April 1948 and died at Hamelin in March 1974.

Hoffmann was less guilty of presiding over atrocities on Alderney than his successors, Lieutenant-Colonels Zuske and Schwalm. It was under Zuske that recorded deaths of Todt prisoners reached their height in the winter of 1942–3. When it became obvious the Allies might include the Islands in their invasion plans Schwalm issued a chilling order stating that 'the concentration camp prisoners will immediately be collected in Sylt Camp and kept under the strictest supervision by SS guard personnel. Attempts at breakout or escape will be rendered impossible. In no circumstances will prisoners be allowed to fall into the hands of the enemy.' The camp commander, Braun, was to act in accordance with orders direct from Himmler.

Subservience to the military increased early in 1944 when the civil commander's authority was reduced from Feld – to Platz – commander, and the military commanders of the three Islands – von Schmettow, Heine, and Schwalm were made Festungs – commanders. D-Day was followed by the complete isolation of the Islands as a result of the successive captures of Cherbourg, Granville, and St Malo. They became fortresses under siege with civilians imprisoned inside subject to the laws of war. This produced severer policies and changes in personnel which left the Islands under the rule of a dedicated group of Nazis determined to hold out at the very least to the end of 1945. Then the Islands were stripped for action by the removal of the Todt organization and concentration camp inmates, reinforced by naval units and personnel, and required to play an operational role on the flank of the battle for Normandy. German submarines were repaired, and naval craft escaped to the Islands from French ports. The military were involved in offensive action to help the Island of Cèzembre hold out, and in attack on Granville.

Under attack, fearing invasion, and furious at Allied victory in Normandy which cut them off, the mood of the German occupiers changed, and even von Schmettow had to realize that he was first and foremost a soldier at war. In July 1944, another event occurred which made the Nazi officers more determined to be savage if necessary to ensure that the Islands held out. The Bomb Plot to kill Hitler by officers and aristocrats failed, and it was well known that some in the Island administration like von Aufsess had relatives involved on the fringes of this conspiracy. Von Aufsess told Duret Aubin, the Jersey attorney-general, that he wished the plot had succeeded, and then pledged him to secrecy.

As soon as D-Day took place the Fortress policy began to operate, and Coutanche was given a proclamation by Heine, the fortress commander, setting the new scene in stark perspective: 'I expect the population of Jersey to keep its head, to remain calm, and to refrain from any acts of sabotage and from hostile acts against the German forces, even should the fighting spread to Jersey. At the first signs of unrest or trouble I will close the streets to every [*sic*] traffic and will secure hostages. Attacks against the German forces will be punished by death.'

On the day of invasion German troops appeared in full battle order, and Berlin Radio incorrectly announced British parachutists had landed. The artillery roared into action against Allied planes. Guards were placed on all essential strong points, the telephone service closed, schools shut, and all social gatherings were forbidden. Mrs Cortvriend noticed Germans looking worried for the first time. By coincidence, von Schmettow had been summoned to a mainland divisional commanders conference at Rennes on 4 June, and was in Granville on the way back as air raids on the Islands began. However, he came across in a boat through the raids and landed on 7 June.

Von Schmettow was loyal to his supreme commander, and sent a wireless message to Berlin declaring that, 'The three Island fortresses conscious of their strength and following the example of other fortresses, will faithfully hold out to the last. With this in mind we salute the Führer and the Fatherland'. When the Americans made two half-hearted attempts on 9 and 22 September to start negotiations for surrender by reopening the cable to France, and then by direct parley with a major from Eisenhower's headquarters, von Schmettow abruptly rejected them, worried that his own position was under threat. Until June 1944 control had been exercised by the military government in St Germain, but clearly war prevented this administrative system from operating. On 25 October 1944 control was invested in Marinegruppe West under the command of Admiral Krancke who from the comparative comfort of Bad Schwalbach and under orders from Admiral Dönitz was to insist on the no-surrender policy which would involve the Islanders and German troops in months of prolonged suffering.

The storm petrel heralding this change was Vice-Admiral Friedrich Hüffmeier, naval commander in the Channel Isles region, who arrived on 30 June to replace von Helldorf as von Schmettow's chief of staff in view of the increased naval role in affairs. Hüffmeier was the former commander of the *Scharnhorst*, and in spite of his avuncular appearance he was a ruthless Kriegsmarine Nazi determined to hold the Islands at all costs, and deeply suspicious of the existing generals whom he saw as being too close to the Island rulers. At the end of July his first report to Krancke stressed that nothing was being done to strengthen the Islands for a long siege by bringing in more supplies or evacuating the civilian population. Von Schmettow was certainly pessimistic because by this time the blockade was cutting mail supplies, and an order for long-range planes to supply the Islands could not be carried out. Von Aufsess noted that, 'the first long term report on the besieged fortress has been drawn up. We can hold out until the end of December. After that famine is inevitable.' Indeed another estimate said that only 45 days supply was left.

Hüffmeier had three solutions: cut supplies to troops; cut supplies to Islanders; then cut-off all supplies to Islanders and force their evacuation or supply by the British or their mass starvation on the Islands. Keitel, Jodl, Dönitz and Krancke supported these severe proposals, and after a second report from Hüffmeier spoke of defeatist tallk in the garrison,

OKW acted on 18 September and Keitel issued a directive cutting civilian rations to a minimum, saying that if supplies still proved inadequate the civilians would be *abgeschoben*, i.e. pushed over the British, a vague phrase whose purpose was made clear in a further clause stating that: 'An Order will follow for the complete stopping of rations to the civilian population, and for measures to inform the British government that this has been done.'

Next day the Swiss protecting power was informed of the German plan to withdraw supplies and a long-drawn-out battle to persuade Churchill to send relief began with tragic consequences for the starving Islanders. The policy naturally won the strong backing of Nazis on the Islands so that Heine could warn that all private stocks might be confiscated on Jersey by military necessity. Von Aufsess was shocked by a document circulated by someone in Military Intelligence saying that, 'the civilian population following a brief ultimatum to Great Britain, should be abandoned to starvation straight away. They should be rounded up in camps, where they would be cut off from any further food supplies.'

Von Schmettow knew he was being watched by military intelligence, and he decided to make it clear to the Island governments that he backed a tough policy. This he did in a letter to Coutanche in Jersey on 25 September, also sent to Carey on Guernsey on 23 October when the bailiffs complained about decreasing food supplies, and dared to warn von Schmettow he might be held accountable after the war for unnecessary restrictions on supplies. 'The necessities of war', said von Schmettow, 'cannot be disregarded'. They were now cut-off and 'I can no longer provide for the civilian population'. Even if things came to the worst, he said, and a calamitous situation arose for the population 'this would not in any way alter the case', and Britain would be to blame in the first place as the besieging force. Coutanche's and Carey's fond belief that they were dealing with civilized men vanished, and von Schmettow made this very plain ending, 'I must also abstain from personal conversation' following criticisms made of German policy. A non-fraternization order for all troops soon followed.

In his 1945 New Year message von Schmettow told the troops they had a hard year ahead of them, and there would have to be more sacrifices. The Inselkommandant had done all he could to use the forces at his disposal offensively to help the Normandy front, and the Kriegsmarine. During the siege of St Malo von Schmettow sent the hospital ship *Bordeaux* to the besieged city on 7 August escorted by two other vessels, and brought off some 600 wounded as well as about 90 unwounded troops. The Commander in St Malo was able to order vessels to leave for the Channel Islands and nine did so. He was determined to hold out in the fortress of St Servan, and ordered troops on the Island of Cèzembre under the command of Oblt. Seuss to fight to the finish. Requests for help reached the communications bunker on Guernsey, and von Schmettow despatched two ships with supplies. One boat returned, but the other one went aground in the night, and was sunk by the Americans off Cèzembre next day.

This action enabled Seuss to reject an American offer of surrender, and the men had to stay there two nights while the Island was bombarded by the USAAF. A vessel with ammunition was then sent from St Helier and the men from the second boat taken off together with wounded, and 22 unwounded Italians. Nightly visits were tried to help sustain the tiny garrison who were subjected to bombardment by a French battleship, the dropping of napalm bombs, and aircraft rocket strikes. Hüffmeier ordered the *Bordeaux* out a second time, but it was captured and taken to Portland. Hüffmeier radioed not to surrender, but bad weather prevented the next relieving force and on 2 September the garrison surrendered 15 days after the fall of St Malo and a siege which cost the Germans 300 casualties.

Just before Christmas a number of Germans managed to escape from their POW camp near Granville, and in an American patrol boat reached St Helier with details of the harbour and the American positions. A model of the port was constructed and a raid in force planned by von Schmettow and Hüffmeier. It was scheduled for the night of 6/7 February but had to be called off, and so by the time it did take place on the night of 8/9 March Hüffmeier was able to claim the credit. The ships used were six mine-sweepers, three artillery carriers, two landing-craft, three MTBs, and a tug, and 600 men were involved.

Five ships took up positions to hold off relieving forces, and two mine-sweepers entered the harbour under the covering fire of three others. Meanwhile, MTBs landed assault parties of engineers to destroy installations, naval ratings to place charges on moored ships, Luftwaffe men to immobilize the anti-aircraft guns, a party of 12 to destroy the radar station, and a prize party. A force of infantry created a diversionary attack on the Hotel des Bains to cover these forces. The Germans controlled the port for an hour and a half in spite of American attacks. Moored ships had their mechanisms smashed, and port installations were demolished. A British coaster, the *Eskwood*, was towed out, but found to contain few supplies. Only the attack on the radar station failed. Prisoners were taken, including a party of Americans in their pyjamas from the Hotel des Bains. Attempts by naval forces to stop the raid failed with an American submarine chaser and possibly another vessel being sunk. On their way back the force put out of action a signal station on the Chausey Islands, and returned in triumph having lost one dead and five wounded and but one ship. They had taken 30 prisoners and released 55 Germans. Dönitz convinced Hitler that it was all Hüffmeier's doing, and Hüffmeier replied that he could hold the Islands for a year, and planned a second raid in April.

In spite of von Schmettow's efforts, Hüffmeier continued to undermine him in his reports, and at last in February 1945 orders came that von Schmettow was to retire on health grounds. Changes in personnel then took place. Hüffmeier took Major-General Dini as his chief of staff, and, as he clearly could not command 319 Division, Major-General Rudolf Wulf was flown in from the Russian front. Heine was promoted to Major-General and became Hüffmeier's right-hand man. The Platzkommandantur was also shaken up. Heider was replaced by Captain von

Cleve, and Captain Reich took over in Guernsey. The task of these dedicated Nazis was formidable since the German army was going to pieces as it starved slowly to death. Soldiers died trying to get sea-birds eggs on the cliffs or poisoned themselves eating hemlock. Sedition in the forces had to be severely repressed, and this led to attacks on Hüffmeier and Wulf by troops maddened with despair and hunger.

Hüffmeier and his colleagues were determined to deal with those officers they believed wanted to surrender. By now von Aufsess was terrified he would be arrested, and had planned his escape from Jersey. He wrote later that he had identity documents as a French labourer, bearing his photograph and duly stamped by his own office. His fellow conspirators were young local people, two men and a girl whose sailing boat lay in Gorey Harbour. With his help they fitted it up with two outboard motors, a supply of petrol and a week's rations.

Von Cleve was suspicious of von Helldorf and von Aufsess, and said they should be shot. Von Helldorf was placed under house arrest, and on 28 April he was banished to the Island of Herm. Von Aufsess was then transferred to Guernsey on 14 April disrupting his escape plans, and he remained desperately worried to the end of the occupation.

Having squashed discontent in the administration, Hüffmeier set out to restore the garrison's morale with the issue of 30 pages of new standing orders. Drilling began again, and proper guards were mounted outside German headquarters buildings. When he doubted the loyalty of Russian troops he sent them to Alderney and Sark, and on Alderney there was a court martial in April 1945 after which two soldiers were executed. The Islanders were also cowed by severe orders ending with one issued on 3 May which stated that: 'The German authorities are determined to maintain and have the power to enforce the maintenance of law and order until the end of the occupation. There must therefore be no public marches, assemblies or demonstrations. Those who transgress this order will be most severely dealt with ...'

Had the Islanders known it, behind the scenes more drastic measures were often debated. Von Aufsess noted that at one discussion on taking hostages he was the only one to oppose the idea, and on 12 April von Cleve ordered the drawing up of a list of 100 hostages although in the end only 50 names appeared. The extremists wanted to provoke the people so they could finish them off. One German told von Aufsess he wished a soldier would be killed 'then all would go better', and one night in February 1945 pro-Nazi officers ordered troops to daub swastikas on hundreds of houses during the night in order to provoke retaliation.

Hüffmeier addressed rallies of the troops in the Forum Cinema in St Helier, and the Regal Cinema in St Peter Port on Hitler's birthday. He even went to Sark to rally troops there. In Jersey he finished by saying, 'Passionately filled with the belief in the justice of our National Socialist conception of the world in the age breaking upon us, from our present pain, and with the certainty of German victory, as Commander of the defence of the Channel Islands I will carry out plainly and without compromise, strictly but justly, the mandate given to me by the Führer.'

Perhaps Hüffmeier did not realize that before he could even make this speech intense security preparations had to be made against his own troops. In Sark he ordered troops to pile their arms to one side, and told them they would be sent to the Eastern front if they did not resist. Court martials and guard duties continued to the end, and at his last parade Hüffmeier ordered troops only to salute with the Nazi salute when they met the British.

German military government in the Channel Islands had been lenient in some respects: at first, when they thought the occupation would not last; later, because it suited them to build good relations for the benefit of the garrison; and most frequently when they were dealing with people in their own class among the Island rulers. But their occupation rule was in the end as destructive, futile, and negative as Fascist and military rule was in the rest of Fortress Europe. The goodwill and work of those like von Aufsess and Knackfuss, was never more than icing on the cake. The real substance of occupation was a military machine maintaining itself in power by overwhelming force, threatening savage penalties, and using secret police informers and quislings. There was a change of personnel for the worse in 1944, but even the so-called moderates like von Schmettow were loyal to the orders of the Führer to stand firm.

Morrison's report as always continues to make extraordinary reading because he concluded after talks with Carey and Coutanche in May 1945, 'I was told that on the whole the behaviour of the Germans had been correct, particularly in the early days ... Early this year however, when Vice-Admiral Hüffmeier took over the command from General Schmettow, there was a stiffening of the German attitude, but apparently without a great deal of difference to the practical outcome.'

To tens of thousands of starving Islanders and soldiers this would have seemed a strange conclusion about the five years of military rule they had just experienced, although the Island rulers would have tended to agree with the Home Secretary.

5

The Island Governments and the Germans

If Hitler's forces had come to Britain in 1940 who would have been the co-operators and collaborators in the ruling class to fulfil the Vichy role of their counterparts elsewhere in Europe? The British ruling class was not put to this test, but it seems unlikely they would have behaved any differently from their European counterparts, particularly as many in the Conservative party had expressed support for Hitler in the past, and there were several pro-Fascist and 'peace' groupings in the establishment.

On the Channel Islands, part of the ruling class was faced with the problem of collaboration or resistance and chose a path described by Cruickshank as 'passive co-operation'. Herbert Morrison, in May 1945, hurried to stress that the Island rulers had 'succeeded to a remarkable extent in getting the best possible treatment from the Germans commensurate with the avoidance of any semblance of collaboration', and this has always been the official line. It was still supported by Cruickshank in his history when he stated that 'it would be difficult to voice any criticism of their conduct of affairs', stressing 'they did so much that was right under circumstances of the greatest possible difficulty'.

Collaboration has become a politically ugly word. It had many meanings shading into one another like the colours of a rainbow, and it was brought about by a variety of motives. Those who collaborated might be gullible, frightened, indifferent, or greedy rather than politically committed. In everyday life collaboration was more a matter of economic gains and social advantages than overt support for German actions or ideals. It was often a matter of turning a blind eye, failing to complain or help resistance, perhaps betraying opposition by informing, lying low and profiting from the black market or German contacts. Such acts are hard to prove in peacetime, but evidence of their committal lies in the preservation of office and livelihood by virtually all the Island rich and rulers during a period when ordinary Islanders suffered the full miseries of German rule.

Nazi subversion policies were well tuned to produce among conquered peoples, organizations and rulers willing to co-operate provided they might 'endure the war, without thereby forfeitiing any of their patriotism'. This phrase occurred in a German report in September 1941 about their rule in the Islands, and neatly encapsulates the policy of 'golden bands' described in the last chapter. The Island rulers faced with this policy came from a narrow wealthy class little accustomed to democratic ways, and it was easy enough for them to mix with people of comparable rank and position from abroad. Hitler ensured the Channel Islands officers and administrators were often drawn from aristocratic, conservative Bavarian and Prussian circles so that men like von Aufsess and von Schmettow might get on with people like Coutanche and Carey.

It was made clear to the Island governments that if they obeyed German orders their own lives would continue relatively undisturbed. They would get the perks and privileges of office, and, if they wanted them, of the black market. They would be free from prosecution for such offences as having a wireless, and would secure exemptions in such matters as billeting or deportation. Their jobs would be safe and their property left intact. It is understandable that almost to a man the Island government officials preferred to co-operate on these terms rather than face the consequences of resistance: the sack, the threat of punishment, or possible use as a hostage. With individual exceptions, and a small number of protests at particular acts, the Island rulers in Sark, Guernsey and Jersey did as they were told for five years. They helped individuals on some occasions, and claimed the overall impact of their policy was to benefit the Islanders by leaving them in office to do their best for their fellow citizens, and reduce German hostility and possible severity.

They could rightly point to a lack of any support from the United Kingdom which left the Island governments isolated and vulnerable. Proud though they were of their ancient liberties and traditions, Island governments were little more than county council officials in a large English county, appointed with no thought that they would have to take major political decisions, or deal with a massive German occupation. Any actions they took might lead to reprisals of the kind they were familiar with in neighbouring France.

In December 1943, an order was issued reducing the Island butter ration by half, and members of the Guernsey administration complained. The Germans insisted on the cuts, and the Island government accepted them. The Reverend John Leale, attorney-general and acting president of the Controlling Committee wrote to Carey, the bailiff, to explain their action. He said that, 'Had the Committee refused to carry out the order it must have ceased to function either by its resignation or by its dismissal, it being too optimistic to think that the Occupying Force would overlook a flat refusal. Others would have had to be found either by the States or the Germans to take our place, and the newcomers' first duty would have to be to do what we refused to do. Rightly or wrongly the Committee came to the conclusion that either resignation or refusal – while they might savour of the heroic – would lead nowhere and would be detrimental to the Islands' interests.'

The decision to act in this way 'rightly or wrongly' had certain consequences. Not only did they carry on the government efficiently and enforce occupation law as required, they issued a string of orders urging people to obey the Germans, report law-breakers, hand over escaped prisoners, oppose escapers, and commit no sabotage. They may have protested in private, but in public they were seen to carry out orders including illegal reduction of rations, enforcement of labour on military sites, prosecution of Jews, and the carrying out of deportation. They made little effort to protect the property of the evacuees entrusted to their care, and rarely provided legal representation at trials of Islanders before the Military Court. Once on the slippery slope of 'passive co-operation' there was no attempt to distinguish between actions and laws they might reasonably be expected to carry out, and those that were degrading or oppressive. It is hard to see this as other than a form of collaboration. The Island rulers played a part, by their example, in encouraging ordinary Islanders to collaborate in various ways as black-marketeers, informers, and Jerry bags.

The German garrison was dependent to some extent on the goodwill and labour of the Islanders for its maintenance. This put the Island governments in a position to bargain, or at least to test the waters of German disapproval. Apart from Sherwill and Le Quesne no officials were imprisoned, and the latter arrest was seen by German officials as an error. There was a certain amount of belt-tightening in the governing class, but by and large they lived a privileged existence throughout the occupation. For them the policy worked. It was a model and moderate occupation. What is far less clear is the degree to which the policy actually helped the Islanders as a whole. There is little evidence that occupation was other than a frightful experience for many, and a miserable one for all except those openly collaborating, involved in the black market, or in government circles.

When the lieutenant-governors withdrew in June 1940 the Home Office issued the following instructions to the Island rulers: 'It is desired by His Majesty's Government that the Bailiff shall discharge the duties of lieutenant-governor, which would be confined to civil duties, and that he should stay at his post and administer the government of the Island to the best of his abilities in the interests of the inhabitants, whether or not he is in a position to receive instructions from His Majesty's Government.'

As a result Carey and Coutanche assumed new roles as heads of the executive, and consulted their fellows on how to organize the government on a wartime footing. This was the only instruction known to have been received by the Island rulers. All that happened when the Germans took over was that the Island Commander exercised a power of veto, and the Island greffier or registrar was required to register as laws both Island and German orders. Alderney was of course deprived of all government with the departure of Judge French, and Sark received no instructions. The Germans simply stated that orders by the Island Commander 'will automatically have effect on the Island of Sark.'

The government of the Islands were in personnel and structure, antiquated and undemocratic, in some parts feudal and autocratic, and this meant that under the Germans the same narrow circle retained their hold on affairs. They continued to exercise their paternalistic role which admirably suited German purposes. The bailiff, Victor Carey's first order after Occupation read: 'The public are notified that no resistance whatever is to be offered to those in military occupation of this Island. The public are asked to be calm, to carry on their lives and work in the usual way, and to obey the orders of the German Commandant'. The adoption of this line by all prominent members of Island governments was certainly some justification for ordinary people on the Islands contemplating resistance to decide that it was futile under such circumstances. As Frank Falla said, 'it was made clear that anyone who stepped out of line could expect no sympathy, understanding or help from the local government'.

While the Island authorities were willing to support German orders publicly, and co-operate with the Germans in catching escapers or saboteurs, they were equally unwilling to oppose in public German violations of the law and the Hague Convention. They sometimes seem to have forgotten who were the enemy. John Leale, for example, told the States that, 'There must be no thought of any kind of resistance. Should there be any resistance, we can only expect that the more dire punishment will be meted (out). I say this, the man who even contemplates resistance should the Germans come is the most dangerous man in the Island and its most bitter enemy.'

Those who resented what happened and committed acts of resistance like smuggling out information, or spreading news about German defeats, came to despise this paternalistic government and press for reform. In 1944 an MI9 report referred to the way certain people were benefiting from the black market in high places which von Aufsess said involved many deputies and jurats from the Island states or parliament. The report remarked that, 'Probably as a result of this graft a new party has been formed on the Island called the Jersey Democratic Society. This is not a resistance group. It is a movement with a post-war aim. It leads the campaign for the abolition of Jersey's feudal system, and independence, by publishing and distributing illegal pamphlets.'

At the end of the war, an attempt by the Jersey Democrats to have the conduct of the Island government investigated was ignored by the British military government, and the old system was quickly restored, although changes making it more democratic were introduced later.

In everyday life the Islanders remained under their traditional form of government made even less democratic by the Germans. The Island parliaments or states had little power to initiate laws, and had only a minority of directly elected members: in Guernsey for example, it was 18 out of 57 deputies. There were also archaic restrictions on who might stand for the states. Jews, atheists and freemasons were excluded in Guernsey. In the states sat other groups of members like the jurats who were elected by the sitting members for life, and tended to control the government departments. The states were forbidden to hold any kind of election, and were summoned only rarely to bolster severe German orders, or unpopular measures to which the Island governments had agreed. Civilian government therefore rested almost entirely in the hands of two new bodies set up by Carey and Coutanche. On Guernsey, a controlling committee was formed on 21 June and met four days later, and on Jersey a similar body called the superior council met on 24 June and assumed full powers three days later. Each executive body consisted of seven or eight jurats and Crown officials with their assistants and secretaries. Each member presided over a small government department responsible for key functions amongst which probably the most important was the essential commodities committee presided over by Sir Abraham Lainé in Guernsey and Philip Le Masurier in Jersey.

There was one joint body called the purchasing commission formed on 16 August 1940 which worked well throughout the occupation. This body consisted of a German official, and two representatives from Guernsey and Jersey. The scheme was got off the ground by Raymond Falla, the agricultural committee chairman on Guernsey assisted by William Hubert, a Guernsey seed merchant, John Jouault and Touzel Bree, a farmer of Breton stock, who was Jersey agriculture committee's chairman. Falla made the first of many journeys in ships flying the German flag to Granville where the commission established an office at the Villa Hirondelle, with a bilingual clerk provided by the Germans, and under somewhat primitive conditions (their money was kept in a wardrobe). Their job was to purchase essential supplies and to arrange shipping, and to do this it was necessary to deal in the French black market as well as making legitimate purchases. A false set of books was kept to show the German authorities, and in this way after shipping had been improved by employing a firm of brokers all manner of goods were transported in one small boat ranging from 'underpants winter weight, ankle length', through putty, yeast, insulin, seeds, to replacement violin strings. Hubert and Falla returned to Guernsey and were replaced by Philip Mahy and George Vaudin who together with Jouault became the permanent officials assisted sometimes by Falla, Louis Guillemette from Guernsey and Mr Rumbald from Jersey. All these men risked prosecution for their black market dealings. The conduct of other aspects of government was to prove less satisfactory.

Guernsey was the worst-governed of the two main Islands because it was the poorer of the two, and yet contained German headquarters and those involved in running Alderney and Sark as well as the garrison. Conditions deteriorated more rapidly than is often realized, and as early as September 1941 Mrs Tremayne wrote after a visit there by her daughter, 'They are well on the way to starvation. She says it is pathetic to see the hungry faces of the people waiting in the queues for rations, and these include even some of the old colonels resident in Guernsey and well-to-do people ... There are Germans in the Post Office, the Press office and *Star* Offices overlooking everything and everybody. People are afraid to speak in the streets, the Gestapo [Feldpolizei] is everywhere, two and three abreast.' Victor Carey, a lawyer and member of an old Island family, had become bailiff in 1935 rather surprisingly in view of his age. By the time the Germans arrived he was 69, and as an old man was naturally fearful and anxious to avoid any trouble. Although he gave his place in day-to-day supervision of the Controlling Council to others, he remained bailiff and orders of both Island government and the Kommandantur were published under his name. His upbringing and conservative nature led him to employ a courtly official tone which looked subservient, even though he disliked the Germans perhaps more than some of his colleagues.

However, even if his orders were required to be published by the Germans, there was no reason why he should not have taken greater care with some of the words. In August 1941 he referred to escapers as being from 'enemy' forces, and on another occasion offered a reward of £25 for information about the chalking of V-for-Victory signs. Frank Falla said he knew of at least one case when this reward was claimed, and as a result an elderly and crippled man, Xavier de Guillebon, who chalked the signs on German bicycle seats was sentenced in July 1941 to a year in prison. Nor did the Island authorities complain when John Martel, his defence counsel, was excluded from the trial. It would have been better if such orders had been published under the commandant's signature alone.

Ambrose Sherwill was placed in charge of the controlling committee on the advice of Guernsey's attorney-general. He was dismissed and then imprisoned in October 1940 for his involvement with the concealment of four British agents, but was allowed to resume his former post of attorney-general, and from July 1942 to attend the controlling committee once more. A few months later he was among British subjects deported to Germany where he became camp leader at Laufen. Sherwill, a Devonian, had obtained his entry into Island ruling circles by his marriage to May Carey. He became attorney-general in 1935. The way in which he was punished in 1940 in spite of his encouragement to agents to surrender, his complete backing for obedience to German rule, and his broadcast on Radio Bremen may well account for Sherwill's persistent determination thereafter to see the Germans in the most favourable light. He told the police chief, 'I can see no way of avoiding' conformity with German wishes. In the background, too, was the fear that his son John with intimate knowledge of the Island, might be used in a subsequent raid.

But his willingness to co-operate brought him some reward in September 1942. The deportations were supposed to include all British-born subjects on the Islands, and very few exceptions were made even among the elderly and sick. Knackfuss asked Müller if women and children should be included, and was told no exceptions could be made, but von Aufsess in the Kommandantur deliberately left Sherwill's wife and sons off the list. May and the two boys continued to live at Havelet House in a flat while the upper part of the building was given over to billeted troops who in this case, unlike so many others, behaved 'with perfect consideration'. Although there were other cases in which the Germans relented, like that of Doctor McKinstry, the favourable treatment given to Sherwill and other members of the Island governing class was yet a further example of double standards.

Another prominent member of the Guernsey government exempted in 1942 was the man who succeeded Sherwill in charge of the controlling committee, the Reverend John Leale, formerly financial adviser to the committee until his permanent appointment in January 1941. Although Leale was a Methodist minister of cultured tastes, he was also an extremely rich man. From the first he argued 'there must be no thought of any kind of resistance', and strongly condemned sabotage as foolish. He adopted the line that both sides were bound by the Hague Convention which forbade any actions by an occupied people against their occupiers and after the war he said he could not recommend anyone for honours who had helped escapers or damaged the Germans because it would violate the convention. There was no validity in this argument, as a resistance news-sheet pointed out in June 1942, because while the Germans could not point to any major violations of the convention by the people, they had broken it whenever it suited them to reduce rations, confiscate property, or enforce labour.

Jersey was better governed than Guernsey. The bailiff, Alexander Coutanche, was an able and ambitious member of an old Jersey family, and had been a deputy for St Helier since 1922. Called to the Jersey bar, he rose to be attorney-general and bailiff in 1935 aged only 43. He had been closely involved in developing the tourist trade, and in the opening of a new airport at St Peter's. Von Aufsess found him congenial company, but also remarked on his 'coolly calculating' nature. His bland memoirs say nothing about his personal views or role in the occupation. Although he is on record for complaining about various measures like deportations, or ration reductions, it is clear he endorsed the policy of co-operation. He told Norman Longmate he did not believe they could have done anything else to help 'the general cause'. When questioned about anti-Semitic orders he claimed there was nothing they could have done to help, that the significance of these and other measures was not then appreciated.

Charles Duret Aubin, the attorney-general, was probably the second most important figure in Jersey Island government. A large and rather ponderous man in speech, von Aufsess nevertheless saw him as a modest and intelligent person, and the two got on sufficiently well for von Aufsess to tell him about his dislike of Hitler, and his intention to escape. The bailiff's secretary was Ralph Mollet who faithfully supported the co-operation policy. On one occasion he was in church at St Saviour's when the clergyman, Canon Clifford Cohu, asked the congregation to sing the National Anthem. This was strictly forbidden and, although Germans present made no objection, Mollet reported it to Duret Aubin who in turn told the Dean who warned Cohu to be more careful.

Could this group of men have done more to distance themselves from German policies and encourage resistance? After he had stayed with Carey and Coutanche Herbert Morrison did not think so, and his report to the cabinet said, 'the Island officials had discharged their difficult responsibilities during the Occupation in exemplary fashion'.

This was simply untrue. They had surrendered to pressure. The Germans warned them they would remove from office any official who failed to conform to orders from the commandant. If an official did not obey orders he was entitled to have charges in writing submitted to him, and to a hearing at which he could put his case. No official availed himself of this procedure. The removal of Sherwill and others in 1940 had been sufficient warning for most. Doctor McKinstry, who was critical of German policies was threatened with deportation in 1942, as was Doctor Symons in 1944. The Germans also threatened general action against the administration. Carey told Mrs Cortvriend that one reason why he had issued the reward notice about V-for-Victory signs was because the Germans threatened to deport some of the jurats to Germany. When the *Bulletin of British Patriots* criticized the Germans, ten members of the States were briefly imprisoned as hostages.

Administrators and lawyers are experts at creating delays and smokescreens, and Island officials could have used their outdated procedures and legal niceties to create endless difficulties. They must have realized the Germans valued their signature on orders, and their public pronouncements against escape, or sabotage. This fruitful co-operation benefited German military occupation and could have been made into a bargaining counter. The Island rulers knew they were treading on dangerous ground. When they signed the anti-Jewish orders it was agreed that only the preambles should be published over their signatures rather than specific details of anti-Jewish measures.

Apart from a handful of individual cases, and a number of delays in implementing measures, their complaints were ineffective even in the palmy days before June 1944, and none after that date. They denounced escapers as foolhardy, and sabotage as pointless. Several times they urged Islanders to act as informers. The Germans imposed collective penalties illegally after the Nicolle-Symes landing, cable-cutting sabotage, the commando landing on Sark, and the publication of the *Bulletin of British Patriots*. They threatened to take hostages and to deport people, and did so in certain cases. They confiscated bicycles, cars, motor cycles, cameras, and wirelesses among other goods. When the Island governments objected to confiscations in May 1942 their protest was ignored. Reductions in food rations were carried out illegally as a reprisal and when Sir Abraham Lainé, who had a good record of complaining, used the word 'reprisal' Dr Kratzer reprimanded him. Coutanche and Carey published the order making the reductions stating 'it is no sense a punishment against the civil population'. Forced labour was demanded for the fortifications and nearly 200 Islanders conscripted. Leale complained that this violated the Hague Convention. The labour was used, and then in August the Germans replied and agreed not to take any more 'to perform fortification and entrenchment work' after they had used what labour they needed.

What made the policy even more regrettable was the degree of goodwill towards the Germans in personal relations. Although Coutanche said that there was no 'social intercourse', there was in fact a good deal as von Aufsess' diary shows, and von Schmettow himself broke off cordial relations late in 1944. Sherwill, Carey, Hathaway, and Leale all spoke of courtesy and consideration between themselves and the Germans. In one speech Sherwill said of relations: 'These are not merely on a correct basis, but they are cordial and friendly. It is most important that they should remain so. Let no one jeopardize this by unseemly or unruly conduct.'

This sort of relationship had a number of results. For breaking laws, like sheltering British agents or listening to the wireless, which sometimes led to death and long imprisonment for other Islanders, they received minimal punishment. Although some of them or their relatives were deported others were granted exemption. Small though such kindly gestures as not digging a trench across Coutanche's lawn, or getting Hathaway's glasses repaired might be, they were privileges not extended to others, and a constant reminder that withdrawing co-operation would render their lives as unpleasant as those of most Islanders.

In October 1944 a case involving Deputy E. Le Quesne, chairman of the labour committee and a member of the Jersey superior council, highlighted the situation and its inequalities. The Feldpolizei arrested him for listening to a wireless. The police had not consulted the Platzkommandantur so Le Quesne was tried, and given seven months for an offence, which in other cases had led to deportation to a German prison. Von Aufsess intervened, and then a 'foolish blunder' was made because after only two weeks Le Quesne was released. Such behaviour on their part, said von Aufsess, 'leads to the accusation that we have one law for the highly placed and another for the ordinary citizen'.

Well-off Islanders who fraternized with Germans inviting them to their houses, dining with them, lending them books, riding and playing sport with them, were assured of favourable treatment. Von Aufsess wrote as late as September 1944 that 'there are still many rich people' in Jersey. Mrs Hathaway admitted to entertaining Germans from all three Islands. Von Aufsess often visited Miss White at Samarez Manor who lost only two valuable items during the occupation. Another of his friends was Mrs Riley of Rozel Manor where in April 1945 they ate cakes of pre-war quality, while Mrs Tremayne was writing the same week, 'I don't think there are any potatoes or bread, it is slow starvation'. Was it callousness or indifference to people in another class that allowed Mrs Riley to entertain a German in this way?

The gathering of wood was illegal and people were prosecuted for doing so. One afternoon von Aufsess came across a mother and daughter gathering kindling. He helped them carry it home, a fire was made, and soon 'we were all sitting round the glowing hearth ... like friends'. They shared the contents of Red Cross parcels, and although fraternization had now been banned by von Hüffmeier, Mrs Fielding and her daughter, were allowed by von Aufsess to visit him at Linden Court 'making a discreet entrance through the back door'. This happened in February 1945. On several occasions Mrs Tremayne indulged in outbursts in her diary about the friendliness of people towards the Germans which made her 'positively sick'. On Guernsey, Mrs Cortvriend described the atmosphere of denunciation and betrayal as 'revolting' referring particularly to anonymous letters about people breaking regulations by listening to the wireless, or obtaining more food. 'When the existence of traitors among us became commonly known [she wrote] we learnt to tread warily, to look over our shoulders when passing on the news, not only from fear that the Germans might overhear us. We began to avoid certain people and to be cautious of our remarks before any of whose trustworthiness we were in doubt, and this feeling was to many of us one of the most repellent experiences we had ever known.'

No one had done more to denounce collaboration and encourage resistance in Europe than Churchill, and after the war he paid tribute frequently to European resistance. In spite of all attempts to stop it there had been resistance and sabotage on a small scale in the Islands unaided by those in positions where help would have been invaluable, or by organizations specifically set up by Churchill to help such resistance, but this small band of British resistance heroes and heroines was left unacknowledged. It would surely have been natural for him to visit the only part of the British Isles to suffer occupation.

The Guernsey Liberation Council, an unofficial body, wanted to ask Churchill to visit the Channel Islands, but the governor turned down their request in March 1946 saying someone equally distinguished had already been asked. In November 1947, Churchill again refused to visit the Islands and made no promise about any future visit. As Prime Minister in direct contact with Sir Stewart Menzies of MI6 receiving details from their European agents, MI9 agents, SOE operatives and MI5 vetting of escapers from the Islands, Churchill must have known a good deal about the ruling class who in many cases had run occupation government and were fully restored to their former power. A war office summary of information provided by escapers up to October 1944 pointed out that there was widespread discontent among ordinary citizens with the conduct of state officials and many wanted the Islands to be incorporated in England after the war as an ordinary county. Such demands were still being made in the summer of 1945 to the British military government. The report said that many officials were accused of passivity, inefficiency, overwillingness to co-operate with the Germans, and profiting from the black market. Even though, as the report said, ordinary citizens could not know all the circumstances surrounding Island government activities, evidence of such activities may have influenced Churchill's decision not to visit the Island.

Part 3

Collaboration

6

The Forces of Law and Order: The Black Market

Although no specific attempts were made by British Intelligence to find out what was going on in the Channel Islands, reports filtered through in other ways from escapers or people on the Continent in contact with the Islands able to convey information to SOE or MI9 operatives. Among such reports was one on Jersey in 1944 dealing with collaboration among ordinary people which seemed to be on a widespread scale.

The report referred to dealing in the black market which 'is due to the meagre rations issued and is practically universal from the highest to the lowest. Jurats, Deputies etc. are not above it and are some of the worst offenders. Farmers are making large sums of money by holding up supplies and then selling them at very enhanced prices to those who can afford to pay. Those who have any stocks of unobtainable commodities are selling what they have at exorbitant prices.' The report highlighted, secondly, the work of informers described as 'quislings' assisting 'the Gestapo' by 'informing on their fellow citizens. Among their activities is informing about people who have kept wireless receiving sets. It is understood they are paid by the Germans for each person they hand over.' The report said Irish and Italian hotel workers were particularly prone to informing. Finally the report gave details of fraternization by local women who had been 'prostituting themselves with the Germans in the most shameless manner', some of whom had become informers.

Collaboration by ordinary people is much more understandable than by those in authority. Had they passed over opportunities to help the Germans they were the most likely to suffer retaliation from the German law and order forces. It is important to remember that law courts, police, and prisons were subordinated to the German will, and alongside them appeared some of the apparatus of the police state inaccurately referred to as 'the Gestapo' in contemporary accounts although that particular force was not permanently on the Islands. To Islanders all German police are the same, so that when some arrived on Sark after the commando raid in October 1942 Mrs Tremayne commented that, 'the Gestapo are still here, questioning everyone about the landing of the British'. Some understanding of the forces of law and order, and the laws themselves is necessary before looking in more detail at civilian collaboration with German rule.

There can be no doubt that the legal position of the Island courts and police as far as their conduct is concerned is unassailable. Given the decision by the Island governors representing the King to co-operate, and the home office request to Crown civil servants to continue at their posts, the Royal Courts had to continue functioning, and apply the law under the terms of the German occupation as well as dealing with ordinary crime as before.

Similarly the police as Crown servants continued to function as before and this inevitably involved them in house searches, acting on information received, and carrying out laws punishing people for a wide range of 'resistance' and other activities under the ever widening network of German regulations. Although there were cases in which the police appeared overzealous in enforcing German regulations, and other occasions when they profited from their privileged position, the force seems by and large to have acted fairly. In a few cases they secretly opposed the Germans, and two policemen, Inspector Albert Lamy on Guernsey, and Sergeant T.G. Cross on Jersey were among the few Islanders given occupation honours after the war.

The reaction of the police to their new role was noticed by Edward Chapman, when the order came for police and prison warders to show the same respect for German ranks as they did for English ones. 'They were for the most part, ex-soldiers of the 1914–18 war, and bitterly resented this humiliation. At the beginning all of them took their medals off their tunics, but later, as an act of resistance, they replaced them. I remember a fine old chap called Bill Carrier, an ex-professional footballer who ... barely concealed his contempt for the Germans. When they came on a visit he would dourly touch his cap to their commander and only just obey their orders. But as soon as the Nazi had turned his back he would wink at us, and give the V-sign.'

The courts were organized differently on the two main Islands with Alderney and Sark being subordinated to Guernsey Royal Court in the matter of appeals. In Guernsey there were the Full Royal Court which dealt with civil and criminal cases, and the Ordinary Court for civil matters which heard appeals from the Magistrates' Court concerning minor criminal matters. In Jersey the Royal Court, called 'the Superior Number', dealt with civil and criminal matters, and acted as a court of appeal from the Inferior Number. For criminal matters there was an Assize Court and for petty cases, a Police Court. In St Helier the Royal Court House was in Royal Square, and in St Peter Port it was situated in Manor Street.

The Germans created their own network of courts for offences they deemed triable by them. In any police state, particularly one under military rule, the destination of cases and form of trial were determined in the end by the arbitrary decision of the commandant. In some cases before the commandant's Court defence lawyers were permitted; in others they were excluded. The commandant's Court consisted of a military judge assisted by two officers, a prosecuting counsel, and an interpreter. When Germans and civilians were involved in a case this was tried in the commandant's Court. Additionally each of the services had its own court for purely military offences, and crimes by members of the Organization Todt whose officials and workers were tried in the particular military court belonging to the branch of the services they were working for at the time of the offence. Consequently Todt officials and workers received severe sentences.

Occupation meant a rapid rise in prison population. The Island penal system was antiquated and small, and even before the occupation long-term prisoners were dispatched to Winchester Prison. According to Ramsey at least 4,000 custodial sentences were passed during the occupation, and this produced an impossible burden for the existing system. Edward Chapman was imprisoned until October 1941 in the old jail in Patriotic Street, St Helier, which only had accommodation for 60 prisoners. As the severity of the occupation increased so did the prison population, and by January 1945 von Aufsess was commenting that 'fines and gaol sentences continue to rise at a fantastic rate'. To meet the problem in St Helier the Chelsea Hotel was taken over and its hundred rooms converted into a holding prison by cutting slits in bedroom doors, and fastening barbed-wire over the windows.

In Guernsey the jail was in St James Street, and a similar holding prison was created at Birnham Court in Queens Road. As early as September 1942, the prison was so full that people had to wait to serve their sentences until there was a vacant cell. Two Sark lads who stole hens from the postmistress were sent to Guernsey, but could not be imprisoned due to shortage of accommodation. Inevitably, as shortages affected the Islands both food and heating were in small supply. In Alderney both military and civilian prisoners were confined at the Court House prison in New Street, and in cases involving less than three months, summary justice was carried out by the military court. Prisoners were housed three to a cell and on average two-thirds of the inmates were German military; the rest were civilians or Todt workers engaged on the fortifications.

Confusion was created for ordinary people by the number of different police forces. Apart from SS guards in Sylt Camp on Alderney Himmler's police forces do not seem to have reached the Islands unless a few of them were called in for special occasions such as the commando raid on Sark. In October 1940 Feldgendarmerie 131 for military policing, and Feldpolizei 312 for civilian policing arrived on the Islands, and after a temporary withdrawal were fully established on orders from St Germain in June 1941 and warned not to show 'unnecessary mildness'. The Feldpolizei offices were at Silvertide, Havre de Pas, in St Helier, the Albion Hotel, Queen's Road, St Peter Port, and the Jubilee Old People's Home in St Anne on Alderney.

There were three other police forces on the Islands: units of military intelligence whose main job was to report on the loyalty of the garrison, and who were commanded towards the end by Major Gebbhardt; an auxiliary police, the Hilfspolizei, called in during 1944 to help enforce food regulations and Hafenpolizei, or customs police in the harbour areas.

The Wehrmacht could make arrests itself when it caught anyone in a criminal act, or behaving suspiciously, and even civilian staff on the Kommandantur who were not in uniform received military training, and carried pistols.

For hundreds, if not thousands, of Islanders occupation brought experience like that of Frank Stroobant nearly caught dealing in black market cigarettes. A friend offered him cigarettes which he bought and then sold off to his friends. One afternoon an unknown Guernseyman came in and asked for some for one of the Todt workers. Stroobant sold him two packets, and before long a Todt worker and a Feldpolizei turned up and carted Stroobant and his assistant, Harry Ferguson, off to the police station where they were separated, interrogated, and imprisoned in overcrowded cells. He found himself spending two nights on a straw mattress with two blankets. During the day he was paraded before various possible dealers and asked to pick out who sold him the cigarettes, and then in front of three men who were asked if he had ever bought anything from them. His premises were closely searched. Then without comment he was released.

The functioning of the German police forces cannot be properly studied because of a lack of records and this prevents any full assessment of German brutality or Island collaboration. As for the Kommandantur records, fewer than a dozen files survived in Jersey. In Guernsey several hundred remained, but many of the more interesting files on Jews or criminal activities are not among them. Those few documents located by Solomon Stekoll at the Yad Washem Holocaust Archive in Jerusalem bearing on Guernsey administration, or among War Office papers relating to MI9 reports, are therefore of particular interest. These show co-operation and collaboration to have been widespread; full Feldpolizei records would no doubt have revealed the real extent of prosecutions, and details of informers. The disappearance of these records impedes the historian today: then, it prevented prosecutions of quislings and Germans alike, and both groups had much to gain by their disappearance.

Farmers were particularly affected by regulations designed to stop them keeping back produce for the black market or themselves, particularly meat, milk, potatoes and poultry. In Maugham's view fines in the civil courts were very high, and he cites a number of examples. Money values have changed out of all recognition, but it is a good idea to keep in mind that in those days a working man's wages were usually between £2 and £3 a week. On the same day in August 1943, one farmer was fined £6 for not registering pigs, and another fined £100 for filling in a potato return incorrectly. For neglecting to register three calves a farmer was fined £85, while failing to declare five pigs led to a fine of £200. A farmer who killed a horse for its meat was fined £500. Such fines fell on farmers already forced to distort their production under German orders, unable to export their traditional crops, and in many cases having had to give land for fortifications.

Fishermen were subjected to severe laws because their boats were the vehicles for escape, and resistance work. From the start, fishermen were restricted to a mile from shore, and two when they were escorted. In September 1940 came the first total ban on fishing, and when it was lifted all boats had to leave from the main harbours, and were only allowed to land at specified points. They were not allowed out in misty or poor weather, although later the Germans were to force them out into seas sown with mines. In August 1943 there was a second total ban, and after this bonds were introduced which had to be placed with the harbour police for both boats and their crews. No one was allowed to crew who had relatives in England or was unmarried. Boats had to be painted in bright colours for easy identification. Such regulations destroyed men's livelihoods, and the confiscation of boats and tackle was ruinous.

Ordinary folk were affected by a curfew from eleven at night until six in the morning. Blackout regulations were enforced, and with the failure of gas and electricity towards the end of the war night must have held fresh terrors. Every time there was minor sabotage or landings by British forces curfews were tightened, and at one point Sark Islanders were confined to their houses 12 hours out of the 24. In March 1944 breaking the curfew was made punishable by death. The curfew made for all kinds of difficulty and misery. Confined to cold and lightless houses there was little to do but retire to bed. Those who had business at night like some workers or doctors took their lives in their hands, and for elderly, ill or pregnant people without telephones the ban on movement could well be dangerous.

Molly Finigan recalled an instance when a simple regulation caused much distress. All weapons except souvenirs had to be handed in, but some Islanders wanted to keep their sporting guns. Her grandfather kept his prize rifle while handing in another one. A year or so later the house was searched by the Feldpolizei, but they failed to find the gun hidden in a barrel of sawdust. Great anger was expressed by Molly's parents because her grandfather had exposed them all to arrest, but they did not dare to hand it in, and had to endure extreme worry during future house searches. A search for weapons had been ordered in Guernsey in March 1941, and Carey issued a typical order begging people to search 'every nook and corner'.

Wartime life in Britain was also closely regulated, but in the case of the Channel Islands, the orders and restrictions were almost entirely for the benefit of the enemy, and therefore doubly irksome. Among these regulations were those forbidding attack on or criticism of their forces, receiving information from anywhere except the censored press, helping escapers or Allied POWs, damaging German property, playing the National Anthem, using cars for private purposes, travelling between the Islands, moving in prohibited areas particularly on the coast, violating food regulations, concealing any of a wide range of commandeered goods, and foraging for fuel. By the last year of occupation there were so many rules that von Aufsess commented, 'soon there will be nothing left we can forbid to the people except to live', and every diary kept during the occupation reflects a sense of oppression produced by the police presence. In July 1941 Mrs Tremayne said, 'it is just one year since we were made prisoners', and she often referred to life in the Island 'prison'.

The majority of German punishments were financial, but interrogation in itself was a punishment in cases where violence was used. Individuals certainly suffered personal violence during the judicial process. Hubert Lanyon who distributed copies of an underground journal called *GUNS* was beaten up at the Feldpolizei headquarters in St Peter Port, losing two teeth in the process. Charles Machon, concerned in the production of the journal, suffered from ulcers, but he was denied his special diet during interrogation even though his mother brought it to the gates. He was interviewed in an overcoat in an overheated room, and then flung into a cold cell. People were taken for interrogation on the least suspicion, and released without explanation. In January 1942 Julia Tremayne reported that a Mr Baird had been taken off Sark: 'We don't know exactly what for.' He was an American but used to report at German headquarters every week. It appears he said in one of his Red Cross messages that there were two or three hundred troops in Sark, so we think that must be the reason. He has asked the Vicar to take charge of his house as he never expects to get home again.'

Sometimes special groups were rounded up for questioning. In June 1944 retired officers living in Jersey were taken from their beds in the middle of the night to the Feldgendarmerie headquarters and asked simplistic questions before being released with no explanation given.

Few Islanders escaped a frequent feature of Feldpolizei activity – the random search of private houses. Sark was particularly prone to house searches because of the two Commando raids and the murder of a German doctor in April 1942. His batman was closely questioned by the Feldgendarmerie, and fled into hiding. Several weeks later his body was found at the bottom of a well with a note saying he did not commit the crime, but had been driven to kill himself because he was suspected. It later turned out that the real culprit was a soldier who had been refused a medical certificate, and wanted to avoid Russian service. The Germans then dug up the body, and had it reburied in the military cemetery on Guernsey. The crime unleashed the Feldpolizei on the Island, and on the day of its discovery Mrs Tremayne's house was searched early in the morning. For ten days all Sark men had to report twice a day at the Kommandantur including old men and invalids. When it was rumoured that the batman was not guilty, Mrs Tremayne dreaded what would happen next. 'We are daily expecting another search of our houses, they are looking for a mallet or a certain kind of stick that was used, a gold watch and a missing wallet or any other clue. Norah says "Mother, will you burn that diary you are writing before they search again", but mother says "no, not on your life" ... So I have found a safe cubby hole where even she cannot find it, and as shooting seems to be the penalty for most things I must make my cubby hole very safe.'

Mrs Cortvriend described a house search on Guernsey which filled her with fear because of her diary, their wireless and a camera, followed a few days later by a second search.

Wartime brought rationing and shortages to everyone in the British Isles, including the Channel Islands, but with different results. In Britain rationing helped to produce a fairer society, bring decent food to all for the first time in history, and improve the quality of people's diet. Yet even under such favourable circumstances there was a black market.

Rationing in the Channel Islands was not part of welfare reforms, but a way of distributing ever declining resources of every commodity of daily life: food, fuel, and clothing and it is only to be expected that a more extensive black market than that in Britain would operate. In the Islands health suffered instead of improving: hospitals were short of basic supplies, and the most vulnerable in the community, the children and the old, were particularly hard hit by privation and starvation. Average daily calorie intake was down to 1,700 by 1944. The desire of Islanders to frustrate the regulations was borne out of necessity as well as a search for profit, and it would be absurd to blame them for benefiting from the black market. As Maugham wrote: 'I have no hesitation in saying that, in Jersey, the black market proved a boon and a blessing to large numbers of people, many of whom I am well assured, would not be alive today had it not been for the additional nourishment and strength which they derived from ... their only channel of supply.'

A farmer who slaughtered a beast illegally, or kept back part of his crop, could help his own family, sell directly to those who could afford to pay, or sell to a wholesaler through whom ordinary Islanders could make their purchases. The Island courts and the Feldpolizei tried to prevent the operation of a black market, by prosecuting firstly possible suppliers for breaches of regulations, and secondly those involved in actual transactions. Prosecutions rose steadily: in Guernsey, for example, from 40 in 1942 to over a hundred in 1944, but with only limited success.

Unfortunately, there were other sides to black market activity. Large profits were made by some people out of the necessity of others. Some black market dealers were prepared to steal to acquire goods for sale to the public either from German or Island stores. In one case, when two youths were arrested for stealing tinned goods and whisky from the Jersey food control commission, one of them was said to have a bank balance of over £800 (perhaps £8,000 today), although he was only sixteen. Others hoarded goods in order to force the price up and take advantage of people's misfortune. One day von Aufsess was taken by the Feldgendarmerie, 'into a room piled to the ceiling with black market goods found in the possession of a French doctor here. I was furious. A basket of huge hams, a ton of salted beef, boxes full of flour, a hundredweight of potato flour, sugar, oats by the sack, and in addition twenty hundred weights of potatoes.'

The German presence added a further dimension to black market activity. In some cases items plundered by Germans were sold to Islanders. The Germans bought goods cheaply in France and sold them dearly in the Islands, and the Organization Todt followed the example of the Wehrmacht. In von Aufsess' view, 'the troops engage far too much in black marketeering and wangling of supplies'. Transactions of this kind between Islanders and Germans were illegal under Trading with the Enemy Acts, and some attempt was made after the war by levying War Profits Taxes to punish some of those involved. Sadly von Aufsess' indignation was not matched by his own conduct. He dined at black market restaurants, and at Christmas 1944 was well supplied by a black market dealer, Lieutenant Wetzstein.

'The main black market', said Cruickshank, 'was run by greedy and unscrupulous Islanders for their own profit and the benefit of other greedy and unscrupulous Islanders'. There seems little doubt that the Island rulers best placed to bend regulations or lay their hands on goods were among the chief offenders, providing once again a good reason why they were not anxious after 1945 to call for prosecutions. Von Aufsess commented that in Jersey, 'I fear that many States officials do not, in their position, set the example they should. Current rumour credits them, with the exception of Duret Aubin, of generally dabbling in the black market, and taking advantage of their privileged position.' Von Aufsess had recently been visited by one of the suspects, Jurat M., and 'viewing his well nourished appearance I surmised he must have a well stocked larder'. Inevitably some public officials took their cue from their superiors, as a case involving no less than 18 Guernsey policemen and a civilian arrested in March 1942 showed. Led by a police sergeant, the men robbed German stores of a wide variety of commodities including tinned meat, sausages, butter, lard, grain and logs. The Feldpolizei treated them roughly during interrogation, beating them severely, and they were tried before the commandant's court. After being sentenced to terms between four weeks and four and a half years, the accused were then indicted before the Royal Court presided over by Carey who had harsh words for the offenders saying 'I am filled with shame. It is revolting to think how you have abused your position. I cannot imagine what all the foreigners in the Island ... think of you.'

Whatever may be said about the value of the black market for ordinary people, this was not its main purpose, and they were not always its main beneficiaries. Edward Chapman and Anthony Faramus were involved in the black market in 1941 when Chapman came out of prison. They operated from a hairdresser's run by a local bookmaker called 'Sandy', buying goods from the Germans and selling them at twice the price to Islanders. They helped to supply pubs with drink, and sold cigarettes at seven and six a packet. They got to know certain German officers. When the Island police tried to arrest Chapman one night, German marines tried to free him, but the Feldpolizei joined in the brawl and he was captured. However, one of the officers telephoned the police station, and he was released.

Helping Germans and being helped by them was dangerous in wartime because blackmail was never far away. The Germans needed information, and usually obtained it from among the Island population closest to them. The Germans could overlook crimes, cancel sentences, provide jobs, dole out bribes, and give rewards, and in the hard days of occupation there were not a few who found themselves working for the Germans, some out of necessity, but others for more squalid motives.

Some Examples of Black Market Prices

Item	Per	1940 £ s. d.		1944 £ s. d.
Butter	lb	1 6		1 5 0
Sugar	lb	4½		16 0
Fruit	Tin	1 0		1 10 0
Birds Custard	Tin	1 2		4 2 6
HP Sauce	Bottle	1 0		12 0
Soup	Tin	1 4		12 0
Whisky	Bottle	14 0		10 0 0
Candles	Packet	10		1 18 0
Eggs	Each	——		7 0
Tea	lb	2 8		25 0 0
Potatoes	cwt	6 0		6 0 0
Bisto	Packet	9½		1 3 0
Soap	Tablet	——		6 14 7
Rabbits	Each	——		1 15 0
Cooking Fat	lb	11		1 15 0
Herrings	Each	——		1 7
Cigarettes	Packet of 20 Craven A	1 1	Each	2 1
Bicycle		5 0 0		50 0 0

The legal rations available per week came to 3s. It is difficult to compare money values. In the first place the currency then was 12 pennies in a shilling, and 20 shillings in a pound. A shilling equals 5 pence in today's money.

The best way is to compare these prices with wages. In 1940, a farm worker got £90 a year, a skilled engineer, £148, and a Battle of Britain pilot started at £340 a year. A bungalow cost £250 and a 10 hp de luxe Vauxhall car £169.

7

Working for or with the Germans: The Informers

In one of the museums devoted to the war years on the Islands are displayed some wartime letters from informers. In the cold light of day, these anonymous documents in the German Occupation Museum in St Peter's, some of which sent fellow Islanders to their deaths in Germany, still arouse feelings of contempt and shame. One began by asking why a particular man had a ton of anthracite delivered when other people had no fuel, and went on to urge the Germans to 'call and see his stock of food in bedroom cupboards and billiard room, and see what you think of it'. This letter was sent to the Feldpolizei, inaccurately described on the envelope as the Gestapo, at their Silvertide headquarters in St Helier. Another letter sent to the Commandant at Victoria College House said: 'Please search Brompton Villa, Great Union Road for at least two wireless' hidden under floor boards, loft and cellars.'

The informers are a category of Island quisling for which no writer has a good word, and nearly all accept they were not isolated individuals, but part of a substantial group. Cruickshank is not sure if such activity was collaboration, and without any real evidence suggests they acted out of personal animosities and spite. In reality, motives for informing were extremely varied: the hope of personal gain, the wish to stand well with the Germans, fury at injustice in the distribution of food or the exaction of penalties, concealment of their own illegal activities and a wish to avoid being involved in reprisals. All such acts clearly helped enemy forces, and were therefore illegal in Britain under the Treason Act passed in 1940, but this act did not apply in the Channel Islands, and therefore none of the informers who had acted directly or covertly were ever punished.

It was believed, spies operated by standing in queues to listen to grumblers, and there can be no doubt that foreign staff in the surviving hotels were willing to inform on residents or fellow staff. This had occurred, it will be recalled, in the case of Mrs Green and her remark about the rice pudding, and Mrs Cortvriend reported another case of a waitress imprisoned as a result of being informed against by a member of the staff.

The Germans did all they could to encourage informers, and some Island government pronouncements seemed to indicate giving information to the Germans was a duty. This must have been a powerful inducement or a partial justification to some at least of the informers. Victor Carey's condemnation of cutting a German cable near the airport included the statement that, 'it is the duty of any individual who has any information with regard to the perpetration of this act of sabotage to inform the police immediately.' His public request regarding V-for-Victory signs is well known. He offered a reward: 'to the person who first gives the Inspector of Police information leading to the conviction of anyone not yet discovered for the offence of marking on any gate, wall or place whatsoever visible to the public the letter 'V' or any other word or sign calculated to offend the German authorities or soldiers.'

The truth about the extent of informing will never be known. According to some Island writers, the total of such people was to be numbered in three figures rather than two. Post office workers in Jersey claimed to have stopped several hundred such letters, and Inspector Albert Lamy on Guernsey said he destroyed many sometimes warning those involved. In a few individual cases there can be no doubt. John Ingrouille was betrayed by a well-known mother and daughter who were seized on Liberation Day and had their hands tied before soldiers rescued them. Mrs Chalus, their daily help, betrayed Connie and Robert Vaynor for having a wireless. Several informed on died in German camps as a result of receiving sentences for listening to the wireless like Cohu, Tierney, Nicolle and the Painters. Even on Sark informers operated, and Sibyl Hathaway recorded, 'I know for certain that we had one Quisling on the Island because the German Commandant told me she had helped to select the people she most disliked for deportation.'

The most well-known case of an informer's activity is the betrayal by 'Paddy' of those producing the underground news sheet *GUNS*, which led to the death in Germany of two of those convicted. He was a friend of Charles Machon, and took copies he obtained from him to the Feldpolizei. Later, he was seen with the Feldpolizei as they raided Machon's house in the Victoria Road district of St Peter Port. Even Herbert Morrison had to admit the role of Irish itinerant workers in supporting the Germans, and wrote that 'most Irish labourers had no compunction about working for the Germans'.

Military Intelligence reports said there were nearly 400 Irish potato-pickers stranded on the Islands, who 'constitute a serious threat to law and order' and on liberation 'should be interned until repatriated'. A German spy on the Islands before 1939 had met some of the Irish working in the quarries and found them friendly towards Germany. After occupation, several of them went to Germany to work. In return the Germans treated the Irish well.

The treacherous role of informer was one way in which Islanders worked for the Germans. In another way, nearly all made a contribution to the Island economy and hence to the income and lives of the occupying forces. Article 52 of the Hague Convention said that an occupying power could demand labour 'in proportion to the resources of the country and of such a nature as not to involve the inhabitants in the obligation of taking part in military operations against their own country'. This was a false distinction because anyone working was allowing the Germans to transfer their own labour to war activities, and because the Islands were in a battle zone the operation of air raid precautions and emergency services were as much in the Germans' interests as those of the citizens. Nor was it easy to distinguish work that was purely military from work that was civilian. For instance, German sea walls were useful sea defences as well as anti-tank devices, and works like the Beaumont power house on Jersey, or the water supply for St Anne on Alderney, were generally beneficial. The Island governments tried to preserve the distinction in Article 52, and on a number of occasions quarrelled with the Germans over particular pieces of work. Coutanche complained that the raising of St Aubin's Bay wall protected a road used by military convoys, and therefore Germans must do the work. On another occasion, when a gun emplacement was flooded, international law was preserved by the Jersey fire brigade pumping out enough water to prevent anyone drowning, but not enough to save the ammunition.

Such nice legal points could not survive grim reality. The Islands had to bear occupation costs unaided for two years with an unfavourable rate of exchange in occupation marks. Little money was available for public works or the wages of public employees. The Germans made major demands on Island resources, and distorted the economy with some of their agricultural demands. The absence of many men in their twenties and thirties threw the burden of fending for dependants on a smaller, older work force, and compelled women to seek work in a depressed labour market. By the end of 1940, the labour department in Jersey estimated there were 2,300 out of work.

Naturally, the Germans were delighted to replace their own nationals with voluntary Island labour. By Christmas 1940, the Germans were able to withdraw large numbers of civilians in posts like secretaries, telephonists, kitchen hands, waiters, and even medical staff replacing them with Island workers. Numbers employed grew, and in Guernsey alone by early 1943 over 2,000 were directly employed by the Germans giving a possible total for the Islands of 4,000. In Alderney, the evacuated civilian population was replaced between the spring of 1941 and June 1944 by several hundred Island workers who made life pleasant for the garrison.

Almost all those forced by poverty to work for the Germans probably heartily disliked what they were doing, but they had no alternative. Only in 1945 did some of them begin to show their feelings. Von Aufsess noticed the electricity works manager who had been co-operative had now turned surly perhaps because 'his feelings have been worked on by would-be patriots or with the end approaching he is getting worried about having co-operated with the occupying power up to now.' Many Island workers toiled alongside Todt slaves and saw the brutality. Sometimes they were its victims. Gordon Prigent argued with the Germans on his building site, and found himself in Norderney.

The Germans had plenty of slave labourers, and their usual way of persuading Islanders to work for them was to offer better terms than Island employers. Although Richard Johns, in charge of the Guernsey labour department, warned Organization Todt against wage differentials claiming it would help to bankrupt the Islands, the Germans held off for a few months, and then began to offer £1 1s. 4d. a week extra combined with larger food rations and special allowances for those willing to move to another Island. Islanders therefore worked in almost every conceivable capacity for the Germans.

Two places where Island workers were most needed, where there could be no doubt that they were breaking the Hague convention, and where they ran the risk of being killed by British air attack, were harbours and airports. A demand for labour at the airports for levelling new runways and hangar building clearly broke the convention, but Island labour departments had no alternative but to comply. In Guernsey about 180 men were employed in this way. In wartime it was inevitable the RAF killed British allies in bombing attacks on West European countries. A rather muddled notice was issued by the Island authorities saying that no one would be required to work at the airports, 'if flying conditions are such that there is a danger of attack from the air'. This would have been hard enough to define, but the notice went on to increase pay to 'time and a third' and admitted 'that it is impossible with the best will in the world entirely to eliminate all risks'.

It was in 1943 that the Germans, under pressure to complete their fortification programme, introduced more widespread forced labour when unemployed shop assistants and glass-house workers were taken on for such purposes as ammunition-cleaning and trench-digging which clearly violated the convention. Knackfuss, the commandant, issued an order stating: 'In order that the States shall not have to choose and engage the necessary persons themselves, it has been agreed that the States shall only report to the *Feldkommandantur* the groups of people to whom this compulsory employment applied. We reserve ourselves the right of completing the lists by referring to the card index file of persons with present place of employment added.'

There followed a period of administrative double-speak while the work was carried out. After three weeks Leale complained, but his letter was not replied to for six months. Knackfuss stressed workers had been given the opportunity to refuse even though the forms for this had been printed in German, and very few are recorded as having taken advantage of this let-out clause. Most of them were desperate for work, and orders early in February 1943 had established favourable conditions for such workers. Knackfuss never accepted that the convention had been broken, and work of a military nature was demanded on other occasions.

On Alderney there were no more than a handful of civilians, and the need for labour was great. In spite of tough conditions, the army billeting office established there to recruit labour never had any difficulty, and from early in 1941 until the summer of 1944 hundreds went from other Islands to work on Alderney and service the daily life to the garrison. Mrs Tremayne heard as early as July 1940 that attempts were being made to recruit labour to 'clear it all up and put the houses and hotels in order, also gather in their harvest and bring it back to Guernsey for our use'.

Among those who stayed were four individuals who were on hand to greet British forces when they landed. Frank Oselton returned to farm with his cattle, George Pope acted as a pilot and did a little farming, Clifford Bichard was the foreman of building works and presided over the construction of a pay office and new bakery for the Germans, and Peter Doyle worked as a handyman, and pilot. Their testimony was to be vital in 1945 when alleged atrocities were investigated, and, apart from Pope who made exaggerated claims he could not substantiate, none of them appeared to be willing to give evidence about brutal German policy on the Island.

Three groups of workers went to Alderney: farm labourers, those involved in maritime matters like pilotage and salvage, and those required to service Wehrmacht and Organization Todt facilities. The agricultural workers arrived early in 1941 having been directed there by Raymond Falla and Richard Johns. They cleared the land and collected 200 tons of straw. Crops were then planted and cultivation carried on until the summer of 1943. Four farms – Island, Mignot, Rose and Mill – were the main ones brought back into use, and working with Italians, Moroccans, POWs, and other camp inmates they managed to raise 250 tons of barley, oats, potatoes and vegetables. Some 40 workers were involved in the harvest that year. Pigs, cows, and a flock of 300 sheep with a Scots shepherd, Thomas Creron, were also tended on Alderney. A small number of Guernsey fishing boats were ordered to operate off Alderney with more severe restrictions than those imposed on all Island fishermen, and once again their catch was exclusively for German use.

The harbour commandants, Jacobi, Parsenow and Massmann, required expert maritime labour to pilot boats, maintain harbour works or check wrecks, and called on French and Dutch volunteers as well as Islanders for these tasks. Braye Harbour was subjected to considerable changes to accommodate convoys from Cherbourg every ten days. A spur was built to accommodate a bunker and guardroom, a boom with a gap in the centre was placed across the harbour from the end of the main breakwater to Bibette Head which proved difficult to maintain in high seas and the appalling winters of 1942-3, and 1944-5. A steel pier with a wooden deck was added to the original stone jetty, and cranes installed.

Storms were responsible for the sinking of several ships like the *Xaver Dorsch*, a dredger, a barge, and a harbour guard vessel, and after the winter of 1942-3 the Germans decided to recruit workers to salvage these wrecks.

A group was formed under John Matthews from marine workers on all three Islands, amounting to some 30 or more including several from Sark. Mrs Tremayne heard the men were told 'it was either Alderney or Germany', and this is borne out by Matthews' own account of their recruitment. The team were ordered to leave at once for Alderney and refused. After discussion, the Germans had to give way because they needed the equipment and skills of Matthews' men. They were told their task was to try and salvage a trawler, and that they would be given proper living quarters, Navy diet, and adequate leave. The party them embarked on the *Alfreda* and sailed to Braye where they were met by Captain Jacobi. They worked with German and French divers, but after a week it became clear the trawler could not be retrieved and was likely to break up where she lay wedged in a rock crevice. The marine workers remained on Alderney from May to October 1943.

The complete departure of the Island population left Alderney for some months largely uninhabited. Property decayed, and boatloads of German sightseers from other Islands and Cherbourg began to loot deserted houses. Doors and windows were smashed, and valuable goods, including a collection of silver trophies won by an Island farmer, were stolen. Other property was dragged out and left to rot in gardens. The Island governments were responsible for the property of evacuees and made some attempts to do their job by recruiting 40 Guernsey men to make the properties safe. With the decision to fortify the Island, and establish camps and a large garrison, Sonderführer Herzog was ordered to requisition property and prepare accommodation for the coming forces, and this led in the spring of 1941 to substantial maintenance gangs of electricians, plumbers, and builders going to Alderney. Looting was stopped and the church plate of St Anne, for example, was sent to Guernsey for safekeeping, although the church was later desecrated by its use as a butcher's shop and wine store. Then, as the garrison grew, more Islanders went over to work as waiters, cooks, drivers, and domestic servants. The exact number is unknown but Mrs Cortvriend referred to 'several hundred' disembarking at St Peter Port in June 1944 when air raids forced the Germans to remove almost all civilians from Alderney.

Islanders on Alderney worked closely with prisoners on the Island, and were in daily contact with Todt workers and those from Sylt camp. When the Island was liberated in May 1945 not only was eyewitness evidence available from the four men who met the British troops, but in MI9 lists the government had names of those from Guernsey including power and sewage workers who were government employees and remained on the Guernsey payroll while they were on Alderney. One document listed 13 names.

The workers were billeted in St Anne and fed at a communal canteen in the Victoria Hotel where they received the same food as the Germans. They had access to shops and soldatenheims, and were able to buy luxuries like biscuits and sweets. Oselton and other Islanders said they were well treated by the Germans. Perhaps there was reluctance on their part to get Germans into trouble for crimes that did not directly affect them. There was every reason after 1945 for keeping quiet about working for the enemy.

8

'Boots for Bags': Fraternization by the Island Women

Ginger Lou ran frantically across Howard Davis Park in St Helier, her smart day frock awry, her silver fur cape slipping, and her perfectly done red hair dishevelled, as she dodged this way and that between the bushes. It was a fortnight after the Liberation of the Islands when this scene was witnessed by a local doctor. A crowd formed, and she was dragged from a shrubbery, her clothes nearly torn from her, and bits of fur left clinging to the bushes. Car lubricating oil was smeared over her before she was rolled in the dust of the park by the shouting mob. Extricating herself, she ran to the doorway of a nearby house, where she cowered until the police arrived. Later she appeared before magistrates who gave her a small sum of money and put her on the boat to Weymouth.

'One of the Jerry bags had got her deserts', some might have said in 1945 when memories were fresh. Certainly Ginger Lou had been a flagrant example of the breed. French by birth, married to a local tailor, she had taken up with a German officer in the first year of occupation, and for five years received all the perks of her squalid position. She had been given another Islander's house, and was driven wherever she pleased. She had the best clothes and make-up. She took precedence in queues at the hairdresser's and in food shops. She was not the only Jerry bag to be caught. A local writer noticed on the evening of Liberation that: 'regrettably scenes took place this evening when one or two of these women were severely handled, and possibly but for the intervention of troops would have been murdered'.

Such scenes were enacted in many European countries at the time of liberation, and in some countries, like Denmark, retrospective laws made it a crime to have profited from the occupation in any way so that well-heeled collaborators could receive their punishment.

There is no doubt that such fraternization was widespread in the two main Islands even if it did not affect more than several hundred women out of many thousands. A report to MI9 in 1944 observed that, 'local women, chiefly Jersey-born, have been prostituting themselves with the Germans in the most shameless manner. There are quite a considerable number of these women all over the Islands.' A later report commented that D-Day had made no difference to these relations: 'Informants are amazed at the ostrich-like attitude of the local quislings, both male and female. Ever since D-Day they have continued their nefarious practices and seem quite unconcerned with the fate awaiting them. The women are especially blind and are continuing their association with the Germans to the bitter end.' The reports referred to the problems of abortions, unwanted and illegitimate children, and widespread venereal disease resulting in part from these liaisons.

Naturally reports from the Islands stressed the great bitterness about many of these women. Feeling is so strong said one report: 'that the girls will find that certain groups of people will probably round them up, shave their heads and treat them as similar French girls have been treated by French patriots'. It was stressed the local police would turn a blind eye to attacks on these women after liberation, 'because murder will be done, and public opinion in general will approve'.

Fraternizers comforted the enemy in time of war in return for privileges at a time when most people were suffering, and they brought dishonour and misery to their families. In some cases men returning were prepared to accept a new member of a family, like the baby boy born to a girl called 'Louise' taken in by her family and adopted by a childless sister, he later became a sergeant in the British Army. Advertisements sometimes appeared in local papers reading 'Wanted – someone to adopt a baby due on [such and such a date]'. In other cases, the presence of such babies no doubt caused much bitterness and fury. One girl beaten up by her father for returning to breakfast in her lover's car denounced her father for possessing a wireless, and he received six months!

The contemptuous phrase 'Jerry bag(gage)' was an evocative one. Boots the chemist attracted German attentions because they employed particularly attractive girls on their make-up and perfumery counters. In St Peter Port, the Germans were lured by the Boots girls sunbathing on a roof during their lunch-hour. In St Helier 'Boots for Bags' was chalked in the road, and Reginald Gould, the manager, sacked some of the more obvious goodtime girls. The Germans compelled him to reinstate them, and when he appealed to the Island authorities the solicitor-general advised Gould to obey the Germans. The Goulds were among those deported in 1942–3. The girls were sacked in 1945.

But before dealing with the sorry events of female fraternization, it is important to set them in the context of occupation conditions, and the position of women in society in those days. Few were traitors or informers, some were hard luck cases, others goodtime girls, and there were also genuine love affairs resulting in marriages after the war. Doctor John Lewis who was in charge of the Jersey Maternity Hospital referred to a girl called 'Louisa'. She gave birth to a boy. A year after the war, her German lover returned, her house was sold, they married at the Roman Catholic church and she left for Germany.

It would have been impossible for 30,000 Germans to descend on the Islands without causing social disruption. Abortions, divorces, illegitimacy and venereal disease statistics increased under the stress of war. Even though the German forces were far better behaved than Allied forces in Britain inevitably, wartime disrupted family life, and added to pressures on women. For five years, Island women were shut up in a drab, grey, penny-pinching atmosphere of privation and slow starvation. Mrs Cortvriend suggested many of the relationships were simply a release from intolerable boredom. Island women who had men serving in the forces had infrequent news, sometimes no news at all for five years, of their relatives. There were no leave-time homecomings, and no letters besides a standard Red Cross form. Many women had also been separated from their families by evacuation of all or some of their relatives, and in some cases a woman might be left without children or husband when in 1939 she had both. When the hotels of St Helier and St Peter Port filled with a company of healthy, strong and uninhibited young Germans, themselves condemned to the boredom of occupation life, and without even a brothel of their own until 1942, it was a temptation that a good many could not refuse. The relationships, as Norman Longmate points out, were usually due neither to German lust or Island looseness of morals, but to the war itself. Those girls who kept a low profile were forgiven, and they and their children were accepted into Island life, because, apart from the criminals and the officers' molls, it was recognized that what had happened was to some extent inevitable and natural.

It was not treachery, but the possibility of small gifts of soap and scent, or sweets and toys for the children, combined with a straightforward desire for sex, which mainly motivated Island Jerry bags. The Islands were holiday resorts, and to Germans fresh from campaigns, particularly in Russia, or from the tensions of occupation life in other countries, they were places to be enjoyed. Unlike the seedy British holidaymaker who often sat nearly fully clothed on the beach in those days the Germans were soon seen, semi-naked and bronzed, on the beaches and in the lanes, and although this affronted a more elderly woman like Mrs Tremayne it proved to be popular with younger women. In July 1943, she wrote, 'Grand Grève Bay has been opened for bathing, but more for the troops than the civilians, lots of the Sarkees go, all those who have have turned pro-German.' Their friendly approach to children, their gifts and money, their singsongs, their good looks, and camaraderie in wartime proved as popular as similar GI characteristics did in Britain. If Guernsey girls 'have gone crazy with the German soldiers', it was not entirely surprising.

From the first months of occupation good relations prevailed between many Island women and the Germans. Mrs Tremayne wrote in her diary she would like to stab them in the back, but even she admitted from time to time that their behaviour was correct enough. Other women attended the first dances held by the Germans, and these were reported in the censored Island press and in German forces magazines as highly successful. Islanders continued to attend, particularly at festive times of the year and the various functions for celebrating Hitler's birthday. German bands and touring theatrical groups from the Strength Through Joy movement visited the Islands to provide entertainment. Germans coming to the Islands, from an ordinary soldier like Gerhard Nebel to an officer like von Aufsess, recorded their pleasure at the relaxed and friendly atmosphere they found. Von Aufsess noticed the women would surrender readily enough 'provided this can be effected in proper privacy',

Procession entering the centre of St Anne on Alderney in 1942

Braye Harbour seen from Fort Albert. The *Xaver Dorsch* and other vessels were damaged by gales and air attack in this harbour where John Matthew's Sark party were to carry out salvage work

Two of the hundred French girls who came to Alderney as Todt workers, some of them to be mistresses for the officers, and others to work in brothels. There were four left in May 1945

Todt workers constructing the Mirus battery on Guernsey which mounted four 12-inch guns with a radius of 37 miles. They were fired ten times from April 1942. The battery was named after Captain Mirus who was killed in an air attack on his way to Alderney in November 1941

Todt workers in Guernsey being fed at a camp. These were among the 2,000 employed on the Mirus battery at Le Frie Baton

The entrance gate to Sylt camp opened in August 1942 and closed in July 1944. It was run from March 1943 by the SS, and the scene of considerable numbers of deaths and of starvation and torture

The remaining foundations of Norderney camp destroyed by the Germans in July 1944. Under Karl Tietz, Adam Adler, and Heinrich Evers, this camp saw brutal killings and torture by Organization Todt guards

and he thought their lovemaking 'simple, effortless and swift'. Chapman saw Jersey women getting on well with the Germans, but it was equally true of Guernsey or Sark where women, 'have the soldiers in their houses in the evening and the soldiers take the children for rides in their cars'.

According to Maugham there was a particular problem with billeted troops in some houses 'where the family included girls and young women, the conduct of the Germans, at times, was odious. Any attempt to restrain them by force was the immediate signal for the drawing of a revolver or a bayonet, and was almost certain to be followed by some trumped up charge.' There is no direct evidence of Maugham's rather frightening picture. When Germans were billeted in his own house all he noticed was that they 'tried to make friends with our maids'.

One MI9 report said girls 'of all classes' were involved with the Germans, but it was not until the publication of von Aufsess' diary that the extent of good relations between officers and Island girls became clear. Officers from the armed forces, the Feldpolizei and the Todt organization were able to find girlfriends. Throughout von Aufsess's diary, which covers 1944 and 1945, the worst years of the occupation, he referred to girls he knew including 'gay, pert Ella', Lucienne, who 'has a great crush on me', and Elaine who he met with her mother, and who he said was very much in love with him. At one point he referred to Heider's girlfriend who was 'the sheltered only daughter of wealthy parents', and elsewhere to von Helldorf's affair with a servant girl. He described parties with French and Island girls when 'the firelight lit up our flushed and happy faces'.

Other members of the German hierarchy also had their girlfriends. It was alleged that one girl was mistress of the Feldpolizei chief, Inspector Bohde, and lived with him at Havre de Pas, and that another girl had a child by a member of the Feldpolizei. On Alderney several officers set up house with French whores. Zuske lived with a woman from Evreux called 'Marianne' and one of his staff officers with another woman called 'Paulette'. Stürm, the Feldpolizei chief on Alderney, lived with a woman who left the Island to bear his child and then returned to him. Other women were less lucky. An officer brought his girlfriend to the Limes Nursing Home on Jersey one evening desperately ill after a failed abortion. Her life was saved.

Von Aufsess' diary bears out the MI9 report that said the girls continued their fraternization even when liberation was on the cards. In April 1945 Heider and von Aufsess were transferred from Jersey to Guernsey, but they soon found a 'pair of saucy, common young things' for whom they gave a party only a fortnight before liberation when they were all in 'rollicking good humour', and worse the wear for drink. Heider slept with one of the girls, and the other came to von Aufsess' room and 'made such overtures to sexual intercourse as I have never before experienced'. He did not say whether or not he succumbed to this temptation.

If the majority of these cases did no actual harm, it might perhaps be argued that there is little to condemn in what happened. But there were grim consequences: abortions, illegitimate births and venereal disease affected considerable numbers of people. In September 1944, Doctor Symons on Guernsey reported medical conditions in the hospitals were so bad that they were becoming 'medical sick houses'. Drugs were in short supply, as were all essentials like catgut for sutures or surgical spirit. Overworked doctors and overburdened health facilities had to cope with the consequences of fraternization at the expense of ordinary patients.

Venereal disease was widespread on the main Islands. On Alderney in 1942 40 women among Island workers were found to be suffering because the VD epidemic on the Island had spread from French whores to the civilians, and it was necessary to ban women workers from the Island. Even then some managed to remain 'who are no better than they should be' according to a MI9 report. This report went on to discuss Jersey where 'From his hospital experience [the] informant knew of many advanced cases of disease ... It was not unusual for the General Hospital to have as many as fifteen women under treatment every week, some cases being slight but some serious.'

So widespread was VD, said another report, that it might constitute 'a further menace to our forces' when they liberated the Islands. By the middle of 1942 some 80 cases were reported in Guernsey alone, and the situation had become so serious that a joint meeting was held between von Oettingen of the Feldkommandantur and Sherwill. It was agreed to make contracting the disease a criminal offence subject to a £100 fine and imprisonment. There was even discussion about setting up an isolation unit for cases on the Island of Herm. In October an order signed by Symons and his German counterpart appeared stating that: 'Sexual relations either with the German soldiers or with civilians are strictly forbidden during the next three months. In case of non-compliance with this order severe punishment by the Occupying authorities is to be expected even if no infection takes place.' Those with the illness were brutally despatched to the Russian Front, and Doctor Lewis treated an Austrian doctor, and an Italian conscript who came to him for help to save them from this fate.

There was a rise in abortions and doctors charged two guineas more for babies born to a putative German father than to an Island one. Exaggerated figures for illegitimate births in the Channel Islands circulated during the war, and even though these proved untrue the actual figures were alarming enough on Islands with a population of 66,000 and in days when bastardy and bearing a child outside wedlock were regarded overwhelmingly as immoral. Even allowing for some activity on the part of Island men, published figures show increases from 5.1 to 11 per cent on Jersey and from 5.4 to 21.8 on Guernsey in the percentage of live births recorded as illegitimate during the war years. Of 539 recorded illegitimate births a substantial number were of German origin, and this figure takes no account of births at home or in nursing homes. Nor are figures for abortions available as they were illegal.

One reason for the French women and the involvement of Island women with Germans was that it was not until 1942 that the network of brothels were set up in St Peter Port, St Helier, and St Anne. Their presence gave rise to much ribald amusement at the queues of waiting customers, and at the demand of the Germans for the prostitutes to receive the same food allowance as heavy workers on the Islands. There was also a dispute involving the Island doctors who the Germans were anxious to recruit for medical inspection of inmates and customers at the brothels. The overworked doctors were ordered by the Controlling Committee to inspect the brothels twice a week but in the end the Germans nominated their own doctors for this job.

The last three chapters have considered three forms of collaboration. Frank Falla, one of the most hostile writers about the war years, estimated a very small percentage of Islanders were involved. As far as working for the Germans for wages or helping them to benefit from the black market this was untrue. Exact details of informers are unknown, but it seems that they were numbered only in hundreds. Fraternizing between Island women and Germans was widespread, even though the number of illegitimate children was less than contemporary opinion believed. The difficulty in assessing collaboration is that it was never defined in law. No collaborators ever stood trial, and details of accusations made in 1945 still remain secret.

Part 4

The Dangerous and Lonely Decision: Resistance

9

Espionage and Undercover Information

Immediately after the war a flood of books came out dealing with resistance in occupied Europe and Britain's role in supporting it. The work of the Commandos, Small Scale Raiding Forces, MI9 helping escapers and evaders, SOE arming, and financing foreign resistance and particularly the courage of individual agents who had taken off from airfields like Tangmere and Tempsford for Nazi-occupied Europe were all admired.

Britain's role, described by the distinguished French historian Henri Michel as decisive in every aspect of resistance, seemed beyond reproach as did the conduct of those who organized and took part in resistance. In Europe resistance was given the highest possible profile since it indicated that basic human rights and self-respect had been maintained in a world where European civilization had turned into a charnel house.

Claims of all kinds were made about the value of this resistance. It had helped rescue and protect evaders and POW escapers. It had carried out sabotage of the Nazi economy, and of particular sites vital to German war effort. It had provided intelligence vital to D-Day. By raising armed forces, it had tied down large numbers of German divisions in Western Europe which could have gone east if the population had been completely cowed. In 1944 and 1945 it played a vital military role in disrupting communications. It paved the way for the return to political normality, and helped to discourage collaboration and purge the body politic of Fascism. Besides these practical contributions there was the simple fact that resistance killed Nazis while others were doing their bidding.

Henri Michel wrote, 'there was not a single occupied country which did not give birth to its clandestine resistance', but this was untrue. The Channel Islands produced no organized resistance either by the British government, so keen to foster and praise it elsewhere, or by the Island governments. Writing in 1971 Norman Longmate commented that, 'it is hardly a matter of pride that the Channel Islands should have been the only enslaved country without a resistance movement, though one can feel grateful that as a result they were spared the murders, massacres and atrocities which marked German rule elsewhere'.

During the 1970s, attitudes towards the success or even the wisdom of resistance began to change. As memories of Nazi rule faded, and wartime heroism and patriotism became less immediate emotions, historians probed the case for resistance. They said that by creaming off many of the best men and women, and in the process killing a high percentage of them, secret armies and resistance forces deprived the regular forces of much valuable talent: the Channel Islands raids, for example, produced little tangible success, and led to the death of some of those involved. It began to be stressed that bravery was not an individual matter: it involved others because the Germans took reprisals against the innocent. In Sark, Julia Tremayne said the second raid brought them more misery, and on occasions, such as evasion by Nicolle and Symes or the cutting of cables, the Germans acted harshly on the Islands as a foretaste of what might happen if resistance got going in a substantial way. In France at Romainville prison, where a number of Channel Islanders were to end up, a supply of hostages was kept to be drawn on every time a German or Vichy official was killed.

The Germans were skilful operators of the police state, and employed informers and native Fascists anxious to betray fellow countrymen. They were equally skilled in refinements of execution and torture, and resistance enabled them to put these ideas into practice. Historians suggest the Gestapo and the SS were nourished by resistance, and lives were sacrificed for little purpose other than individual protest.

Close study of resistance showed, too, a mixture of motives. There were the brave, disinterested, and patriotic; there were also time-serving politicians, criminals who enjoyed breaking the law, and sadists who enjoyed killing people. Some were there, as M.R.D. Foot wrote, 'for the tobacco and the rumours of easy women'.

On the Channel Islands, Ambrose Sherwill's plea in August 1940 to refrain from provocative behaviour, adhere to the 'strictest conformity' with German orders, and make the occupation 'a model to the world' was heeded to the end by the overwhelming majority of Islanders. In a sense the official line adopted by Coutanche, Carey, and Leale seems to have anticipated the shift in historians' views because they argued resistance was futile, dangerous, and counter-productive. Their view is strongly endorsed by Charles Cruickshank who wrote, 'It is manifestly impossible that there should have been in the Channel Islands anything like the resistance movements which developed in the larger countries occupied by the Germans.' He described the action of discouraging resistance as 'simply plain commonsense', and agreed that such people as escapers placed innocent lives at risk by their actions. Just as the Island governments hushed up what resistance there was and ill-rewarded the resisters, so Cruickshank largely ignores the courage and significance of unofficial resistance which did lead Islanders to take the lonely decision to oppose the Germans.

There are arguments on both sides in the Islands as elsewhere in Europe. Something on a similar scale to European resistance was impossible: the weight of the German presence, and the difficulty of escape were strong arguments. The Channel Islands were not a country, but only part of one, and neither their local government nor Whitehall had given any indication that resistance was to be encouraged or favoured. Without direct help by MI9 for escapers, or SOE with sabotage, resistance was hamstrung by British government action, and could only be amateur and piecemeal. Officially the Islands were in a war zone subject to military law, and it seemed likely that the death penalty, so often alluded to in notices, would be enforced. It was certainly passed on a number of occasions and, with the disappearance of Islanders to prisons in Nazi Europe, resistance was unwise. If the relative moderation of the Germans and their good relations with the Island rulers were taken into account, it seemed wisest not to disturb this balance by acts which at best could be pinpricks to German power. Larger measures would only provoke savage reprisals and the deaths of innocent Islanders. It was official policy not to resist. It was illegal under the Hague Convention for occupied people to take reprisals. The last Royal Order had told the authorities to carry on the government to the best of their ability. Other arguments pointed in a different direction. Small acts of resistance were not trivial. A myriad of such acts added up to a substantial burden on the nerves and resources of the occupiers, diverted resources, and prevented propaganda from further reducing the will to resist. In an atmosphere where Mrs Tremayne setting out one afternoon to chalk up V-for-Victory signs lost her nerve, every little act had some significance. As Mrs Cortvriend pointed out, however estimable individual Germans were, collectively they were cogs in the German war machine, and 'to oil a cog was to increase the machine's efficiency'.

A price had to be paid for lack of Island resistance: the suffering inflicted went unchecked and unpunished, and the German war machine functioned without interruption at the expense of the Allies.

Obtaining intelligence was a major risk for resisters, and in the case of the Channel Islands was of two kinds: until the summer of 1944, details of the garrison were needed; thereafter details of the food situation had to be smuggled out. Brave men did this at great risk to themselves. Major Crawford-Morrison, organized the most important of the groups concerned with military intelligence. In his official position as ARP Controller he had a car, and was able to hold meetings without arousing suspicion at the Picquet House (later National Westminster Bank) in Royal Square, St Helier on Saturday afternoons when crowds assembled to hear the German band outside. William Crawford-Morrison, and his main helpers the two brothers, Majors Manley, and Major L'Amy, worked away for years until they had acquired a schedule of military fortifications on Jersey. Some of the information was gathered personally by such simple expedients as asking the Germans to notify him of their times of artillery practice so he could warn people of possible damage or noise, or on another occasion memorizing a map of German defences on the wall of von Schmettow's office. Crawford-Morrison also operated a network of agents, some of whom worked as drivers or servants for the Germans. One was the gardener at Knackfuss' residence at Linden Court, Frederick Cook. As states surveyor, L'Amy was able to move freely about the Island and spy on German positions. Their information was filmed by Stanley Green, the local cinema projector operator.

Getting information off the Islands proved difficult, but some was entrusted to escapers, and when Crawford-Morrison and his wife were deported to Biberach he decided to take a copy of the information with him. Although the Germans searched his coat and shoes thoroughly, they did not look in the lining of his flat cap where the plans were hidden. When some of the internees were repatriated to England Crawford-Morrison entrusted the material to one of them, and it reached the British secret service. After he had gone the Germans curbed ARP activity and clearly had their suspicions, but Major L'Amy continued the work helped by Monsieur Lambert, the French consul on Guernsey, who was involved in a number of resistance activities which he would not discuss after the war because he had violated his diplomatic privilege. Information had been obtained about naval defences on Guernsey from a Frenchman, Xavier Golivet, who was an electrician worked for the Germans. Lambert agreed to help him escape if he would take the information, but a boat had to be found.

Lambert approached two brothers, John and Thomas Le Page. They had no near relatives, so there was no risk of immediate reprisals. They agreed to take Golivet and his dangerous cargo out. Lambert made a waterproof container for the documents which could be dropped overboard if the boat was searched. The Pages knew the French Consul because when their own fishing boat had been damaged in a collision with a German patrol vessel he had given them the *Etoile de Marin* which the brothers had improved by inserting a 6/8 horsepower engine. Golivet began to go out with them on fishing trips so that suspicion would not be aroused. Night after night in January 1945, Lambert, Golivet and the Page brothers waited for the coincidence of fog and tide they needed for a successful evasion of the tight German fishing regulations. Eight nights passed, but on the morning of 23 January conditions were perfect. It was neap tide, and mist had reduced visibility to about two miles. Shortly before eleven that morning Golivet and the Pages arrived at Albert Pier. While discussions were taking place with the Marine Guards Golivet slipped into the public toilet where Lambert handed over more documents.

As usual, the Pages were required to give details of their intended trip, and said they were going east to pick up lobster pots, and would then turn southwards. They left harbour and sailed towards the Great Russel where they turned north between Herm and Sark to avoid the German patrol boat. At two o'clock the mist lifted, but by then they were ten miles off Sark and were undetected. Darkness fell as they passed Cape de Flamanville, close inshore, and shots rang out. The boat came in on a sandy beach where they were surrounded by American troops who took them to Cherbourg. Their boat was brought in, and a plane sent off to circle the Island to let Lambert know they had succeeded. The Pages were then sent to London where they presented their documents and an up-to-the-date report on the food situation.

L'Amy continued to smuggle information out of Jersey, and in February 1945 five boys, two brothers called Le Gallais, C.A. Luxon, and two others, possibly called Foster and Avard or Havard, were entrusted with this. A boat was obtained from one of L'Amy's informants, William Gladden, a boat-builder living at St Martins, and petrol for it was found by one of the Island doctors. An old furniture van was used to move the boat to Fauvic Beach, and, as there was no horse available, the boys pulled the van themselves past unsuspecting Germans. They left Fauvic Beach on the evening of 22 February, and arrived in France next day. The firing of a gun at a prearranged time from the mainland informed L'Amy they had arrived safely.

William Symes, cousin of James Symes the agent captured in October 1940, owned the Dive in Fountain Street, St Peter Port, a waterfront pub frequented by fishermen and Frenchmen forced to work on the Island. Symes smuggled out information which reached the Maquis and MI9 operatives in France and Spain. But he was caught, and taken to Cherche Midi prison in Paris for interrogation. He was sentenced to imprisonment going first to Compiègne, and then to Romainville from which, after travelling four days naked with about a hundred other prisoners in cattle trucks, he arrived at Buchenwald where he found Stanley Green.

The consequences of being involved in military matters were sharply revealed in the case of a young boy, James Houillebecq of Jersey, who went around picking up weapons and soon had quite a store of them. Others boys were involved, but his parents managed to destroy a list of their names when their house was raided. Houillebecq died later in Neuengamme concentration camp a few weeks before his eighteenth birthday.

In the autumn of 1944 it became vital to get information to London about food shortages. Even though the Germans had said they would notify Switzerland, the protecting power, nothing had happened, and permission had not been granted yet for the bailiffs to approach the Red Cross directly. For once the names of Island officials appear in the ranks of resisters when it was decided to get vital information from Guernsey to London in November. Frederick Noyon, a widower and retired sea-captain, agreed to make the attempt from St Sampson's. His nephew Steven wanted to go with him, but Fred would only take Bill Enticott because he feared reprisals against Steve's parents. Sir Abraham Lainé agreed to provide the information through an intermediary, Deputy C.H. Cross, and on the night of 2 November Noyon collected the material from Cross' house.

Friday 3 November dawned. German artillery practice meant that fishing was not permitted that day, so Noyon went to the harbour police to get a permit saying he was going to drop a net in the next bay, and then sail on to St Peter Port for engine repairs. At one o'clock they set off from St Sampson's, jettisoned an old net in the next bay in case they were being watched from shore, and carried on towards L'Ancresse. At 4.30, mizzle came up. In the mist and gathering dark, the boat altered course for the Channel, and hoisted sail. The aim was to make for Poole in Dorset, but 30 miles north of Guernsey they were intercepted by an American ship which took them back to Cherbourg where their papers were examined. Nine days later they arrived in Britain, and delivered their papers at the war office. For once the government allowed a coded message to be sent

SOE fashion to Guernsey. It said 'Personal message to George. The answer is Yes'. As far as is known it was the only such message sent in connection with espionage.

Part of any successful occupation policy was to deny information to the occupied likely to encourage resistance by censorship of various kinds. The libraries were purged. The newspapers were censored. The *Guernsey Evening Press* proprietor was a co-operative supporter of the Germans, and made no effort to circumvent the operations of successive censors, Kurt Goettmann and Horst Schmidt-Walkoff, although on Jersey, Arthur Harrison of the *Jersey Evening Post* proved more difficult to control. As early as July 1940 in Jersey the *Deutsche Inselzeitung* was produced for the troops, and the editor told Leslie Sinel that it was the first German paper issued in Britain 'for the time being'. In July 1942, it was joined by the *Deutsche Guernsey Zeitung* copies of which reached Sark next month. 'An awful German pictorial on a par with our *Picture Post* is on sale at all the shops showing the British defeats,' said Julia Tremayne and quoted some headlines like 'Britain facing Hunger', and 'Second Front would be Churchill's wildest gamble'. The German news, she wrote in February 1944, was always appalling, and it seemed the local newspaper might stop altogether through lack of paper leaving them with only the German version of events. Any genuine news from the mainland was heartening to Islanders, as Mrs Tremayne wrote in July 1943: 'We all feel a bit more hopeful this week, scraps of news come through saying we are doing well, although this German rag is full of boasts and brag.'

Mrs Tremayne referred to the paper as 'Haw-Haw' headlines. She recognized it for what it was, but it must have been hard to resist the official story deprived as Islanders were of any accurate information from Britain. Those who resisted by breaking the German news monopoly were doing valuable morale-boosting, and for that reason the Germans were particularly severe on those involved in clandestine information circulation from the BBC broadcasts in printed bulletins.

The first temporary ban on wirelesses as a result of the Nicolle-Symes Mission was described by Mrs Tremayne as 'a day of mourning'. The order was issued in October, and confirmed in November 1940, although they were allowed their wirelesses again in time for Christmas. In December she recorded, 'Great joy, we have the wireless back', and at her last normal Christmas for five years, she heard the King's speech and drank his health in port wine.

This temporary ban was followed by the complete confiscation of all wirelesses in June 1942. In fact, confiscation did not prove quite so sweeping. The Irish were permitted to keep their sets. German officials kept theirs, and Frederick Cook was able to listen to Knackfuss' in his kitchen at Linden Court. On Alderney, Clifford Bichard, the foreman, was able to listen to one kept by his German room-mates. Members of the Island governments were allowed to keep sets in secret – von Aufsess listened to Ralph Mollet's regularly, and he expressed alarm, it will be recalled, when the Labour representative, Le Quesne, was arrested for having a set. On Sark, Sibyl Hathaway described how: 'We hid our set in a trunk left behind by one of our friends … and went to the length of packing it in an old moth-eaten carpet to which we added moths from time to time. We only dared to listen to the 9 p.m. news, and there were four of us, Bob, our farm bailiff, Bishop, his wife Jenny and myself.' Elsewhere it is claimed this secret set was kept in a chicken run. What Hathaway did not mention was that the German doctor left his own portable set for her to listen to during his visits.

The order was a violation of the Hague Convention because, although the Germans cited Article 53 as covering their action, this clause made it clear it was transmitters not receivers that were illegal. Julia Tremayne's set had broken down, but she had listened to neighbours, and when all wirelesses were taken away 'we hear no news, except German news, so just try to imagine our thoughts about you all'. She believed the sets would never be returned. 'There is not one in the Islands now and you may be sure the Germans will only give us 'Haw-Haw' stuff. The rumours are alarming, and if we believe them we should be in the depths of despair. Before long she said she felt 'more resigned than ever to our prison life', and this was the Germans' purpose.

Detector vans were in use, but in the main the Germans relied on Islanders handing in their sets. Many failed to do so, and at a stroke became liable to prosecution for the rest of the war, resorting to all manner of tricks to hide sets and spread information. Wirelesses were hidden beneath floorboards, in the bottom of armchairs, in unused water tanks, or in specially constructed cupboards like one made by the Cortvriends. Many were the tales of narrow escapes during the frequent searches. A small set was concealed by one woman under a tea-cosy which she carried round with her pretending it was a teapot while the Germans searched her house. The manager of a St Peter Port bank heard of a woman who had kept a set, but was now frightened and wanted to get rid of it. He took the set and concealed it in the basket of an errand-boy's bicycle he was using. As luck would have it, he had to cycle past Germans, but he got the set to Barclay's Bank, and hid it in the strongroom. To his horror, the bank was subjected to a detailed search, but fortunately for him the searchers were too lazy to go downstairs, and he was ordered to bring the boxes up being able of course to keep the one with the wireless back. Others faced with searches had to lose their sets. One woman plunged hers into the suds of the weekly wash just in time, and another tipped hers into a septic tank.

Possession of a set led to three months in prison and even death. So many were convicted they had to wait their turn to serve sentences in Island prisons. On Jersey, they would have been even more surprised to know the assistant matron of the women's wing in the prison listened to a set in her sitting-room. But all traces of comedy vanish when the fate of some Islanders is considered. It was seen that when Canon Clifford Cohu of St Saviour's in Jersey, visited the general and maternity hospitals he was able to impart information he could only have got from BBC broadcasts, and it is likely that one of the women fraternizers betrayed this fact. It is said that Cohu had a set concealed in the organ loft, and he received information from a cemetery worker, Joseph Tierney, who in turn heard the details from John Nicolle listening to his own set. The

Germans surprised Tierney at the cemetery, and although Nicolle escaped to his father's farm nearby, he was arrested. Others were soon roped in including Joseph's wife, Eileen, Mr Mourant, a local farmer, and officials at the hospital. Some received short sentences.

Three were sent to the Continent. John Nicolle died in a camp near Dortmund, Joseph Tierney died at Celle, and Clifford Cohu at Spergau. They were not the only men to die for listening to a wireless. A former CID officer Percy Miller and Peter Painter and his young son Peter were among those who also lost their lives. Jack Soyer sentenced for the same offence managed to escape in France, and joined the Maquis. He was killed in action on 29 July 1944, and honoured by them. Others, like Stanley Green sent to Buchenwald for a wireless offence, managed to survive the war.

Ingenuity produced new wireless sets. At first these were handmade mains receivers, but when electricity was cut off crystal sets were introduced early in 1945 which could pick up Forces broadcasts from France. Telephone boxes were raided for earpieces. A large piece of crystal in the Jesuit College museum on Jersey was used to make over 60 such sets, while in Guernsey a jeweller cut up an old meteorite for the same purpose. Sets were available for £10 according to Mrs Cortvriend, and Mrs Tremayne had access to news from a crystal set somewhere on Sark. In 1945 L'Amy wanted a transmitter, because the number of escapers had fallen rapidly once Hüffmeier had taken over. The set was made by a post office engineer, and installed in a convalescent home at Les Vaux where it was possible to enter the room secretly from below. But before the set could operate, the cipher and call sign had to be smuggled out. Gladden was persuaded to build another boat, and two boys were willing to escape with the material. Plans were laid for an escape in April 1945, but bad weather delayed them, and it never took place.

From clandestine radios producers of resistance news-sheets obtained their information. One appeared on each of the main Islands although both were closed down by the Germans. On Jersey, Herbert and George Gallichan produced the *Bulletin of British Patriots* which took as its theme the illegality of confiscating radios. 'For our part', they wrote, 'we refuse to comply with the confiscation order'. Herbert worked in the food office in the town hall where it was typed and duplicated, while George was responsible for distribution. When no one owned up to producing the paper, the Germans seized ten hostages – an indication of how effective they thought this kind of activity was. The Gallichans then surrendered. George was given a year in Dijon Prison, and Herbert remained in Wolfenbüttel concentration camp until the end of the war.

In Guernsey the underground news-sheet, entitled (perhaps unwisely) *GUNS* (*Guernsey Underground News Service*) circulated from May 1942 to February 1944. Conceived by Charles Machon of the *Guernsey Evening Star*, the others involved included Frank Falla, Ernest Legg, Joseph Gillingham, and Cecil Duquemin. A good many others were involved in distribution, but it was policy only to communicate directly with Machon so that even Falla, for example, did not know Duquemin was involved. On Sark, Wakley the carter and Lanyon the baker were the distributors. The sheet, 13½ × 8″ with a heading bearing the illegal V-sign, came out daily and contained about 700 words from BBC broadcasts. It was dangerous to produce it in the office, and even more unwise on occasions to use linotype. This was sometimes done when Churchill gave an important speech, and an ex-editor, Bill Taylor, took it down in shorthand for them to set up in type. *GUNS*' circulation of perhaps three hundred reached out to all the Islands successfully. Mrs Tremayne praised Lanyon when he was given six months 'for trying to cheer us all up by telling us a bit of news'. They had many narrow escapes, said Falla. 'Once a subscriber passed his *GUNS* to a friend with the written injunction 'burn after reading' followed by his initials. Unfortunately this friend left it in a book which he had read and returned to the library. Happily the next person to take out that book chanced to be a regular receiver of our news sheet.'

Falla was worried about security. On one occasion he found a copy on a market stall, and while ticking off the man concerned turned round to find a German directly behind him. Sadly, copies came into the hands of an Irish informer who decided to turn them in.

On 11 February, the Feldpolizei arrested Machon and Duquemin. A typewriter and back copies were found in Machon's possession, and for a fortnight he was interrogated. Faced with threats to his mother he cracked, and Legg and Gillingham were the next arrested. At last on 3 April Falla was rounded up by a Feldpolizei called Einert, taken home and there handed over his wireless. The five men were tried on 26 April, and their sentences confirmed on 17 May. They were two years and four months for Machon, one year and eleven months for Duquemin, one year and ten months for Legg and Gillingham, and one year and four months for Falla. Machon was deported at once and died five months later at Naumburg. The others were forced to work for the Germans, digging trenches, building a bunker, and loading sand on to lorries. On 4 June, in the company of six Feldpolizei, they were taken to the harbour, and next day arrived in St Malo. Gillingham, too, was to die, and although Legg, Duquemin, and Falla did survive it was only by the skin of their teeth. Copies of material from wireless broadcasts continued to circulate after the end of *GUNS*. In October 1944, Mrs Treymayne wrote that she had 'seen Mr Churchill's speech' which had been lent to her, 'and I dare not say by whom'. She expressed her joy at reading this piece of news knowing that it was genuine.

None of those involved in activities to keep up morale received any award or recognition from either British or Island governments. No compensation was paid to them, and no pensions given to the relatives of the camp victims who died. Even when the British government eventually obtained paltry compensation from the West German government for British victims of war crimes in 1964 none of this was given to those from the Channel Isles imprisoned on the Continent, and a letter from the Foreign Office informed them they would have to wait until the conclusion of a definitive peace treaty with Germany. Few are now left waiting.

10

Public Demonstrations and Secret Politics

Bitterness and frustrated patriotism led Islanders to show their feelings against the Germans in outbursts of personal anger or violence, or by petty acts of resistance. Sometimes these were in secret like listening to the forbidden wireless or reading news-sheets. Others were more public, like the drunk arrested in St Peter Port in October 1943 for calling out 'Balls to Hitler', or a boxer in the same town, who hit a German and received two years in prison. Public criticism or insulting words directed at Germans led to severe prison sentences like that on Geoffrey Delauney incarcerated for the rest of the war or a lawyer, Mr Ogier, imprisoned with his son Richard for defamatory remarks against the Germans, who died in a German camp in 1943.

Cutting communication cables began in March 1941 at St Martin in Guernsey. Such an act achieved very little because repairs could be quickly carried out. Carey denounced such activity as stupid and criminal because it involved others in punishments, and after the war Coutanche expressed the same view: 'I didn't think then, and I don't think now, that it did any good to anybody'. However, German reaction showed they resented it, and feared it might lead to more serious actions. The curfew was extended by two hours, and 60 Islanders were ordered to carry out night patrols of the wire for three weeks. John Boucheré remembered his father and brother were among those forced to do this duty. There was a subsequent cable-cutting episode in the Les Vardes district although on this occasion as no civilians lived near no-one was punished. Other minor sabotage had more tangible results. Charles Roche, airport controller on Jersey, told his groundsman, Joseph Quernard, to cut the grass so closely that it became slippery in wet weather, causing aircraft to crash into each other. It is certainly true there were runway collisions like that on 29 August 1940 and claims have been made for over 20 accidents being caused. Questioned about the shortness of his grass-cutting, Quernard told the Germans that climatic conditions conditioned the length.

To people living under dictatorship such small signs of opposition possessed a greater symbolic importance than their trivial nature might suggest. It is in this light that the V-for-Victory campaign started in June 1941 on the Islands needs to be regarded. It was not simply the childish painting or distributing of V-for-Victory signs: the act represented widespread determination to show the Germans they were unwanted.

They were certainly not 'trivial' acts because, as we have seen, a number of people like de Guillebon, Mrs Le Norman and Mrs Kinniard suffered imprisonment as a result. So did one of the most successful V-sign campaigners, Roy Machon. Roy had been involved in cable-cutting, and used his spare time to make V-for-Victory badges out of coins. He was given six months which he served at Munich, although he was then sent to Laufen internment camp for the rest of the war. His friend, Alfred Williams, continued to make the badges without being detected. The first V-for-Victory signs appeared in the St Martin district near the Hotel Beaulieu. The Germans retaliated by confiscating wirelesses over a wide area, and roping in civilians for a month's night-time guard duty. The signs did not stop in spite of threats from the Germans and Carey, culminating in the issuing of the poster offering a reward for anyone who could help detect the culprits. Mrs Cortvriend said Carey told her he went as far as this because prominent Islanders were threatened with deportation. Although de Guillebon was caught the signs continued to appear chalked on gateposts including the Feldkommandantur headquarters, in tar on the roads, in chalk on German bicycle-seats, made in matches on tables, cut from cardboard and slipped through letter-boxes, left on shop counters and in other public places. Some people even took to knocking with the morse V.

Prosecutions continued, and 19 children from Castel Primary School were hauled before the Nazis with their parents and teachers and threatened for their activities. In the end the Germans infuriated by the outbreak of V-sign drawing throughout Europe decided to use the symbol themselves incorporating laurel leaves and using it as a peace symbol, and this eventually had the desired effect.

It is not surprising that the first serious public demonstration took place when deportation was announced in September 1942. In Guernsey, the German authorities took a relaxed attitude, and permitted farewell parties to take place. Frank Stroobant organized one for some 200 people. During the evening they sang their way through a patriotic repertoire from 'Rule Britannia' and 'Land of Hope and Glory' to contemporary songs like 'The White Cliffs of Dover' and 'There'll Always be an England'. In St Helier, crowds gathered shouting defiant patriotic slogans like 'Churchill' and 'England'. Troops with fixed bayonets were called out, and in parts of the town like Pier Road, Bond Street and Kensington Place young men gathered – several of them from Queen Elizabeth College. Leslie Sinel described how, 'The Germans chased some young boys, and one of them unloosed a beautiful right hook and laid out a German officer; others played football with a German's helmet.' Some 14 were captured and imprisoned at the Gloucester Street police station for a fortnight. They were tried, and although some were let off, others received a month in prison, and a man who was said to have incited them was given three years.

When the first funeral of RAF crews was held in Jersey on 6 June 1943, it provided the next opportunity to indicate what ordinary Islanders felt.

The cortège passed through crowds numbering hundreds, and Coutanche himself attended the ceremony in the Mont L'Abbé Cemetery. This was followed on 17 November by an even larger demonstration of silent patriotism when victims of the HMS *Charybdis* disaster were buried at Foulon Cemetery. Falla was present and described the scene. Many people, he said, were suffering from heavy colds, bronchitis and even pneumonia, due 'mostly to the lack of nourishing foods'. Nevertheless, under grey winter skies, several thousand Guernsey people crowded into the cemetery. Nine hundred wreaths covered the graves, and the German censors had their work cut out removing all patriotic references from the list of details given in the *Guernsey Evening Press*. They stopped all publicity for the funerals on Jersey, and soon afterwards an order limited the number who might attend such occasions in the future. The *Guernsey Evening Press* managed to produce a four-page supplement on the funeral, and the censor ordered that no more than 2,000 be printed. Apparently the order was defied and 5,000 were distributed.

The last time the Islanders were able to demonstrate their feelings was in June 1944 on hearing news of the D-Day landings. According to one eyewitness, 'when the invasion started on June 6th some hundreds of people in Guernsey went nearly mad with joy and excitement singing 'Roll Out the Barrel', and 'There'll Always Be an England'.

The Germans issued orders forbidding all public demonstrations of any kind and Hüffmeier was to repeat these orders up to the last minute in May 1945. The curfew was increased by three hours, and all places of public entertainment closed.

The least likely form of resistance was the growth of a politically motivated opposition determined to use the circumstances of the war to oust those in government who had co-operated with the Nazis, and seize the opportunity to recast the outdated government system of the Islands. Intelligence reports referred to opposition political groupings known as the Jersey Democratic Society, and the Guernsey Underground Barbers. The former, founded by a communist who had fought against Franco, was preparing a campaign for 'the abolition of Jersey's feudal system'. Their main work was to contact ROA Russian troops in the German army, or Russian Todt workers. The group's network which is said to have had nearly a hundred members was involved in sheltering and feeding escaped Russians, and also supplied paper, and other materials for underground news-sheets.

It has been claimed that in 1945 the Jersey Democratic Society, or at least its Marxist members, linked up with Communist Germans in the Wehrmacht, and played some part in the opposition among the troops. There was certainly sufficient evidence of impending mutiny among the ROA troops for the Germans to disperse some of them from Jersey to Alderney and Sark. There was a Jersey Communist Party and they were involved in the decision to erect a memorial in 1970 to Russian slave workers killed on the Islands. The Russians for their part gave gold watches to some who sheltered Russians and have sent Embassy officials to Island liberation celebrations over the years.

As for the Guernsey organization, it never seems to have developed a political content, concerning itself with threats to punish collaborators.

Politically motivated resistance to the German command began under von Schmettow, rapidly increased under von Hüffmeier, and came not from Islanders but from some Wehrmacht soldiers, and Kommandantur officers. Once the Islands were cut off, and fiercely attacked from the air, D-Day had taken place, and the evidence of defeat had arrived on the Islands from St Malo to fill the underground hospitals, the morale of the garrison began to decline. As the months advanced into the icy winter of 1944–45, the rank and file of the Germans began to experience what the Islands had long endured: shortages of every basic item of civilized life, and eventual starvation. The military authorities reacted with severe laws and courts martial when the troops began to take the law into their own hands seizing firewood, looting Red Cross parcels belonging to the Islanders, and thieving every conceivable item. Matters became worse when Hüffmeier announced there would be no surrender, and attempted to restore military discipline with guard duties and kit inspections of soldiers dropping dead on their feet through starvation.

As early as July 1944 an Islander noticed, 'On Sunday night a lot of the troops got drunk and started fighting. It was a political fight and there was shooting going on, we could hear it until the early hours of the morning. It must have been the Nazis and the Slovaks and the Poles. Several men have been taken to hospital in Guernsey badly wounded, so it looks a good sign for us if they are fighting amongst themselves.' Only a week or so later there was another row amongst the troops, and there is 'great unrest'. A fight among German sailors in a Jersey café led to a fatal stabbing. Desertions began. A sailor hid with his local girlfriend, was captured, escaped and committed suicide. A young Jersey girl was sentenced to death for hiding a deserter who was himself shot. The German medical officer on Guernsey advised that morale among ROA troops was very low, and Wulf therefore dispersed some of them. Thirty Russians, unarmed, were sent to Sark, and others to Alderney where two soldiers were executed after courts martial as late as 2 April 1945.

From some source, either Marxists within German forces, or those within the Jersey Democratic Society, seditious literature began to circulate in matchboxes and cigarette packets. One document read: 'Soldiers in Jersey. How long do you intend to take part in this, the biggest deception of all time? How long do you want to stay here and starve? The war is lost.' Another addressed to the 'Soldiers of the Channel Islands' read: 'Pay attention to the following: When the signal is given for the rebellion, tie a white towel or handkerchief around the left arm and follow the orders of your leaders. On principle, all officers are to be arrested and on resistance shot immediately.' The documents urged the soldiers not to shoot saboteurs because every act against the Nazis helped them. 'Free yourselves through a great act of liberation', the subversive document ended.

This did not happen, but there were violent incidents. The first of these is still a matter of dispute. On the evening of 8/9 March, a conference was being held at the Palace Hotel in St Helier, a Todt building used by the Wehrmacht for planning the Granville raids. According to one account a fire broke out, and as the Germans did not trust the fire brigade they decided to put charges round the fire. These blew up demolishing the hotel and killing nine Germans, and further people were injured and property destroyed by exploding ammunition. Another version is that an explosion occurred first killing considerably more than nine Germans, and that the fire was a consequence of the explosion. It is said that an employee at the hotel was warned not to go in that day by someone who knew an explosion was going to take place.

On 18 March, while he was travelling in the interior of Jersey, General Wulf was the object of a bomb attack. The bomb bounced off a wheel and did not explode. Mrs Tremayne noted on 24 March that 'another' attempt had been made to kill a leading German officer. At the same time a store with ammunition and vehicles was blown up causing damage to surrounding property.

The counterpart to sedition in the ranks was treachery in the officers' mess. Hüffmeier and Wulf succeeded in polarizing the officers between fanatical Nazis and those who believed resistance was futile. Von Aufsess, made plans to escape from Jersey, but was then transferred to Guernsey. There he hid his diary behind the wallpaper of an adjoining room. Von Helldorf was confined to his house and then sent to Guernsey. Three days after Hüffmeier's 'never surrender' speech in the Odeon Cinema, von Aufsess and von Helldorf met (according to their post-war statements) to plot the arrest of Hüffmeier. They decided this could be done when he went alone early in the morning to the officers club at Castle Carey Hotel. However, five days after this meeting on 28 April, von Helldorf was banished to Herm, and von Aufsess could do nothing by himself. By the skin of their teeth the German forces survived intact without mutiny, but by May 1945 there were clearly many signs that the force was at the end of its tether. In a row between sailors and a group of German officers a few days before Liberation, order was only restored after a sailor had been executed against the wall of the Jersey Motor Transport garage on the front at St Helier.

11

The Courage and Suffering of the Island Escapers

Three teenagers, Maurice Gould, Peter Hassall and Dennis Audrain, decided to escape from Jersey in May 1942 taking an attaché case containing photographs of German fortifications. The small boat they were in sprang a leak and sank. Audrain could not swim and, in spite of desperate efforts by his two young friends, he drowned. Gould and Hassall managed to reach the shore and were found huddled naked together for warmth on the floor of a deserted bungalow, their wet clothes in a pile beside them. The two boys were sent to prison camps in Germany. Gould died at Wittlich of tuberculosis in 1943, and Hassall managed to survive to the end of the war.

Nineteen-year-old Peter Crill on Jersey had a 12-foot sailing dinghy which he managed to smuggle to a farm near Fauvic Beach at Grouville Bay. The dinghy had an outboard motor and Crill, together with teenagers, Roy Mourant and John Floyd, went round siphoning petrol from stationary German vehicles until they had enough for an escape to France. It was decided they would set out on Saturday 11 November 1944, just after the eight o'clock German beach patrol has passed, and at the same time as another boat containing Norman Rumball, Max Le Sueur and Edward Le Masurier. Rumball was a Westminster Bank official who had with him details of the food shortages. His engine failed and the boat drifted back towards the shore for a time, but later the boats separated and the three boys made it to the open sea. Floyd steered with some difficulty because they could show no light in the wartime Channel and he could scarcely see the compass. When the mainsheet slipped from Crill's hand, Floyd lent over the gunwale to grab it, and in doing so damaged the compass beyond repair. They had to stay in the boat as the wind got up, seasick and soaked, as they took it in turns to bale out. In the morning, Mourant was able to clean the plugs and steering by means of the rising sun they came in sight of land. The engine failed once more, and they had to row. But the shore they landed on was liberated France, and they were free.

Escaping from the Islands was one of the resistance acts condemned by Sherwill who described it as 'running away'. He criticized those who escaped, because they put relatives and hostages' lives at risk, and invited reprisals on those who could not escape. Cruickshank even suggested that some escaped from the base motive of believing that life was pleasanter in Britain than in the Islands.

There were at least 160 escape attempts. This wish of young men growing to military age under German rule to escape, the desirability of passing on detailed military information and accounts of the supply situation would all suggest escapers often had patriotic and unselfish motives for their action, but at the end of the war only two people involved in helping them received any recognition. The escapers themselves received no recognition of any kind. No memorial was erected to those who died.

While Britain's record for helping escapers in Europe was remarkable, in the Channel Islands lack of support from Whitehall or Island government meant escape had to be carried out in an atmosphere of hostility from government pronouncements, and without the equipment and radio links which proved so valuable to escapers elsewhere. The decision to escape thus had to be made alone without the benefit of expert advice, and when it had been made the *cheval-de-frise* of natural obstacles was enhanced by the danger of informers. Sherwill not only denounced early escapers, but added (without any evidence) that, 'In the event of a repetition of any such incident there is a grave possibility that by way of reprisal, the male population of this Island [Guernsey] will be evacuated to France.'

The Island police were ordered to co-operate in every way with the Germans in patrol work to stop escapers. In a statement issued on 28 September 1940, the controlling committee on Guernsey said: 'It must be known to a good many local inhabitants that some eight persons recently left this Island in a boat with a view to reaching England. As a direct result, drastic control of boats has been instituted by the German authorities, resulting in fishermen ... being unable to follow their vocation ... Any further such departures or attempts thereat can only result in further restrictions. In other words, any person who manages to get away does so at the expense of those left behind. In these circumstances, to get away or to attempt to get away is a crime against the local population ... '

Escape from the Channel Islands was fraught with difficulties, but so was escaping in all parts of Nazi Europe. The Channel Islands had the Feldpolizei, and military intelligence, and there were a number of informers, but these threats to escapers were not on the same scale in numbers as on the Continent. It is true the total of German forces on the Islands was very large, but it was no different from the proportion of German troops in relation to the population in Norway or Denmark, and escapes from those countries were attempted, and persisted in after reprisals. The Islands had difficult terrain, tough climate, and rough seas ahead for any seeking to escape; though the risk of the natural hazards of weather, a rocky coastline, and difficult currents and tides was balanced by good local knowledge of these conditions. As in Europe, severe penalties were threatened against escapers, and limited reprisals taken. In May 1942, the Germans threatened to make parents responsible for teenage escapes, and to deport all men of military age, but such threats were not usually carried out.

Escaping from the Islands contained added hazards like crossing patrolled and mined beaches. The strong points, observation towers and searchlights were effective, and sometimes led to tragedy. In the autumn of 1944 von Aufsess commented that, 'attempts by young Islanders to escape to the mainland are on the increase ... Last week a woman was shot when she was caught in the glare of a Very light at night.'

Restrictions in Guernsey meant that all boats were controlled from three harbours: St Peter Port, St Sampson's and Portelet. Engines were limited to 8 horsepower, and only a day's supply of fuel was allowed. All boats were forbidden to put to sea in poor weather; they had to leave at least one hour after sunrise, and return at least an hour before sunset. Harbour police and customs officials were detailed at random to accompany the boats as a deterrent, and German patrol boats followed fishing craft.

However, it is easy to exaggerate the difficulties. The German garrison like any other was inefficient, and escapes were possible. The British commando and small-scale raiding-forces were able to land unmolested, and clearly submarines could have taken off escapers and resisters if the British government had wished to carry out such actions. Even left to themselves many of the Islanders were well able to take out even the smallest boats, and petrol could always be supplemented by oars and sails. Until June 1944 escapers had to make for England some 60 miles away, and while the Channel contained German E-boats, submarines and mines it also contained Allied shipping, and was criss-crossed by Allied planes. The escapes of Guernsey fishermen like Frederick Noyon, William Enticott, and the Page brothers with vital information in November 1944 and January 1945 showed that escapes were feasible.

A spectacular example involving eight young men occurred in September 1944. Now the war was going Britain's way these young men who had grown up under German rule wanted to escape. For some time they had been working for Major L'Amy mapping the German defences. Unable to find a boat, they set out from Pontac in two canoes and a rubber 'folboat'. Their leader was Bernard Cavey. One canoe containing Frank Killer, Hugh Le Cloche, and Peter Curwood sprang a leak and was forced back. Cavey with four others rowed for six hours until they landed on the coast of France, where one of the young men was confined to hospital. The other four eventually arrived in England. The three who had to put back were arrested. Le Cloche remained in prison for the rest of the war, but Killer and Curwood escaped by covering the top of their prison wall with blankets, and using the rubber hose of a stirrup pump as a rope to get away. They were provided with fake identity and ration books and hidden until liberation by a number of people who risked severe punishment.

Mention of such forged documents draws attention to those willing to help escapers. Almost without exception Islanders faced with requests to hide someone or provide help, did so at risk to themselves. In 1940, many people were involved in sheltering British soldiers sent to Guernsey, and later help was given by people like Mrs Pittard on Sark, or the Le Breton brothers on Jersey. Four names are particularly associated with help given to escapers: William Gladden, Doctor McKinstry, the French consul, M. Lambert, and Wilfred Bertram of East Lynne Farm near Fauvic Beach on

La Grouville Bay east of St Helier. McKinstry received the OBE and Bertram the British Empire Medal among the Occupation Honours in December 1945, although McKinstry's award, like that of his fellow medical officer, Symons, was for public service. McKinstry, a witty Irishman, and principal medical officer on Jersey, was one of few officials willing to help Todt workers, and other escapers, and to provide them with forged documents which he could obtain in the course of his medical duties. At one point he tried to help Crawford-Morrison escape with military secrets by providing false X-ray information although this failed to pass muster with the Germans. Gladden was an elderly Englishman living at St Martin's who collected information for Major L'Amy, and sheltered escaped Todt workers. He was a boat builder and provided several vessels for escapers for which McKinstry could sometimes provide petrol. Lambert sheltered Todt workers, including a French boy he found sobbing in the road and hid in his garden shed, and gave escapers information. He sent out a warning of the Granville raid which went unheeded by the Americans.

'Bill' Bertram and his family, deserve pride of place among unsung heroes and heroines of the Island escape routes. He was a former corporal in the Canadian army who had settled at East Lynne Farm with other members of the family: his brother Charles, his nephew John, and his cousin Thomas who lived nearby with his family. They helped at least eight separate escapes, including the two American airmen who successfully got away in 1945. Their bravery in risking death was all the more surprising considering their farm was not in an isolated part of the Island, but on Grouville Bay where the beach was swept by the light from Fort Henry. However, there was a lucky gap in the mines at this point which was of benefit to the escapers. The Feldpolizei visited the farm on several occasions, once nearly catching them listening to the wireless, but happily they remained undetected to the end.

Precise totals of escapers are not easy to come by. In the case of Jersey it was not until the liberation of France that escape became possible on any extensive scale, and then Gladden, McKinstry and the Bertrams played a part which had no parallel in neighbouring Guernsey. Richard Mayne has listed some 80 escapers including Dutch and French workers. Between 8 September 1944 and 22 February 1945, 71 tried to escape from Jersey, and of the 68 Channel Islanders, 47 were successful. Of the 21 that failed to make it, Douglas Le Marchand was shot, six were drowned, and fourteen were captured, although three of these escaped and one made a second successful escape attempt. Many of those involved were teenagers or young men, but there were brave women too, including Barbara Hutchings and Rose Perrin who escaped successfully, Barbara Turner who was captured, and Madelaine Bisson drowned with her husband Ronald in an escape attempt soon after their wedding.

Escapes from Guernsey have been chronicled by David Kreckeler, and in the main took place in the first few weeks after occupation when Islanders took advantage of the considerable number of abandoned boats, and the absence of a large garrison to make good their escape. 78 people are recorded as having escaped from Guernsey, and 63 of these did so between 1 July and 6 September 1940. To these figures of escapers by boat from the two main Islands should be added two who managed to escape from Alderney, and two from the purchasing mission at Granville. There was also at least one Frenchman, Dennis Le Cuirot who escaped in disguise on a Todt workers ship.

Although some parties of escapers from Jersey were completely successful including no less than nine on one night (9 October 1944), tragically others did not succeed. Perhaps the saddest of these was the death of the newly married Bissons, and their two young companions, Andre Gorval and Roy Luciennes who set out from Rozel on 12 November 1944. Their engine failed and they drifted helplessly till they struck a rock off La Saline Bay two hundred yards from the shore. Though they shouted for help in full view of some German soldiers, nothing was done, and permission was refused for the lifeboat to put out. Only a few days later another attempt failed. Peter Noel was captured and imprisoned, while John and Bernard Larbarlastier were drowned.

A few individuals escaped by themselves. Dennis Vibert made his first attempt in November 1940. On reaching outlying rocks 20 miles west of Corbière, a storm blew up and lasted for four days. He tried to return, but his boat struck a rock off St Brelade's Bay and sank although he managed to get ashore undetected. Later he found an eight-foot dinghy, and managed to fit two outboard motors – the boat can still be seen in La Hougue Bie Museum, Jersey. It was hidden at his father's house, and in a garage between the main road and the beach at Bel Royal. In September 1941, Vibert set off again, and rowed for four miles before he dared switch on a motor. An E-boat passed nearby almost swamping him. A storm blew up once more, one motor failed, and the other broke away. For three days and nights without supplies he rowed across the Channel, and on the third night was picked up by a destroyer a few miles off Portland.

Frank le Sueur was another individualist. His first attempt to escape in September 1944 failed, and he was sentenced to eighteen months. Le Sueur was determined to escape, and the first step was to get out of prison. This he did by an ingenious ruse. He pretended to be sorry for his misdeed, and was soon on friendly terms with the German officer in charge of the prison. Le Sueur suggested they should go fishing, and this was too tempting an offer for a German to refuse in days of dire food shortages. As a local man Le Sueur promised him a good day's sport, but said he would have to collect his tackle first. The officer was locked in a shed and Le Sueur went into hiding for a few weeks. He escaped with four others helped by Bill Bertram on the night of 11 November 1944.

Usually, however, escapers went in groups. There was comfort in numbers both at the planning stage, and in handling unseaworthy craft in dangerous waters. This was certainly true of the Guernsey escapes in 1940. The *Dauntless* left Perelle Bay on 1 July with seven people including two women and landed at Budleigh Salterton after 16 hours at sea. The *Dodo II* sailed to Plymouth the same day with two crew, while the *Florida III* ended its successful voyage at Falmouth with a party of twelve. The fourth vessel to leave that same day was the *Mayflower*, which was the most substantial boat to leave the Island during the war. She was owned by Clifford Falla who had canvassed for anyone who wanted to escape, and received a big response. In the end, 28 people joined the escape voyage which began at eleven at night from Grand Havre Bay. The escapers made land at Start Point not far from Dartmouth.

The last escapes from Guernsey that year took place in September, and were responsible for the German threats and Island government proclamations directed against escapers. Frederick Hockey and six men moored a small boat at Hommet Benest, an islet off Bordeaux Harbour, in which they rowed out to *Tim*, a motor boat. *Tim* was rowed to a point north of the Palatte Fougère before the engine was started up for a voyage lasting 19 hours which eventually ended at Brixham. At this stage the British government clearly approved of escapers. The story was published in the papers, and details included in an RAF leaflet dropped on the Islands, presumably to encourage others.

Clearly escapes from Guernsey were more hazardous as there was no alternative to a lengthy voyage across the wartime Channel, but there were some. On 14 August 1943, four men and three women escaped in an 18 foot dinghy, the *Kate*. Like others they had decided it was a good idea to move their boat first to near Bordeaux Harbour. The engine broke down on the way across, but after a voyage of 14 hours they entered Dartmouth harbour. They were closely questioned on conditions in the Islands.

A smaller party of four escaped from St Sampson's on 15 September 1942. The two men involved in taking out the *Whynot* fishing boat were her skipper William Lawrence and his partner, Herbert Bichard. They took the boat north and picked up two French girls, Mlle Broche and Mlle Raymonde who were hidden under a tarpaulin while under observation from the shore. Bad weather lashed the craft for over 50 hours, and they had to work hard at baling out much of the way. Two days later the *Whynot* was sighted off Portland. The escapers were luckily taken on board a patrol boat because they had strayed into the West Bay Bombing practice area.

Two events during 1941 added a new dimension to Island escaping. In June Russia became Britain's ally and in October the first Organization Todt workers arrived. Islanders helped the Todt workers when they had escaped, although in the past both ROA forces and Todt workers had been among those looting and stealing Island property. It is estimated that 20 were hidden on Jersey and in August 1944 the Germans admitted 13 were still missing, although three were caught at St John's soon afterwards. Richard Mayne's father, and the Vaynors were among those who sheltered escapers. Gold watches were presented to some Islanders by the Russians who as late as 1965 honoured one of the Islanders who had helped escapers.

Mrs Louisa Gould ran a grocer's store, and had two sons, one of whom was killed in the Royal Navy in action. Soon after she heard of this, a starving Todt worker, Feodor Bourriy, presented himself at her shop, and she took pity on him. McKinstry provided false papers. He was taught to read and speak English and even joined Boots Library in St Helier and obtained a job. The Gould family were convinced Bourriy was informed on by a woman fraternizer, and although he managed to escape the Feldpolizei raid in June 1944, Mrs Gould was taken, and a Russian dictionary found in the house was enough to convict her. Her sister, Mrs Ivy Foster, and her brother Harold Le Druillenec were arrested as well, and each had an illegal wireless in their house. Mrs Foster got a five-month sentence to be served on the Island, but the others embarked on two journeys of horror that were to end in concentration camps. Mrs Gould perished in Ravensbrück in February 1945, and Le Druillenec, after a nightmare life in six different penal institutions, ended by nearly dying at Belsen. Among others punished for helping Todt workers were Edward and Nan Ross, and Miss Pitolet.

From Alderney there was little chance of escape and the only successful escapes took place in transit away from the island. T. Misiewicz arrested, aged 14, in Poland found himself in Norderney Camp in June 1942, and escaped in December 1943. 'A transport of Russian prisoners were being sent back to the Continent and I got among them. Prisoners were helping each other and some of the Russians whispered to me that when the roll was called that I was to answer to the name of Sokolov ... So I was Sokolov and walked onto the ship and disembarked at St Malo.' Misiewicz was soon recaptured after escaping from the depot at St Malo, and it was only after two more attempts that he finally reached London and was able to join the Free Polish Army.

Details of escapes from one of the death trains which originated in Alderney have emerged from SS records because the commandant of Sylt Camp, Maximilian List, and Kurt Klebeck in charge of the guard detail on one of the trains, were subject to a disciplinary hearing at Berlin in November 1943 following the escapes. The transport concerned was originally planned to have 200 sick prisoners, but 50 died before arrangements could be completed. List described what happened at the SS hearing. 'When this transport was put together on Alderney the one hundred and fifty prisoners were specifically asked if they would rather work or die. I recall that they answered to this that they would rather die. When we walked back to our quarters there was quite a bit of laughter about this.'

List said that he feared tuberculosis among the prisoners might spread throughout Sylt, and therefore the sick prisoners should be sent away 'for extermination' at Neuengamme. During the enquiry Klebeck added that the prisoners were unable to work due to festering sores and dysentery, and confirmed 50 died between making up the transport and its sailing from Braye Harbour on 5 June 1943. On arrival at Cherbourg the prisoners were herded inside three of the wagons.

During the night the train had been in complete darkness because they had no batteries for the lights. Next morning the Germans found the ill prisoners had made a hole in the floor of one wagon through which ten escaped, and two more did so during the confusion of its discovery. A partially made hole in another wagon was also found and shored up. The guards herded the prisoners into two wagons for the journey on to Neuengamme where they arrived on 15 July. By then, another seven had died.

Other escapes of Alderney camp inmates took place in the summer of 1944 when the camps were closed. For instance, 280 prisoners were loaded on the *Gerfried* and arrived at St Malo on 1 July after an appalling voyage. One train took them north towards Kortemark in Belgium where they were to work on manufacturing VIs although they had been reassigned eventually to Buchenwald. A Czech political prisoner who had been on Alderney since February 1943, Robert Prokop, has described what happened on that journey. Some 200 arrived at Kortemark, and on 4 September attempted a mass break out. It seems this was betrayed and over 30 prisoners were shot. Only a few like Prokop succeeded in escaping. He took with him a Slovak guard who had been employed by the SS, but had become his friend at Sylt Camp.

William Wernegau was a German leftist who had been captured by the Vichy French in Algiers, and handed over to the Germans who put him in Sachsenhausen before transferring him to Alderney. He was among those evacuated in June 1944. On this particular train, the SS adopted the unusual measure of putting guards inside wagons with the prisoners, and as there were a good many Russians on the train murder was soon committed. At one station while there was a raid some ten Russians escaped after killing a guard. The Germans warned the prisoners that any further deaths would lead to reprisals. A day or so later two SS guards were strangled, and a further escape took place. 'The SS stood on both sides and wildly shot long bursts with their machine-guns into the train, killing many. Then they simply threw the bodies out of the train and left them there. This last incident occurred near Toul on the night of 26-27th July 1944 where a memorial stands today bearing the inscription "Here are buried seventeen victims of Nazi brutality".' The train continued into Germany with wounded on board. Wernegau himself managed to escape with a Pole, and reach American lines.

Nowhere were the risks of escaping more obvious than on Alderney itself and Wernegau and Prokop describe a particularly horrifying example of a failed escape leading to death in the summer of 1943 in broad daylight in the middle of St Anne. Their account was confirmed after the war by a corporal working in the ration office in New Street. The victim was Willy Ebert, a trustee or kapo, who had escaped and got as far as St Anne Church then in use as a store. 'A kapo climbed onto the roof, smashed a window and opened the door, the SS men entered the Church and Ebert was led out. They beat him with iron bars, but still he tried to run away ... He ran through the graveyard towards New Street, but before he reached the street the SS fired and hit him three times.' Finally, he was dispatched with a shot in the head in spite of appealing to a passing German officer.

Part 5

Occupation Life for Ordinary People

12

War Crimes: Billeting, Looting and Destruction of Goods and Property

Collaborators and resisters made up only a few hundred of the population. For the majority of the people daily issues were of a different kind. Their everyday lives were the subject of some of Morrison's wilder remarks and inaccurate comparisons when he reported to the cabinet after his liberation visit that: '... on the whole the situation at least in Jersey and Guernsey was reassuring, and while of course, the Germans have left behind them a good deal of damage which will have to be put right and the economy of the Islands has been dislocated, the problem of their rehabilitation should be less difficult than was to have been expected. Certainly, as far as material damage, the Channel Islands have suffered nothing that compares with the damage due to enemy air raids in this country, while the health of the population does not seem to have been seriously impaired.'

Yet even his report contained evidence of a different state of affairs. Morrison admitted that 'nobody who has not lived under the Nazis' can fully understand what occupation meant. Writing to Sibyl Hathaway, Morrison referred to 'the trials and privations of the long period of enemy occupation'. In one passage in his report he said that, 'The Germans left many of the premises they occupied in a disgracefully filthy condition.' This coincided much more with what eyewitnesses said in 1945. One has a harrowing description of evacuees, internees, and servicemen returning to the Islands finding 'on arrival that their homes had completely disappeared; others that while the almost unrecognisable shell of their premises remained, their household goods and effects had completely vanished.'

For many people there was only temporary accommodation, and compensation was by no means paid in all cases. House rents, living costs and taxation had all risen, and many of those returning had lost five years income and savings. Hathaway's daughter Amice returned to her Guernsey home to find: 'All the furniture had been completely wrecked; the drawers of chests and tallboys taken away, and nothing but the frames left. Her silver, which was hidden in the roof, had been discovered and stolen. Fortunately her baby Austin car had been concealed in a haystack by her faithful cowman, but it was a sorry sight.' They sat down on a packing-case to view the damage, and Amice turned to her mother to remark that all the Germans seemed to have left was the sun-blinds. She went over to pull one down in the drawing-room and found it decorated with swastikas surrounding pornographic drawings. The Hathaways were able to spend Christmas 1945 in the Boston Ritz while other Islanders struggled to recover from five years plunder of everything in their daily lives.

Economic difficulties began with evacuation. Banks limited withdrawals to £25, and people could not take more than a suitcase or two with them. Savings, securities, homes of a lifetime, treasured and valuable possessions had to be left to the whim of the conqueror. Sometimes neighbours helped by receiving valuables, or taking over the running of shops and other businesses, but in many cases there was no time, and as the ships steamed towards Britain they left behind thousands of fully furnished homes, hundreds of well-stocked hotels and businesses, pubs full of beer, and garages full of petrol. 'One has to be very brave to turn the key in the lock of a home one has had for life and flee at a moment's notice', wrote an Islander.

One of the first tasks for the Island governments was to assume responsibility for this property. In Jersey, the superior council issued orders on 22 and 27 June 1940. Household furniture and effects were to be collected and stored, and arrangements made to collect and dispose of perishable goods. Goods in store were to be retained for 40 days after the return of their owners to the Islands. Land and livestock were in effect nationalized for the duration, although farmers received no compensation for their loss. Special arrangements were made to transfer livestock, agricultural machinery, and petrol from deserted Alderney, although here too no compensation was paid. Sadly, the Island governments proved unable to protect their citizens' property. In October 1943, an eyewitness who lived opposite Lovell's storehouse in St Peter Port commented that: 'The Germans never stopped taking the furniture away in vans from the store to the White Rock where they have special sheds and packers for shipping to Germany. What they are taking mostly belongs to those who left for England, who had stored it for safety or so they thought.'

Island governments were under severe and constantly mounting financial pressure, but they did do something to mitigate the difficulties resulting from the breakdown of legal and financial contact with Britain. They shouldered the payment of pensions payable by the British government. After liberation, the states voted to pay pensions and half wages to all returning civil servants, a privilege which extended to only a few other Islanders in the employ of richer firms like the banks. Otherwise those who were evacuated lost five years wages.

Island governments also agreed that people should file claims for damage to their property for treatment after the war. This often meant property remained in disrepair or near ruin for the rest of the war. Writing in October 1944 an Island official said these claims, 'will have to cover not only damage by bombs, but also damage to property, both movable and immovable, which has been in the possession of the German forces and their auxiliaries. The number of dwelling houses and business premises thus occupied exceed three thousand [in Guernsey alone]. In a considerable number of cases houses were completely demolished, while the erection of fortifications ... has rendered useless hundreds of verges of pastures and arable land.'

Ten per cent in Jersey and 12½ per cent in Guernsey of agricultural land was wasted by the Germans. The official concerned admitted that there would be no compensation for the loss of trade by businesses, like tomato and flower-growers whose trade had largely vanished. Owners of pedigree cattle would get no compensation even though their herds would degenerate due to lack of breeding and feeding requisites. All investments would lose interest in the Island, while Islanders would also suffer from increased taxes and lower wages and thus be unable to save. The disappearance of many materials meant that maintenance of houses and domestic appliances was impossible.

Just at the moment the Channel Islands lost a third of their population they were compelled to pay the costs of the Occupation in conformity with the Hague Convention of 1907, which laid down conditions for the treatment of civilians by occupying forces. They continued to pay until 1942 when the Germans agreed to shoulder three-quarters of their own costs. Occupations costs included the wages of those employed by the Germans, the cost of transport and public utilities, and the rents of requisitioned property. John Leale on Guernsey and Edgar Dorey on Jersey had their work cut out to make ends meet, and in spite of all they tried to do the two main Islands were forced into debt. The budget surplus in Guernsey was converted into a debt of £3,022,400 by 1944. Leale calculated the Occupation cost his Island about seven million pounds sterling, and that the total debt was over four million pounds by Liberation Day. On Jersey the government had a debt of over five million by the same date. Tax was raised to try and meet these difficulties. In Guernsey income tax rose from 9d to 4s in the pound and in Jersey the figures were a rise from 1/6 to 5s in the pound. Higher rates of tax were also raised proportionately. In addition, purchase tax was introduced of a halfpenny for every 6d of goods purchased by a merchant or vendor although foodstuffs were exempted. After liberation, the government in London gave £3.7 million to Jersey and £3.2 million to Guernsey to liquidate their debts as quickly as possible.

Financial difficulties were compounded by the introduction of Occupation Reichsmarks (RM) in July 1940 at a favourable rate of exchange for the Germans. Whereas the RM stood at 11.10 to the pound, the occupation orders proscribed a rate of 5 marks to the pound helping to precipitate the troops' buying spree. Germans and others who used this money had it paid into the banks where it was credited in sterling. The governments of the Islands then bought the RM back from the banks to pay some of the occupation costs. Surplus marks could be used for purchases in France. Twenty, five, and two RM, and fifty pfennig coins were introduced, and these gradually drove out all but the copper sterling coins as silver coins were hoarded or sold on the black market. To meet the gap the Island governments had to produce notes of low denomination. Eventually RM became the main currency, and after fluctuating considerably settled down at 9.36 RM to the pound in September 1942. The final stage was reached towards the end of 1943 when the Germans decided to confiscate the remaining British paper money, and RM became the official Island currency.

Economic disruption meant that by 1945 apart from a credit balance in trade with France the Islands' traditional staples had been regulated and plundered without exception. This was to contribute greatly to the food problems of the Islanders from the beginning of 1941 which reached desperate straits by the summer of 1944. Those charged with control of agriculture and fisheries had a thankless task not least because the Germans persistently interfered in matters where lack of knowledge of local climate, sea and soil conditions could only lead to disasters.

On Guernsey agriculture was run by Raymond Falla succeeded by Michael Wynn Sayer in January 1941. He was among those deported in early 1943 when Ernest de Garis took over. There was also a glasshouse utilization board run by A.M. Drake with little success until he was replaced by Percy Dorey in May 1941. On Jersey, Touzel Bree was in charge throughout. Agriculture was directly affected by seizure of land, and requisitioning of produce either by quotas or by direct seizure. The drying up of the export trade seriously affected farmers, and imports of feedstuffs, fertilizers and machinery ceased.

Typical of the problems besetting farmers were petrol rationing and confiscation of vehicles like lorries. As early as 12 July 1940 Mrs Tremayne heard there was no petrol in Guernsey, and saw farmers coming over to Sark to buy up all the horses. Since ambulances and motor buses were also replaced by horses there was sharp competition, and the Germans were willing to hire out their own horses to farmers. Others were imported from France. Overwork and lack of proper fodder soon meant that some horses were worked into the ground, and in 1942 an observer commented 'the poor beasts are just living skeletons. They are suffering from lack of food, the same as we are'. Oxen were sometimes used to draw heavy loads and Longmate says women and young boys were harnessed to lighter machinery like rollers and harrows.

The fundamental problem was to find a substitute market or replacement crops for the main cash crops on Jersey of potatoes and tomatoes, and on Guernsey of flowers and tomatoes. Exports of tomatoes from Guernsey, for instance, fell from 39,960 tons in 1939 to a mere 5,000 in 1943. The new requirements were to feed the Island population deprived of imports, and also the German garrison. In Jersey the main change was the replacement of potatoes with wheat. On Guernsey matters were more difficult. The terrain was harsher, and a large acreage was taken up with greenhouses. These needed plentiful supplies of fuel and water which grew increasingly short as the years passed, and a decision was taken by the Forestry Board to fell trees for new greenhouses and for fuel. Attempts to grow crops like wheat in the greenhouses failed entirely, although sweetcorn was successfully cultivated.

The German authorities intervened at every turn with bureaucratic forms, detailed regulations designed to prevent farmers keeping produce for themselves, or selling to the black market, and towards the end an agricultural police, the Hilfspolizei, under military orders and armed, patrolling farms to prevent theft and ensure that regulations were obeyed.

Mrs Tremayne managed to keep a few hens she fed on house scraps and potato peelings, but after a month or so she was complaining the Germans had ordered Sark to provide 15 dozen new laid eggs a week. 'We get a few, but I hide them, it will be sure death if I am caught', she wrote with some exaggeration.

On Guernsey, the Germans were angry when production in the greenhouses began to fall off, and in November 1941 ordered the agricultural authorities to provide 50 extra tons of vegetables per month for the next three months, and 70 extra tons a month thereafter for the German forces. A Dutch firm, Timmer Ltd., was found to carry out the work, Island labour was bribed by favourable conditions, and Dutch and French workers imported. The Island authorities objected that the scheme was impossible and obtained a concession – winter production was reduced to 30 tons a month, but in the end, as usual, the controlling committee, with the honourable exception of Sir Abraham Lainé, voted to accept the German demand.

German economic policies were not designed to benefit the occupied but the occupier, and looked only to maximizing production with little knowledge of how this might be obtained. Major-General Erich Müller made this plain enough in May 1942. 'During my tours of inspection I daily have the opportunity of observing the conditions under which the Island population has to live nowadays. I do not underestimate the difficulties, but difficulties are there to be surmounted. If the necessities of war demand the taking away of agricultural land, the remaining portion must be worked more intensively. A slack utilisation of land and greenhouses cannot be tolerated.'

Island farmers would have agreed, but their opportunity to maximize production was proscribed by constant harassment. Regulations forbade farmers to move cattle across various imaginary lines without permits, to lift or dispose of potato crops without permission, to thresh except under supervision, to sell garden produce except at the point of production, and to dispose of entire crops of potatoes and cereals other than directly to the states agricultural department.

The Germans seized private property of all kinds, and Müller declared such seizures were not contrary to the Hague Convention. In July 1942, Mrs Tremayne lamented the possible loss of her sewing-machine, and determined to hide her silver in the garden. Such confiscation continued to the bitter end, and von Aufsess wrote in January 1945, 'Every garden hose, every old canvas sail, every curtain, tin of paint, roll of paper, old car, old tyres, everything but everything is demanded of us which we can still squeeze out of this poor little land.'

A widespread feature of Island life that reflected German confiscations was transport. There were some 12,000 motor vehicles on the two main Islands, and by 1942, apart from a few well hidden ones, these had all come into Germans hands. Between September 1940 and August 1941, vehicles up to five years old were called in, and owners offered a bond promising to pay the bearer the value of the vehicle six months after the end of the war. In fact, the valuation arrived at was usually a third of the actual price, and took no account of inflation. Petrol ceased to be issued for Island vehicles, with rare exceptions like doctors' cars, and tyres were confiscated. During 1942, all remaining vehicles were seized, and in September 1943, motor cycles were confiscated. In some cases, owners were infuriated to find they had to provide a service for the Germans. Their vehicles were requisitioned, but they were left responsible for maintenance and might be called upon to be drivers. On Jersey, 12 cars during the day and four at night were kept in readiness, while on Guernsey requisitioned buses were used to ferry troops to their camps. On Guernsey less than 50 motor vehicles were left in the hands of the populace, and the horse came back into general use.

With the disappearance of motorized transport, the bicycle came into its own. Selling for a few shillings in June 1940, by December they were costing £10, and by 1944 black market prices for cycles had reached £50. To keep them going every kind of improvisation was resorted to particularly as tyres wore out. Hose pipes with rope inserted were commonplace, and Wood noticed various advertisements including one offering an inner tube in exchange for food, and another a circular saw for a tyre. Children and old people suffered most, but the Germans rejected pleas of necessity including one from a schoolboy who would have to walk six miles, and another from a 75-year-old woman who wished to visit her 81-year-old sister. Orders went out to confiscate 150 bicycles in each main Island, and the states governments at first refused. But as usual they caved in when the Germans simply threatened to seize 150 at random, and pointed out the Island officials would be better able to decide on cases of need.

Damage to property was widespread and, apart from the houses of the rich which were treated with respect when billeting was imposed, there was scarcely a property that did not suffer. Mrs Cortvriend described how, 'the appearance of most of the houses which the men occupied was rapidly reduced to that of slum tenement dwellings with broken and dirty windows covered with wire netting. What had once been neat and lovely flower gardens were transformed into heaps of filth and rubble.' Properties taken over by Todt workers were said to be 'indescribable for filth and dirt'. On Guernsey, every cottage and house seemed to have been taken over for billeting, and on Sark Mrs Tremayne was always dreading her removal. She was lucky, and Grand Dixcart remained unoccupied, perhaps because the Germans preferred dwellings on main roads, or close to others, but for thousands of other people life was dislocated when an order like the following arrived: 'The houses ... must be vacated by 16.12.41. The owner is permitted to take away his clothing and family souvenirs only. The furniture and the effects such as carpets, curtains, lamps etc., must be left.'

Island authorities sent out forms to all households to obtain details of rooms, and furnishings, and a copy had to be posted near the entrance door. Householders were told to prepare part of the house for themselves, although the Germans often took this rather than the accommodation prepared for them. Billeting costs to be paid by the Island authorities included the use and repair of the building, its equipment, and any domestic utensils 'which may be considered necessary', and the provision of all main services. It was specifically stated that damage 'will not be compensated for by the German army'. The only crumb of comfort was that householders received a small billeting grant. This amounted to 1/6d per soldier plus a further shilling for each subsequent occupant, and also for provision of a separate sitting-room.

What actually happened when a house was occupied by Germans varied immensely. Officers like 'von Aufsess lived well and treated their properties with consideration; the troops billeted on the Sherwills behaved with every politeness. In spite of their horror stories, two wartime diarists had to record the occupation of their own property, and did not find it too unpleasant. Mrs Cortvriend had 'Oberleutnant B' staying first who gave no trouble, and in the last year of the war 'Leutnant-Colonel G'. Although his Nazi views alarmed the Cortvriends, he seemed to confine himself to reading and giving tea-parties in the garden for admiring younger officers. Maugham had to provide night-time accommodation for 12 soldiers at his farm, and although they borrowed his domestic goods and tried to chat up his maids, their behaviour was not oppressive.

Others were less pleasant. The troops molested women, held wild parties and confiscated food and goods for themselves. A billeting officer's report described a house at Les Roquettes which the first German occupants had treated well while an officer was there, but after he left 'it was turned into a barracks. The sealed rooms had been broken into and everything ransacked. The dining and drawing room furniture had been removed. I took Lieutenant E. to view the damage at which he expressed regret, but said he did not see how compensation could be obtained from troops ... who ... had left the Island, probably for Russia.'

With ever increasing shortages of fuel, houses were subjected to plunder of wooden fixtures like furniture and doors for firewood.

Todt workers were far less welcome occupants than soldiers, not least because they were so grossly overcrowded. Molly Finigan ran a guest-house after the war which accommodated just ten guests. When it was used by Organization Todt, it housed between 40 and 50 ragged, filthy and verminous slave labourers. Floors and sinks were often used as toilets. The buildings were infested with rats, and there were outbreaks of typhus.

Public buildings also suffered, as John Leale pointed out in May 1942 when he complained about the occupation of hospitals and schools. Mrs Cortvriend sadly noted how the school building where her children had gone became one of the first soldiers' billets. Frederick Martin has surveyed the impact of the Germans on church buildings in Guernsey which included nearly all the primary schools. He noticed the closing or occupation of schools at La Fosse, St Martin; Emanuel, St Saviour's (Baptist), St Andrew; Capelles, St Sampson; Delisles, Castel; Forest (Methodist), Vauxlebets and Vimiera (Roman Catholic). The Island government had moved to Queen Elizabeth College, but later surrendered it for billets to try and reduce the pressure on ordinary people. Maison St Louis, Highlands, and Jersey College for Girls were among other educational institutions turned into billets, the first two for soldiers and the third for Todt workers.

The Germans showed scant respect for any but their own churches. War damage affected the town church in St Peter Port, destroying the windows, and other damage was done by machine-gun fire (Wesley Methodist church), or shells (Torteval, Methodist). Churches near the airport, like those at Forest, had to close although the Baptists reopened theirs at their own risk. Churches were used as stores and soup-kitchens. St Andrew's Congregational church at La Villiaze was used occasionally as a brothel and then became an ammunition store. St Anne in Alderney was used as a store and butcher's shop, although the bells were saved, two being found on the Island and two at Cherbourg.

Hotels were a prime target for occupation and destruction. In January 1942 Mrs Tremayne reported: 'The Bel Air Hotel is on fire and almost gutted ... What furniture was saved has been broken up for firewood for the Germans, lovely polished tables and chairs, blankets, linen and silver all gone.' The Germans moved on to Stocks Hotel where a month or so later they smashed up the furniture in the hall and dining-room and broke all the wall tiles by shooting at bottles. In July 1943 officers in the Vieux Clos Hotel got drunk and smashed the furniture and windows while the Bungalow Hotel was demolished completely.

It was in October and November 1941 that the garrison of 300 arrived on Sark requiring billets. 'We had an awful scare', said Mrs Tremayne, when 'all rooms and houses were to be ready for them'. Soon her neighbours were suffering. Mrs Sharp had 27 billeted on her. Mrs Rondel had six or eight in her house and had to submit to various indignities including the burning of her books to light fires. Her house was turned into a wireless station, an anti-aircraft gun crew was sited in the garden, and she lived in daily fear of air attack. Her compliance did her no good because when the troops were relocated she was ejected from her house at a few hours notice. So were many others including the old and ill. Miss Hale, an old lady over 80 who was soon to go blind, was one of those turned out, and Mrs Tremayne described how, 'Every window was flung open and pictures, beds, chairs and tables [were] thrown out and caught on the other side if lucky. I am going down to try and help her. Meanwhile she is surrounded with boxes and packing cases, still as chirpy as robin, and as brave as possible.'

Houses like Mrs Walbroath's were destroyed to make way for a road, while bungalows were smashed to provide artillery positions. Mrs Castle Brown's bungalow was moved and blew over a cliff injuring several Germans.

Scenes of such destruction met returning deportees, evacuees and servicemen as they had the eyes of the residents as they watched their homes destroyed and their island vandalized, virtually all done without punishment, and by no means all put right by compensation after 1945.

13

The Wretchedness of Everyday Life

The daily strain of life, particularly on housewives, was far greater than any experienced in Britain except at the height of the blitz. Mrs Cortvriend said people began to have dreams and hallucinations which were plainly the result of strain, and Mrs Tremayne often referred to hers. In one dream she was at a party eating all kinds of food and in May 1944, 'I dreamt I was in one of Lyon's tea shops eating wonderful spice cakes in great hunks and I saw piles of luscious red strawberries ... Our rations this week: little bit of salt, a bit of coffee, and about three quarters of a pound of flour, it's surely starvation diet for the bread is not enough ...' Old cookery books and novels with descriptions of hearty meals were quite afflicting, and Sibyl Hathaway said that after reading *Gone with the Wind* she felt every sympathy with Scarlett in the scene when she imagined bacon frying in the kitchen and the aroma of freshly ground coffee.

Far too many accounts of wartime life in the Islands imply real suffering due to shortages only began in the autumn of 1944 when the Islands were cut off from France. In fact, the early period of good living conditions expired during the winter of 1940–1. That December, both Leslie Sinel and Julia Tremayne described pleasant Christmas celebrations with roast beef, Yorkshire pudding, sprouts, plum pudding, mince pies, port and champagne.

This situation soon changed. The German buying spree in 1940 and the disruption of agriculture soon began to be felt in shortages, and by the end of 1941 shops opened only twice a week to dispense rations some of which were themselves distributed fortnightly only. Later many shops closed altogether, and there was a rush to buy up the last tins of fruit and other luxuries. By February 1941, Mrs Tremayne noticed there were hardly any clothes left in shops, and during the year many items like tea, coffee, fruit, rice and currants became unobtainable except at black market prices. Bread and potatoes, the main staples of diet, were rationed during the year, and by October an Islander listening to the BBC Kitchen Front broadcasts envied the people in Britain with their very different system of rationing.

During 1941 signs of malnutrition and poor health appeared. Some of the children began to 'look very weedy'. Julia Tremayne said that during the summer she had been 'seedy for weeks, feeling like a washed out rag', and thought they were all beginning to get 'a bit nervy and edgy as things begin to get a little more scarce each week'. By the second winter, fuel rationing was in full swing with coal largely unobtainable, and wood controlled by a permit system. Gas and electricity were rationed to certain periods of the day. Mrs Tremayne had a reasonable Christmas lunch and a delivery of coal and logs, but her Christmas gifts showed the steadily deteriorating situation. She received sprouts, a candle, tea, aspirins, and some currants.

Conditions varied from Island to Island, although it is generally true that Guernsey, the poorer Island, with more troops and Todt workers, and responsible for Alderney and Sark, suffered the worst. There they 'are well on the way to starvation', said a Sarkee, who saw queues for potato peelings (at 3d a lb), and people coming away in tears because they were sold out. Sawdust was sold to be boxed and used as fuel, and people seemed to be living mainly on root crops and potatoes. John Leale told General Müller in May 1941, 'that there has been a most noticeable increase in the death rate and in the number of days lost in sickness in recent months.'

Christmas 1942 found Mrs Tremayne in a distinctly unfestive frame of mind. She had had to sell household goods for food. Domestic goods were largely unobtainable as were clothes and shoes. Deportations and reprisals after the Basalt Operation had made matters worse, and 1942 had been 'the saddest year of my life'. There were no cards, parties or presents, although she found a bottle of wine and cooked a chicken. Above all, there was no wireless to hear the Christmas broadcasts. By New Year, 'all our cupboards are empty'. 1943 was the same: a year of steadily deteriorating rations, and worsening health conditions, in which transport was limited to bicycles and horse drawn vehicles, and 'our clothes are all in tatters'. St Peter Port was like 'a dead city, all the shops are empty, most of them have shavings or coloured papers in the windows to keep up appearances'. Winter brought its miseries as the lack of food, fuel, clothes, and lighting began to take hold. Men started to faint at work, and hours had to be restricted. 'We have been on our uppers for months now', wrote Mrs Tremayne: 'It's very cold and wintry here today, and there is quite a lot of illness about. Heavy colds, bronchitis, pneumonia, due mostly to the lack of nourishing foods. Sugar and fats we miss most terribly … it's a case of slow starvation. We all lack energy, and feel we want to stay in bed, we do at least keep warm there.' At Christmas time 1943 she desperately wished it would be their last occupation winter; Mrs Cortvriend went to hand out her meagre gifts passing the houses of evacuated and deported neighbours, and as she returned in complete darkness she could hear German voices raised in song from the house at the top of her road. The carol was 'Holy Night, Silent Night'. A little further on she met a boy in a blue belted gaberdine coat who reminded her of her evacuated son. He told Mrs Cortvriend they were having sugar beet pudding and a rabbit for Christmas dinner, and they wished each other 'Merry Christmas'.

By March 1944 a note of desperation began to be heard in Mrs Tremayne's writing. 'I believe they are slowly starving us to death', she wrote. Illness was widespread due to lack of food. Potatoes had given out, and the bread ration was insufficient. All they had officially was 3 ozs of butter, 3 ozs of sugar, 6 ozs of flour or oats a week, and 3 ozs of meat, 2 ozs of coffee, and 1 oz of salt a fortnight. There was a daily half pint of separated milk. Winter had seen a reduction in the butter ration. On Easter Sunday 1944: 'Things are daily getting worse in the food line, it is almost famine now and people are looking old and gaunt. Here in Sark we have no fresh meat, not even tinned to take its place, no fish, no potatoes, no vegetables, no flour and insufficient bread. So how can we last much longer?'

In fact, the worst was still to come, and was by no means to be ended by the arrival on five occasions of a Red Cross ship, the SS *Vega*, with individual parcels and other supplies.

To say the Islanders had little understanding of wartime privations, as Morrison did, was to add insult to injury. Nor should it be forgotten that diary writers rarely come from the poorest classes. The poor suffered more for they had no hidden reserves, and no cash for the black market. Many of them were unemployed, or had to cope with extra relatives after the disruption of family life brought about by evacuation and deportation. Molly Finigan paid tribute to her mother for keeping a family extended in numbers by the exigencies of war. 'Food', she wrote, 'that's the main topic I seem to remember from the war years'.

Rationing was introduced in July 1940, and for six months or so the commodities involved and quantities allowed were not unreasonable by wartime standards Rationing then included 12 ozs meat, 4 ozs of butter, 4 ozs of sugar, 4 ozs of cooking fat, 4 ozs of tea, 3 ozs of salt, and 6 ozs of flour a week. But as the years passed the commodities declined and even disappeared, and the amounts were reduced. Meat fell to 8 ozs and by the summer of 1941 to 4 ozs a fortnight. Cooking fat had gone by early 1944. Tea fell to 1 oz by April 1941, and ended in October that year. Butter was cut in December 1943 to 2½ ozs in spite of the usual protests. The ration was not restored to 3 ozs until May 1944, and was to disappear again at the end of the year. Sugar fell to 3 ozs a week although children were allowed an extra 5 ozs. Salt fell to an oz a week.

Milk was rationed from October 1940 on Guernsey and August 1941 in Jersey. Children up to 14, expectant and suckling mothers, and invalids were allowed two pints a day of fresh cream milk, but ordinary users were restricted to one pint subsequently cut to half a pint of separated milk, while the Germans kept the creamed milk for themselves setting up their own dairies where cheese was made. To obtain creamed milk, Molly's mother, walked uphill to St Martins every Tuesday and Thursday pushing a pram containing two large milk cans. Fish rationing began in May 1941 in Guernsey and June 1942 in Jersey. Twenty per cent of the catch was preserved for the Germans and this rose to 60 per cent by late 1944. Catches were always inadequate because of the general restrictions. Potato rationing began in December 1941 with an allowance of 10 lbs each cut to 5 lbs in August 1942 and by the end of 1944 there were none.

Time after time diarists complained about the inadequate bread ration. Rationing began in February 1941 with 4 lbs 10 ozs allocated to each adult a week reduced before long to 4 lbs 8 ozs. Special allowances had to be made for heavy workers, male and female, of 6 lbs 2 ozs, and 5 lbs 6½ ozs respectively. Then from April to August 1943 came an illegal reduction in rations cutting them to 3 lbs 10 ozs. All agreed the quality of bread declined. Molly Finigan said husks and even maggots were found in it, and Julia Tremayne remarked the bread was so atrocious that '... some weeks we need a pick axe to divide it, even the hens leave it.' Later these rations of bread were to cease completely in February 1945.

The effects of this prolonged poor diet are obvious. Everyone on Sark from Sibyl Hathaway to Mrs Tremayne lost weight. Doctor Rowan Revell on Guernsey was worried by early signs of malnutrition including lassitude and dizziness, and although actual deaths from malnutrition were disputed by the Germans at the time, and by some historians since, contemporaries were in no doubt such deaths occurred. In the winter of 1944–5 Maugham said that in January in St Helier, 78 deaths were recorded, the highest figure for 15 years. Lack of proper diet must have made a contribution to lowered powers of resistance with rations providing less than half the necessary calories towards the end of the war.

Some alternative sources of nourishment were available depending on where you lived, and on your income. Although Hathaway, Coutanche, and Carey may have lost weight, it is clear their home lives were considerably less disrupted than other peoples. They kept heating and lighting. Even though Mrs Coutanche had the contents of her meat safe rifled, by and large the ruling class escaped requisitioning and looting. Those who lived by the black market or worked with the Germans for higher wages did not go short; nor did criminals and hoarders unless they were caught. When in January 1945 private stocks of food were forbidden, some remarkable collections of tinned goods were unearthed by Feldpolizei raids. Islanders benefited whenever they could from black market produce. Barter began to play an important part with people selling domestic items in return for food.

On Guernsey, the special aid society established a barter market with a charge of 6d per exchange. Stolen goods circulated, and Todt officials and other German employees brought tobacco or cigarettes to exchange for good quality clothes and even antiques. In June 1941, the states stepped in to ban over 36 items from these markets.

The better-off did help on occasion. Mrs Tremayne referred to several personal gifts at times like Christmas from Hathaway. In 1943 she was given some rug wool, leather and a packet of candles. On one occasion, when she heard all the stored grain and potatoes might be seized, Sibyl Hathaway organized the future seneschal, her farm manager, and a carter, to take a cart to the village hall during the German's evening mealtime when only one man was on guard. They got away with a ton of wheat, according to her memoirs, and this was ground and distributed by the baker with normal rations. Many of the potatoes were hidden in a cellar directly below the Hathaways' drawing-room. Mrs Coutanche provided wood for the Blampieds when they were ill. On rare occasions even the Germans were prepared to be kind. Molly and Joyce Finigan were told by them where they could get thick barley soup at the back of a house at Castle Carey.

After the black market, the main sources of extra food were scrounging and theft, and the use of substitutes which sound picturesque, but were in many cases quite revolting. People looked in dustbins and on rubbish tips for potato peelings. They went to glean from the harvest fields. Molly Finigan remembered collecting acorns for coffee which was also made from parsnips (parffee), dandelions and lupin seeds (roasted and ground). Tea was made from blackberry and camellia leaves, shredded and baked carrots, garden mint, lime blossom, and green pea-pods. Tobacco came from cherry and chestnut leaves, rose petals, coltsfoot and clover. Blackberries were particularly in demand as a fruit, for jam, and for their leaves. Tom Jehan, a friend of the Finigans, whose father was killed in August 1944 trying to defend his potato crop, made pocket money by collecting them.

As vegetable substitutes, nettles, sorrel and bracken were used, and those vegetables that were available found new uses in the form of puddings. As fuel supplies declined food often ended up in an uncooked and runny form on plates. Cakes were made from potato flavoured with dried grapes, and rissoles from swedes and turnips. Seaweed was used for jellies, and every sea creature from spider crabs to ormers gathered whenever possible.

One source of food was received with very mixed feelings. Red Cross parcels were sent on by deported Islanders from their camps in Germany where, by all accounts, the diet at least was better than that in the Islands. When Islanders heard of these parcels, 'it makes our mouths water', and great was the joy when at Christmas 1943 they began to arrive. The vicar sent cigarettes and chocolate to Sark in November, and in January there was an even more welcome gift. I have had, said Mrs Tremayne, '2 ozs of real English Brooke Bond tea sent to me by our vicar at Biberach, what a godsend it was, and almost sixteen people have had a cup of honest-to-goodness tea out of it to gladden our hearts'. In March 1944 she heard that parcels were expected to arrive, and speculated on the odd circumstance that with Britain only 60 miles away their first outside help should come from German camps. These parcels did no more than scratch the surface of want. The next month Mrs Tremayne saw a letter in the paper from a dentist's wife thanking people who had sent bits of nourishing food to her husband when he was ill.

The same day she noted the disappearance of candles. 'God, what shall we do?', she wrote. Life was made more miserable by the gradual elimination of virtually every household good, except toilet paper for which unwanted tomato packing-paper was used. Goods were bartered away, could not be repaired, or simply wore out. Soap was scarce by early 1941 and died out, leading to an increase in skin diseases, and body lice carrying typhus. Salt was virtually unknown by early 1943, and could only be obtained from sea-water in which cooking was often done. Crockery, cutlery, pots and pans, cleaning implements and preparations, glassware, and stationery items were among necessities that became luxuries and then disappeared. Above all, both health and pride were undermined by the situation regarding clothes and shoes. Rationing was introduced in September 1940 after the Germans had brought up much in the shops, but it was of little use. By early 1941 the authorities in St Helier were appealing for clothes for poor children and women. Clothes became unobtainable and were made from curtains and rags.

Cotton, darning wool, and wool itself, except that obtainable from unravelling old or holed garments, were unobtainable, preventing proper repairs. 'Our clothes', wrote one commentator, 'are hanging together with the aid of safety pins'. Householders found vital items of clothing stolen in the night, and one person found all his shoes stolen and had to go to work in bedroom slippers. In one case a man was fined for stealing 2 lbs of wool, officially stated to cost 8s a lb, when the shop price was 24/- a lb.

The loss of footwear was most grievous. There were no waders for fishermen or heavy boots for farm workers. Novel substitutes for leather had to be found by spring 1941. One woman said, 'I am soling my boots with those rubber mats that come off pub counters and have 'Pony Ales' and 'Guinness Stout' written on them, so I must be careful when I kneel not to show my soles.' Ordinary shoes rose from 8/11d to 25/6d a pair. Clogs were imported from France, but they cost 35/-. Otherwise people had to repair their shoes with bits of wood, and the lanes echoed to the rattle of wooden clogs and shoes. Getting a pair of shoes was no easy matter. Mrs Tremayne found her feet wet through at the end of 1943, and applied for a permit to buy a new pair. She was told she would have to wait six months, and when she eventually got them they were men's, several sizes too big.

Behind amusing occupation stories of improvisation, life was in grim reality a wretched business. In September 1941 one commentator asked how with the ending of the paraffin ration, and the reduction in candles they would pass the long winter evenings? In Guernsey by October 1944: 'Most of the people have to stay in bed all day, there is no heat or light of any kind either to warm or cook by, no hot water can be had for toilet purposes or washing dishes, all has to be done in cold.'

By the winter of 1944 there were no batteries, flints, candles or matches. Coal was controlled from December 1940, but became too expensive to buy. The ration ceased in September 1944. Gas and electricity were first rationed, and then cut off altogether in the winter of 1944–5. On Jersey, gas use was restricted in August 1941 to 7.30–12.30 in the morning, and from 5 to 9 at night. On the same Island, electricity was curbed from May 1942 from 7–1.15, and from 7 to 11. In November 1944 it was cut to one period from 6–10.30 in the evening. Gas ceased on 21 December 1944, and electricity on 25 February 1945.

To meet this situation a range of improvised methods of cooking were devised. Margaret Bird described bakehouse cooking when her husband and herself trundled a 14-stone jar containing soup, or a baking-tin holding vegetables in a cloth to the local bakehouse. For a charge of 2d a container, people were allowed to use the bakehouse ovens after the bread had been baked until September 1943. At home there was haybox cooking. This, said Margaret Bird, was most effective. The sawdust that those like Molly Finigan collected was put to good use in a tin with a hole at the side. The sawdust was lit, and gave a good hot top.

For many there was no means of providing hot meals, and the Island authorities acted to provide community ovens and kitchens, and registered people's restaurants. In Jersey, 6,500 people used the ovens, and 1,400 the community kitchens. In September 1944, von Aufsess visited them and thought the contents of the dishes very meagre 'mostly a few potatoes cooked without fat, and some tomatoes here and there'. Here were the poorest Island people on the brink of starvation. In Guernsey matters were equally bad, and when fuel gave out even the communal ovens had to close, Doctor Symons told Carey in September 1944, 'To talk of communal cooking for the whole population or the greater part is only an attempt to conceal the seriousness of the situation … the scattering of a dozen kitchens in different parts of the Island and expecting all, old and young, sick and infirm, to proceed anything up to a mile and more and to carry home the rapidly congealing vegetable stew is puerile.' Towards the bitter end even these meagre services ceased. On 17 April 1945 in Jersey, 11 ovens closed as did the restaurants which 'had been the main dining centres to many hundreds of the poorer class of the people'.

It might have been thought that burning wood would have provided the answer, but the Germans were aware of its value, and as early as July 1941 overruled the system of permits created by the Island governments. A limit of one hundred weight of logs a month was introduced, and as usual systematically reduced until in January 1945 an order prohibited the collection, cutting or gathering of any description of wood even by occupiers or owners. Severe penalties and confiscation of tools were the punishment. Meanwhile the Germans took timber for themselves, and as late as April 1945 Sark was ordered to provide 250 tons of wood for Alderney. 'The lovely chestnut trees just opposite this house are scheduled to come down', wrote Mrs Tremayne. The effects of this order led to criminal attacks on property to get wood in the winter of 1944–5.

Symons told Carey that if something was not done there would be disaster. By December on Guernsey there would be, '… the cold, nearly sixteen hours of darkness, practically no artificial illumination, half-cooked vegetables to eat if lucky, medical services almost at a standstill, no work to occupy the time, for how is work possible under such conditions, the worry and mental distress engendered by these conditions. If there are to be many weeks of these conditions, the lucky ones will be those who die quickly.'

In September 1945 the ministry of health bulletin contained a survey of health and nutrition which concluded that they had not been as seriously affected as had been thought. Certainly this report makes odd post-war reading if reports produced during the occupation are considered because there was no doubt in the minds of medical officers of health like Revell and Symons on Guernsey or McKinstry on Jersey about malnutrition, poor health, nervous illness, epidemics, suffering of old and ill people, the parlous state of Island hospitals, and, with the possible exception of maternity services, of every other medical service. On Sark conditions were desperate throughout the occupation. The doctor left with the evacuees, and a retired Doctor – Pittard – and a nurse-midwife held the fort. Doctor Pittard died and the Island was dependent on the nurse who got appendicitis, and after this there was only the German medical staff. Patients including pregnant mothers, had to go to Guernsey. There was a shortage of medical staff. In Guernsey, Mrs Tremayne thought the doctors should all be given medals after the war because they were 'worked to death' with so few left behind. Doctors had to go with the deportees in 1942 and 1943 still further depleting their ranks. There were no oculists left in the Islands, and few enough dentists.

Lack of proper medical facilities led to unnecessary deaths. Jacqueline Carré broke her leg jumping over a high bank. Removed to hospital she had her lower leg amputed which greatly alarmed her parents considering it was only a fracture. However, gangrene then set in, and the rest of the leg to the hip joint was removed. She was a healthy 19 year old, but died soon afterwards. Molly Finigan referred to her Uncle Reginald who had a bullet removed from his leg, and then died of gangrene poisoning. Lack of disinfectant, surgical spirit, heating for wards and sterilizing units, and shortages of vital drugs as early as March 1942 contributed to bad hospital conditions, and the injured suffered as well as the dying.

Psychological illness was less well studied then, and its symptoms often dismissed as 'nerves', but there can be little doubt that five years oppression brought disaster in its wake. There were suicides at the time of occupation and when Islanders were deported. Others simply lost the will to go on under successive blows. A friend of the Finigans, Clifford Holloway, took his meals at their house as his wife and son had gone with the evacuees. Sadly he heard his son had died on active service, and then his wife died soon after she returned to the Island. Mr Holloway killed himself, and Molly's mother found the body. 'The mental torture from this German occupation is becoming indescribable', wrote Mrs Tremayne as early as September 1942.

There was a positive side to the medical miseries. Both individuals and doctors commented until the summer on 1944 on the good health of many people produced by more exercise, less bad food, and more sleep. Although Mrs Tremayne suffered from nervous depression and bad colds, she often referred to her good health putting it down to the sea air, and spartan living conditions. Her own weight fell from 13 to 10½ stone which was no bad thing for a middle-aged woman. One doctor said in June 1944 that, 'the health of the population has, on the whole, been remarkably good, and much above that which one would have anticipated on the past and present scale of rationing'.

In spite of this Doctor Symons said that, 'the people have only just kept above the danger line' so that further cuts in 1944 would lead to disaster. Moreover, culminative effects had to be taken into account, and by early 1944 people had suffered three years of a diet deficient in almost every aspect. In particular the young and old suffered. Molly Bihet referred to some benefits for children like extra milk and cod-liver oil, but these did not last, and she admitted many were underweight. Statistics show considerable reductions in height as well, and a report by Doctor Revell in 1941 said Guernsey schoolchildren exhibited 'a greater number of pinched, drawn anxious little faces and diminished inclination for hearty play and laughter'. On Sark, the schoolmistress said in the autumn of 1943 that 'all the children turn up like frozen rabbits, full of colds and do nothing but cough and sneeze'.

There is evidence of a rise in death rates, due in part to the rise in the average age of the population following evacuation. Towards the end, however, general death rates were high in the winter months. The average was 13 or 14 per 1,000 before the occupation. During it, they rose to 35.6 per 1,000 in January 1944. It seems hard not to conclude that old people thrown out of their homes, unable to fend for themselves, without cash for black market products, or transport to get to soup kitchens, and too infirm to stand long hours in queues, must have suffered more than younger Islanders.

One of the most vexed questions is whether deaths were due to malnutrition. Widespread symptoms of malnutrition existed. Physically they consisted of loss of weight, tuberculosis, stomach upsets, lengthy septic conditions, neuritis, skin conditions, and a number of cases of enteritis and oedema. Mentally it led to dizziness, inability to concentrate, lassitude and depression. A complaint was made by a Guernsey resident in 1942 that people were dying of malnutrition. The Germans made a great fuss, and insisted on a full investigation. They would only admit malnutrition might have been a contributory cause of death. Mrs Tremayne dramatically referred to old people dropping dead in the streets by the autumn of 1944, and Maugham refers to an increase in sudden deaths from syncope, and fainting fits in public.

Epidemics were largely avoided in spite of the inadequacy of the sewage system, and the lavatorial habits of many of the occupiers. A camp at Rue Sauvage in Guernsey had a privy built over a stream at right angles to the main road in full view of passers by, which polluted water used by the German troops further down its course. From November 1944 the Germans were considering reducing the water supply to save fuel at the pumping stations. When Doctor Symons protested in Guernsey he was temporarily dismissed. Typhoid developed, and there were bad outbreaks in 1941 and 1943 with death among Todt workers, and the closing off as quarantine areas of parts of St Peter Port. Diphtheria increased because vaccine ended, and doctors were unwilling to use untried German products. Apart from some limited imports of medical supplies by the Red Cross: two in 1942, one in 1943 and three in 1944, the Islands were cut off from modern medicine.

Shortage of drugs, fuel and light meant that by autumn 1944 the hospital system was in danger of collapse. Perhaps the most remarkable achievement was that of the maternity services which coped with births without any increase in child or maternal mortality even if anaesthetics were not available by the winter of 1944. Although the managers of Boots in both St Helier and St Peter Port did their best to import drugs from France, or improvise native remedies, by the summer of 1944 there were severe shortages and diabetics died in Jersey General Hospital through lack of insulin. Antisepsis in hospitals suffered from lack of surgical spirit, disinfectant, and even hot water. People were asked to wash their own dressings. It was inevitable that wounds took longer to heal, and septicaemia and gangrene were possibilities virtually unknown in peacetime. Operations were hampered by small but crucial shortages like worn-out rubber gloves, and lack of catgut for sutures. Tomato paper was used to cover wounds, and bandages were made from paper and old bits of cloth. By November 1944, said Doctor Symons, as fuel was reduced to operating theatres, laundries, and cooking facilities in hospitals, 'these institutions can no longer be claimed to be functioning as modern hospitals but rather as medical sick houses'. Hospital staff suffered as well. Nurses' diet was cut at one time to acorn coffee for breakfast, turnip stew for lunch, and no supper at all.

But in the final months for healthy, sick and starving alike there was worse to come.

14

The Last Year and the Red Cross Ship

News of the invasion of Normandy in June 1944 filled many Islanders with conviction that liberation for them could not be long delayed although some thought it would not come until the whole French coastline had been freed. The sounds of the Battle of Normandy were clearly audible in the Islands, particularly when St Malo and Cherbourg fell, and all round them in intensified air and sea warfare in the Channel was evidence enough of a decisive battle. 'I pray and trust there will be no fighting, for the Island folks have suffered quite enough', said one observer. On Sark rumour followed rumour, and in August they heard that British troops had landed in Jersey, 'so we feel the day of rejoicing has nearly arrived'. But it was not to be.

When Julia Tremayne heard a rumour they would be relieved by Christmas she put it from her mind, 'because so many times our hearts are lifted, then flop, nothing happens.' Like so many in Europe who had believed liberation would come by Christmas, she was to be disappointed. By February 1945 she was writing, 'Never have I felt such hunger as I have this last fortnight. Saturday when we got up, there wasn't a bit of bread or anything in the cupboard, these are grim, lean and hungry times for us all.'

It was hardly surprising that neglect of the Islands caused discontent coming as it did after years in which there had been little enough contact or support from England. Bitterly Maugham wrote later, 'we often wondered if any thought of our sufferings, both mental and physical ever occurred to those statesmen in London'. He heard about measures of international relief for various parts of Europe, and no mention of the Islands.

For this neglect there were sound military reasons. Invasion did not take place because of the likely civilian casualties, according to Morrison, but this was not the prime factor. In the past Churchill had shown willingness to discuss and even urge operations involving substantial loss of life.

In the planning stages for D-Day it was made clear the Islands would not be included in any attack because heavy German fortifications would necessitate the use of the equivalent of four divisions and this was wasteful use of manpower crucial to success in Normandy. The Islands were a potential flanking threat as the help given to St Malo, and the raid on Granville showed, but no more than that. It was confirmed in October 1944 that no direct attack would take place. From then it was clear that intensive naval activity in the Western Channel would cut the Channel Islands off from supplies and thus damage the German garrison. On 27 September the cabinet discussed the possible supply of food to the Channel Islands. The chiefs of staff, the ministry of economic warfare, and the home office were not opposed to this. However, Churchill was clear that he opposed aid, and General Brooke recorded that evening that it was decided not to send in any food. When he approved the plan for eventual liberation Churchill scribbled in the margin, 'Let 'em starve. No fighting. They can rot at their leisure'. Referring though he was to the Germans, it was the civilian population who would rot as well.

So the last year was to prove a terrible one. Famine, fuel and medical shortages grew steadily worse helped only a little by five Red Cross visits. The troops grew more violent in their search for food. Restriction followed restriction. Gas, electricity, and telephone services ceased. Even the water supply was affected. German repression increased. By February 1945, firm Nazi supporters were in charge of the troops, and the Platzkommandantur. They discussed seizing all food, and letting the Islanders starve.

The Germans, too, were under siege that last year. The officers shielded themselves from the consequences for a time, but the German forces were steadily disintegrating during the last six months or so of occupation as the proud conquerors became beggars at cottage doors. Mrs Tremayne noticed troops going to house after house asking for food particularly after dark. 'It's pathetic to see them in threadbare coats, and no overcoats, their boots the best thing about them'. Molly Finigan noticed how roles had become reversed. An officer gave her father his binoculars in exchange for some Red Cross chocolate. Among those she saw ferreting in the dustbins was the soldier who had once kicked her for scrounging potatoes.

Desperate for food the Germans tried every expedient. Too late they appointed battalion agriculture officers. Instructions on growing wheat and vegetables were issued. They tried cultivation in the greenhouses, and fished in co-operation with local fishermen to maximize the catch. All available animals were eaten: 'You may find it hard to believe but the troops are actually picking up cats and dogs they find in farmhouses and yards and eating them', wrote Mrs Tremayne. Crops and livestock were taken from gardens and fields, and cows were even milked before their owners could reach them. Eleven soldiers died after eating hemlock in January 1945. Others died trying to scale down cliffs for birds' eggs and plants. Von Aufsess mentioned the first deaths from malnutrition early in 1945, and some figures quoted by Cruickshank showed that of 99 soldiers inspected on Guernsey, 24 were suffering from it. German expedients failed, and even Mrs Tremayne was moved to say, 'It is distressing to see the poor fellows walking about. They only have nettle soup now, they go about in groups with sacks gathering nettles ... it is slow starvation.'

The Islanders began to notice restlessness among the troops, then fighting amongst themselves, and finally open dissent. By February 1945, the soldiers 'speak freely of being taken prisoner and I am sure the majority of them would welcome that'. When troops arrived to cut down Doctor Symon's fruit trees, the officer in charge turned to him at the end and said, 'when the war is over, for God's sake kill every Nazi'.

Sadly the breakdown of discipline and the suffering of the enemy did not help the Islanders. The occupation army ceased to be well-disciplined. After a murderous attack on Mr Jehan and his son in August 1944, the Germans announced severe penalties for looting, and such orders continued to be issued with ever increasing frequency; but to little effect. Death sentences were passed on troops like two soldiers who stole six sacks of flour, and in the end orders were given to shoot on sight at night. In May von Aufsess admitted all attempts to stop soldiers looting had failed.

The Cortvriends found their unripe fruit seized, and root crops dug out from their garden, and M. Lambert, worried one night that two soldiers had overheard his wireless, was relieved when they turned out to be stealing his pears. There were robberies with violence and murder. An elderly man and his wife were murdered for the sake of their Red Cross parcel. Mr Le Gresly was murdered and his sister badly beaten by marauding soldiers.

The Germans also tried to help their troops by requisitioning food. Von Schmettow made it plain that he blamed the British government for shortages because of its air attacks, and the Island governments for not taking precautions 'to make provision for the poorer sort of the population'. Now the Islands were cut off, 'I can no longer provide for the population'. He argued that in a war zone, particularly a fortress, 'all consideration for the besieged' disappeared, and even if the population were destroyed in action or by famine, 'this would not in any way alter the case'.

In the first place the officers had to be provided for. In August 1944, soldiers were sent to Sark to buy up eggs, butter and chickens to take back for the officers. At Christmas over 3,000 chickens were demanded for the forces. Von Schmettow rejected complaints about confiscations.

As soon as the decision was made to send the *Vega* with food the Germans used this as an excuse to increase their confiscations. As the first parcels were delivered an order went out to hand in any stocks of food by 15 January 1945. The same day an order restricted households to one dog with ominous implications for pets. Soldiers and Feldpolizei began house-to-house searches, and according to Mrs Cortvriend these were far more thorough than in the past. The Royal Hotel in St Peter Port lost its liquor supplies, 360 tins of vegetables, and some of the last soap remaining in the Island. Milkless days were introduced, and the ration was virtually ended on 23 April when the Germans demanded, 'that all farmers and cow keepers must deliver, without reserve, the whole of the milk produced by their cows.' The potato ration was cut to 1 lb and then stopped. The meat ration ended in April. Most alarming of all, bread rations were reduced on 3 February and stopped on 14 February. The

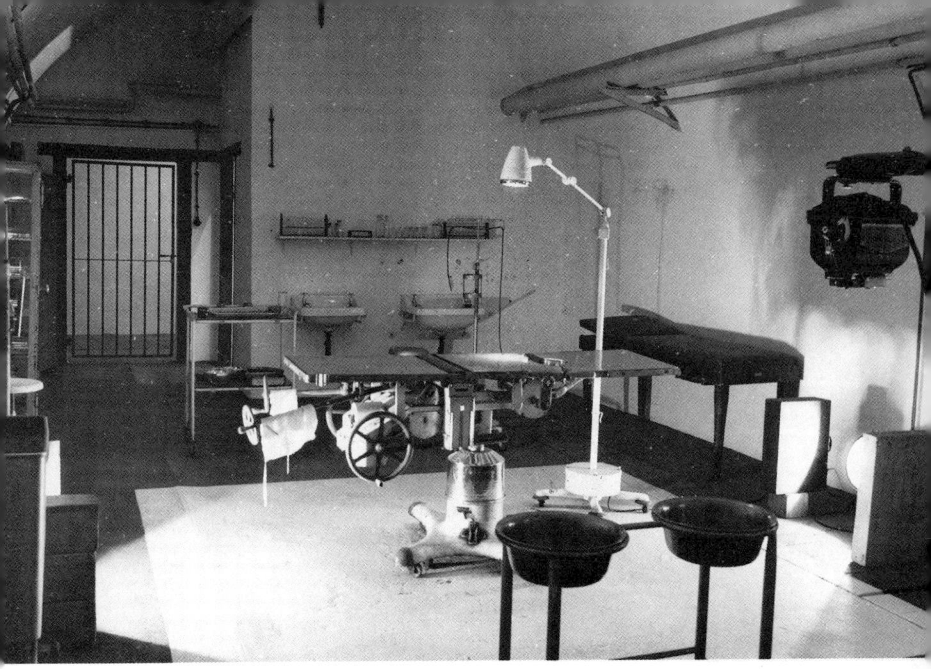

The Underground Hospital at St Lawrence in Jersey. This was used for casualties from St Malo in July 1944. Doctor John Lewis has described operations without anaesthetics which took place at that time when the wounded were held down by four soldiers

Entrance to Hohlgang 12 beneath St Saviour's Church on Guernsey used for storing ammunition and transport

The Dead 1. The graves of Todt workers on Longy Common removed in 1961. Of 509 identified graves, 387 were on Alderney

The Dead 2. German military graves on Alderney removed in 1961. Only 113 German graves at Fort George on Guernsey were left out of a total of 568 on the Islands

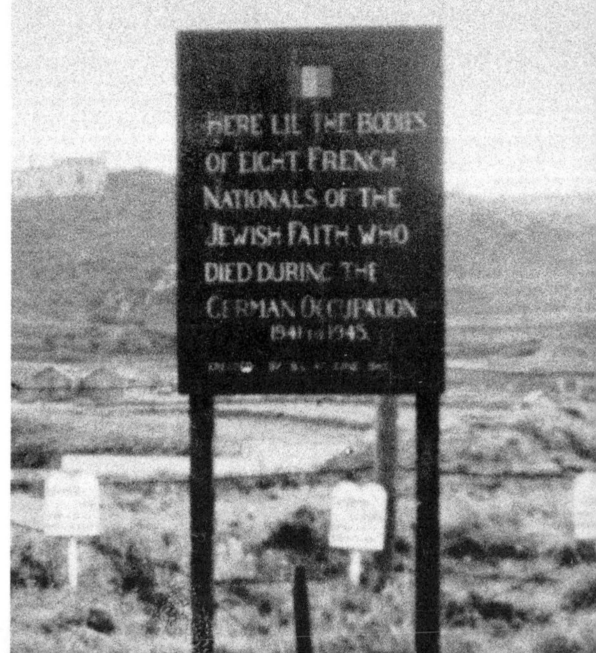

HERE LIE THE BODIES
OF EIGHT FRENCH
NATIONALS OF THE
JEWISH FAITH WHO
DIED DURING THE
GERMAN OCCUPATION

The Dead 3. Eight Jewish graves on Alderney where 300 Jews were imprisoned, many of whom died in Sylt or Norderney camps or in transit away from the Island. Three were removed for private burial, and five reburied at St Ouen, north of Paris

Baron von Aufsess, chief of administration in the Kommandantur on Jersey from January 1942 to April 1945

The conference between bailiffs Coutanche and Carey, the Red Cross representatives, Colonel Iselin and M. Callias, chaired (*left*) by Vice-Admiral Friedrich Hüffmeier at Rozel on 28–9 December 1944

Collecting Red Cross parcels from a designated store at St Peter Port, Guernsey

Liberation Day. St Peter Port, 9 May 1945

Islanders were without bread until 12 March. The first orders to surrender cattle went out the day before liberation. By the time the Red Cross ship arrived, things were so bad that its five visits could do little more than provide temporary relief, and parcels designed to last three weeks were usually exhausted within a week.

Vital public utilities ceased to function. Gas ended in Jersey in September, and in Guernsey in December. Electricity ended in January 1945 together with the telephones. In March, water supply was cut to two hours in the morning and two in the early evening. To make sure this order was kept, 'the Germans sent out pairs of soldiers to cut off bath water supplies and lavatory flushes. They were equipped with heavy hammers and wrenches and their primitive methods of cutting off lead pipes caused floods in several houses.' The aim was to restrict water use to a basic supply for drinking and kitchen washing up, and the Germans told people to use their gardens as toilets. It froze almost continuously through December 1944 and January 1945. Yet it was at this very moment that the order banning the collection of fuel was issued. On Sunday 12 January 1945 von Aufsess witnessed the following scene in St Helier: 'The townspeople's assault on any trees within reach in their frenzied search for fuel today escalated into what almost amounts to a popular uprising. Following yesterday's felling of some of the wonderful old evergreen oaks along Victoria Avenue ... this morning the people turned out in strength and armed with saws and axes descended on the avenue in hordes.' A nine year old boy searching for wood in the Parade Gardens in St Helier knocked over the side of a shelter and was buried alive in February 1945.

The bringing of relief to the Islands was bedevilled by administrative wrangling. By the end of August both Carey and Coutanche had drafted appeals to the Red Cross at Geneva and the Swiss minister in Berlin. At the beginning of September, Coutanche sent a document to the Commandant which von Aufsess said contained, 'a barely veiled threat to bring the guilty persons to justice after the war, if the civilian population should suffer.' Von Schmettow did not reply until late in the month when he said the responsibility for feeding the population was Britain's. Churchill then delayed matters for a month on military grounds.

October was therefore a month of desperate waiting on the Islands. The first escaper with information about conditions had reached London on 23 September. Yet, when the cabinet discussed the matter on 16 October they were still unwilling to accept Morrison's request that the Red Cross be approached. Churchill said the Germans should be warned they would be charged as war criminals if the population starved. All the Islanders knew was that nothing was happening, and on 21 October Carey at last plucked up courage and sent a sharp message to the Commandant accusing him of requisitioning a disproportionate amount of local produce for the troops and failing to maintain the civilian population. Von Schmettow replied two days later refusing the request, denying the accusations, and repeating that 'the besieger alone bears the responsibility for his compatriots'.

In Jersey, Coutanche asked Norman Rumball, a former member of the Granville Purchasing Mission, and an employee of the National Provincial

Bank, to take copies of his memorandum to the Red Cross with him when he escaped early in November. In Guernsey, a group of officials twice urged Carey to take action, and, when he would not, Sir Abraham Lainé, C.H. Cross, and Doctor A.W. Rose decided to act on their own initiative, and Frederick Noyon and William Enticott escaped with details of Island shortages. By then the Germans had won, and the British government been forced to climb down. Complaints from MPs, and action by the Channel Islands Committee in Britain reached the cabinet, and strengthened Morrison's hand. Yet when the matter was raised on 6 November Churchill still dug his heels in, but in the discussion he was overruled and it was agreed to approach the Red Cross providing the German commander was warned of his responsibility, and told not to reduce existing rations. This decision was sent via the Swiss Minister on 7 November, and the Germans replied on 23 November agreeing not to reduce rations, and to give safe conduct to Red Cross vessels. The Islanders reacted with delight to the news. 'Hurrah. A ship is really coming with relief', wrote Mrs Tremayne at the end of November, but sadly there was to be yet another 'month of delay before the *Vega*, a Swedish vessel, sailed from Lisbon on 20 December carrying 100,000 food parcels from New Zealand and Canada, 4,200 invalid parcels, and consignments of medical supplies. On 27th of December hundreds of hungry, badly clothed, chilled to the bone people gathered on White Rock to watch the arrival of the *Vega* at St Peter Port. The food was given out in Guernsey on Sunday December 31st. Goods for Sark were loaded on the *White Heather*, and were distributed on 3 January 1945. The *Vega* then left Guernsey for Jersey on Saturday 30 December, and supplies for Jersey were handed out before it left St Helier on 4 January.

Meanwhile, Island officials were having their first contacts with each other and the outside world carefully supervised by German guards. Coutanche and his wife were allowed to go to Guernsey with von Aufsess, where they were lodged at the Grange, and were able to meet the Careys. Von Aufsess invited them to have dinner, and they had a pleasant meal of roast lamb washed down with burgundy. Next day the Careys too were invited to the Royal Hotel. Coutanche was able to lunch (with two soldiers outside the house) with John Martel, the attorney-general. Over two days, a meeting was held at Rozel with the Red Cross representatives. The two bailiffs said that flour, fuel, and Red Cross message forms were important priorities. The Red Cross representatives said there was no room for fuel on the ship, but promised to send 500 tons of flour which did not arrive until March 1945.

On 8 January, Churchill minuted the minister of production about relief supplies for Holland, Belgium, Italy, and the Balkans. Those, like Maugham, who were angry because they heard of aid to Greece and Italy before any was sent to the Channel Islands were justifiably annoyed by the neglect, and January 1945 passed without a Red Cross ship.

On 14 February Mrs Tremayne remarked it was six weeks since Red Cross parcels had last come, and they had been told they would come every month. The parcels themselves lasted for about ten days. The *Vega* arrived again on 7–11 February, bringing Red Cross letter forms, cigarettes, and tobacco, medical supplies, clothes and shoe leather, but no flour. For a short time there were good things to eat. Mrs Tremayne made herself a pot of tea, and drank off five cupfuls. The ship in March brought flour at last, and bread became available once more. Fuel was carried for the first time. The ship came again in April and May, and earned the deep gratitude of the Islanders in the last three months of occupation. A letter written on behalf of the girls and boys at the Intermediate School in St Peter Port in March 1945 to the President of the Red Cross well summarizes their feelings: 'For three weeks we have been without bread ... But now people look more cheerful because the relief ship, the *Vega* is expected in two or three days time, laden with flour for us. Today, as I went to the grocer's shop to fetch my fourth parcel I met many people wearing smiles on their faces and wheeling small carts carrying their parcels home.'

Part 6

Hitler's New Order in the Channel Islands

15

The Todt Workers and the Death Camps

During the war the Channel Islands became a small corner of Hitler's empire of camps. At Nuremberg in 1945–6 when the war trials started, the British attorney-general, Sir Hartley Shawcross, estimated that 12 million had perished in Nazi Europe, half of them Jews. The multiplicity of camps, the transfers between them, the exaggerated records of zealous officials, the destroyed records of guilty ones, the confusion and secrecy make it impossible, even in a small area like the Channel Islands, to be sure how many came to the Islands, and how many died. The only concentration camp on the Islands, Sylt on Alderney, appears to have been discreetly passed over in SS Records and the Organization Todt records for the Islands have largely vanished.

On the Channel Islands there were subsidiary camps, camp areas like a particular street, work site, or building taken over, and frequent shifts in the population between slave workers, prisoners of war, and other categories. In theory there were a number of different categories of camp. There were concentration camps. There was the hutted world of the slave labourers. There were POW and internment camps. But, in practice, inmates moved between these camps, jurisdictions were blurred, and conditions varied immensely. In some camps the Red Cross was present, and the Geneva Convention was applied; in others there was nothing but brute force, and a violation of every civilized standard. In the Channel Islands, as elsewhere in Europe, slaves, POWs, politicals, Jews, and common criminals were mixed up in the network of camps.

Amidst so much horror and suffering in Europe as a whole it is not surprising the presence of one subsidiary concentration camp on Alderney, and about thirty other camps on the Islands was not front page news in the immediate post-war years. The SS occupation of Sylt camp lasted from March 1943 to July 1944 and the maximum number of prisoners was about a thousand. The Todt camps contained perhaps 16,000 slaves at their maximum extent, reduced by half by the end of 1943, and dwindling to a thousand after D-Day. The treatment of prisoners in Islands camps was not raised at Nuremberg and the British held no trials of those involved apart from a kapo, or trustee, and seven Germans, whose names have been kept secret by the German authorities, who were tried for killing prisoners in transit away from Alderney. There have been frequent denials of atrocities, or any substantial numbers of deaths.

Of course the camps were not an Auschwitz, but they were part of the same system. The numbers involved were smaller, and therefore the number of deaths was comparatively small. But however lenient German occupation as a whole, there is no evidence that the SS or Todt saw the Channel Islands camps as special cases for kid-gloves treatment. The death rate in Sylt in the 15 months it was under SS jurisdiction seems to have been one third of the prisoners: a figure in line with its parent camp in Germany. The treatment of Todt workers witnessed by Islanders was exactly similar to that elsewhere in Europe, and so were camp conditions. The death rate among them might well be expected to run parallel, and there is some evidence that it did. It is not an exaggeration to speak of some of the Island camps as death camps.

With the exception of Sylt for fifteen months, these camps were part of Organization Todt run until his death in a plane crash in 1942 by Fritz Todt. This organization was responsible for the Siegfried Line, the underground V-weapon factories, and the Atlantic Wall of which the Channel Island fortifications accounted for a twelfth of the resources involved. In 1942, Albert Speer became head of the Todt Organization, and armaments minister as well. He was directly involved in using slave labour for production as well as construction, and to feed his empire, Fritz Sauckel was made plenipotentiary for labour in March 1942 with the job of providing workers. Although there was a conflict of aim between Speer who wanted to keep workers alive to boost production, and others like the SS who wanted to work them to death as quickly as possible, in practice Speer's humanitarian pretensions had no effect.

Among the SS camps was Neuengamme, situated some miles north of Hamburg, and by 1942 having as many as 50 subsidiaries including work sites. It was the parent camp of Sylt on Alderney, and this link with the Channel Islands came about as follows. In October 1942 Baubrigade 1 was formed from a mixture of Russian and other nationalities drawn mainly from Sachsenhausen concentration camp. It was sent to work at Duisburg and Düsseldorf, and in February 1943 was transferred to Alderney. It seems the intention was that the thousand or so prisoners should go there to be worked to death, and when their usefulness was at an end they would be transferred to Neuengamme for extermination. The new commandant, Captain Maximilian List, an early member of the SS in 1930 who had seen service at Oranienburg and Sachsenhausen, arrived in Alderney on 5 March 1943. Existing Todt workers were dispersed to other camps, and the familiar striped uniform, cropped heads, numbers, and coloured identifications of concentration camp prisoners were seen in the Island. List installed himself in a chalet-bungalow with a fine view down the Val de L'Emauve and connected to the camp by a tunnel passing under the perimeter fence. He remained there until spring 1944, and was therefore in charge during the period of maximum deaths. His two lieutenants were Georg Braun and Kurt Klebeck. Klebeck was the official deputy, but was involved in inadequate guard arrangements which led to prisoner escapes in transit to Neuengamme, and was recalled soon afterwards. George Braun, an incurable syphilitic, therefore became List's successor. Clearly a strong Nazi, it was he who issued an order in May 1944 that prisoners were not to be taken alive by the Allies, and there is some evidence that a tunnel was specially prepared for their extermination. It is said that neither Braun nor Klebeck survived the war, but List almost certainly did survive and was never tried.

The camp staff were under the command of Otto Högelow, later replaced by Staff-Sergeant Götze. Högelow certainly survived the war because he was called as a witness in the only trial affecting Alderney camp staff. The German authorities tried to conceal his identity on the trial record, but he was identified by the prisoners present at the trial.

Sylt was a typical small concentration camp. There was a wired inner enclosure with about ten wooden huts for the prisoners. The camp was protected with concrete sentry posts, a concrete guard-room below ground level, lights and corner towers. Six bloodhounds came ashore in March 1943, in the charge of a junior private from Stettin. Prisoners were employed to work outside the camp, and this led to petty clashes over jurisdiction with the Todt organization. The officer in charge of the OT workers complained to the Island commandant about excessive beating of prisoners on his work sites and in return List accused Todt officials of being soft on Jews. The SS were able to get their revenge because there was no punishment lager for Todt workers on Alderney, and they were sent to Sylt. At the end of their stay, the SS refused to give up the prisoners. There was much squabbling as a result of which wretched Todt workers endured eight months in the concentration camp.

Because Sylt was to some extent a transit camp for workers, there were frequent transports off the Island among which was the notorious one in June 1943 during which 12 escaped. Seven Sylt prisoners died on their way to Neuengamme on that occasion, and in assessing the death rate of Alderney SS prisoners such deaths in transit should be included. In bad conditions on the *Gerfried* and the *Schwalbe* inmates were transferred to St Malo between 24 June and 1 July 1944 to travel on from there to their eventual destination of Buchenwald. Desperate camp inmates tried to escape at Kortemark, and near Toul. Over 50 of these were killed. The remaining prisoners did not reach Buchenwald. Instead they were marched to Sollstedt, and Mauthausen where an American advance prevented their liquidation. It was during this march that the kapo, Gustav Fehrenbacher, and seven SS men carried out killings for which they were put on trial. Fehrenbacher was convicted of killing two prisoners at Sollstedt, and given eight years.

When the decision was made in October 1941 to fortify the Islands the intention was to carry out a 14-month crash programme. This was delayed by material and transport difficulties, but by the end of 1943 the work had been more or less completed, and half of the workers involved had left the Islands. It was mainly carried out by Organization Todt and by January 1944 their building programme had constructed 484,000 cubic metres of fortifications and other works. Railways were constructed and roads widened and both old and new Island quarries brought into use. Todt was in theory a civilian organization responsible to Speer in Berlin, but for practical purposes it was the Wehrmacht inspector of fortifications west who was the ultimate authority, and Todt came to function under his commander in the Channel Islands, Major May. The organization level of the Todt administrative structure was based on the chief construction office in St Malo, and after February 1943, Cherbourg. Each Island was an *abschnitt*: Alderney became Adolf, Jersey, Jakob, and Guernsey, Gustav.

Many Todt officials were administrators or technical experts, and had little to do with the camps, but Todt was responsible for its own security, although in view of the brutality it is not surprising that prisoners referred to their guards as SS. Each Island had a punishment lager: in Alderney this was achieved by transferring prisoners to the SS in Sylt. On Jersey, Elizabeth Castle was the lager. On Guernsey the *straflager* was housed opposite Les Vauxbelets College in a compound with towers, searchlights, and machine-guns surrounding a house called 'Paradise'. Wood said that, 'in charge of "Paradise" was a brutal sadist, a huge man, who delighted in trussing up his victims with a length of rope, beating them about the head and body, and then leaving them dangling in the hall from the banisters of the staircase'.

One prisoner executed on Guernsey is known by name. Two Todt workers Franzeph Losch and Marcel de Bois, seem to have operated a transmitter to the United Kingdom (another matter on which British secret service histories remain silent) for nearly two years from April 1941. De Bois had fortunately gone on leave when the Feldpolizei arrested Losch in the act of transmitting. He was executed by firing squad at Fort George on 16 June 1943.

At Norderney the *lagerführer* Tietz employed a muscular black Senegalese to beat prisoners and, was not above joining in himself. 'Every day the Camp Commandant made a habit of beating any man he found not properly standing to attention or who had not made his bed properly or did not execute a drill movement properly.'

Tietz was removed from office for black market activities in April 1943, but Adam Adler and Heinrich Evers were quite as evil. Francisco Font who was in Norderney, later recalled beatings by Evers as well as dousing with cold water. At Christmas 1943 he deliberately destroyed prisoners' mail in front of their eyes. According to Steckoll it was Evers who killed the only Chinese Todt prisoner who was then discreetly buried in the military cemetery at Le Foulon in grave number 104. Ki-Lieng Tien was lashed by the familiar stick which broke three of his ribs, and took 20 days to die.

It is usually stated that there were four camps on Alderney: Helgoland, Norderney, Borkum, and Sylt. Each camp was designed to take about a thousand prisoners and all were full in May 1943. Then numbers declined, and one by one the camps were destroyed, and the huts broken up for firewood. But there was a fifth camp at Hauteville in St Anne known as Citadella containing African POWs.

In Guernsey there were purpose built camps like that at Rue Sauvage, and areas of existing housing in St Peter Port which were taken over as camps. Richard Mayne has listed ten Jersey camps. Some of these like lagers Udet and Molders were camps in their own right; others like Prien or Ehrenbreitstein were sub-camps, and some like Schepke or Wick were set up on specific work sites. The list is not exhaustive because in August 1943 a camp for African POWs was opened at Pier Road, and they were involved in work on defences. Prisoners were to be found in places 'not strictly camps' including Melbourne House, St John, West Park Pavilion, and Elizabeth Castle.

The majority of workers were housed in conditions which made their hungry, ill-clothed, and back-breaking existence even more wretched. There was some hospital provision at Avenue Vivier in Guernsey, and Rosemount in Jersey, but the buildings were poorly staffed to cope with the victims' construction accidents, typhus and other contagious diseases, and air raid victims from port areas. Medical affairs on Alderney were handled by the Kriegsmarine medical officer, and there was a single ward in Norderney staffed by Russians. Francisco Font said lice, diarrhoea and dysentery were widespread, and the only medicine ever doled out was aspirin. At Sylt List and Klebeck had one remedy, to send 'the sick prisoners away from extermination'.

Sixteen thousand or more foreigners pouring into small Islands in the mono-cultural days of the 1940s created an immediate impression among the inhabitants who tended to confuse races and the status of those they saw behind barbed-wire, marching in rags, sitting numbed on lorries or back to back on open cars on the railways, or toiling in all weathers at fortifications. The German forces themselves brought Austrians, Russians, and Italians. Among the Todt workers there were 27 different nationalities at one time or another. Mrs Tremayne's daughter Norah, visiting Guernsey, reported back to her mother rather confusedly to say the Island was full of what she called, 'Russians, Jews, Niggers, Americans, Italians, Poles and Swedes'.

Nazi racial ideology naturally extended to contempt for black people as their propaganda directed at black American troops was to show. When the Germans captured French black troops in the summer of 1940 this hatred was given free reign. In the latter half of 1942, over 5,000 of these Algerians and 2,000 Moroccans were among Africans still in German hands in France, and some of them found their way to the Channel Islands. Nearly all left in January and March 1944, and on liberation only five Africans, two Algerians and three Moroccans were left on Alderney, but at liberation there were still 88 North Africans on Guernsey.

The main group of Africans arrived in Jersey in August 1943. One hundred and fifteen were housed in a camp at Pier Road together with 24 transferred later from Citadella Camp. Their camp commander, Sergeant Mohammed ben Mohammed from Marrakesh, proved an excellent leader of men, and maintained morale and probably the best standards of cleanliness and efficiency of any camp on the Island. There were North African Todt workers on Jersey earlier than this as among the first deaths of Todt workers which occurred in February 1942 were four Algerians who ate hemlock by mistake. At liberation there were stated to be three Algerians and one Arab on the Island besides the POWs at Pier Road.

The Africans worked on the railway bridge over the English Harbour, the building of tunnels, and the petrol dump at Avranches Manor, and as POWs they were entitled to pay at the rate of 50 pfennings a day. The Germans sometimes seized this money, but ben Mohammed insisted his men form a common fund with some of it to purchase supplies.

Because they were POWs of an ally, and readily identifiable by colour, the Africans attracted considerable help from Islanders, and when they left ben Mohammed wrote an open letter in the *Jersey Evening Post* to thank the Islanders. Much of this help was channelled through Leon Dubras who negotiated the purchase of cosmetics, toothpaste and soap at Granville. As liaison officer with the Africans, he was able to channel complaints to the Red Cross as conditions in the camp worsened during 1944.

Margaret Ginns has studied the Africans in some detail and besides Dubras and Gouedart mentions a considerable number of other helpers including stall holders who gave them free produce, farmers in St Clements, shopkeepers who did things like repair their clothes, people in the General Hospital, and even the Jersey Bowling Club who sent them playing cards and skittles.

There were 300 French Jews mainly confined in Norderney Camp, their presence on Alderney recalled by a carved Star of David, and the named graves of eight of them later given a permanent memorial. Monsieur Albert Eblagon was one of these Jews who survived who described to Solomon Steckoll his introduction to Alderney at three o'clock in the morning when, 'in darkness we were forced to run two kilometres to Camp Norderney, while the German guards stabbed into our backs with bayonets while also kicking us all the time.' How many Jews died is a matter of dispute, but there can be no doubt that many did in transit from the Island when their usefulness as workers had been exhausted.

Tragically it was the British who would be responsible for the deaths of some at least of these departing Todt workers. On 3 July 1944, the *Minotaure* set out from St Helier with several hundred Todt prisoners on board. On 4 July the *Minotaure* was attacked by British light craft. The bows of the *Minotaure* were nearly blown off, and the ship drifted towards St Malo. It is estimated that half, perhaps 200 or more drowned, including French Jews.

Military Intelligence documents name three Dutch firms contracted to Todt employing Dutch harbour workers and at liberation there were still 38 on Guernsey, and 36 on Jersey. Attempts by Solomon Steckoll to obtain a list of Dutch Todt workers who died in the Channel Islands failed although he was able to establish that among prisoners killed in the break out at Toul in 1944 from the death train were two Dutchmen, C. Van den Oever, and G. Wulder. Among those seeking to escape from the Islands there were Dutch names, including Kosta who failed, and Quist who succeeded in the autumn of 1944.

In France the Germans found Republican Spaniards in refugee camps who had fled Franco's regime. Some arrived in December 1941, and early in 1942 over three hundred were brought to the Channel Islands. Many of them were withdrawn in August 1943 to be replaced with Italians, but at liberation there were still 35 on Guernsey, and 56 on Jersey. They were quartered first by the airport in the open air with only pieces of corrugated iron for cover and then constructed their own camp on Grouville Marsh. One of the Spaniards was Francisco Font who was sent to Alderney and found himself in Norderney in October 1943. He worked at Braye Harbour as a bricklayer 12 hours a day watching with horror the treatment of French Jews and Russians in the camp. He was moved to Jersey in June 1944, but after the loss of the *Minotaure*, transports had stopped, and he remained there to the end of the war. Later he married Kathleen Fox and returned to live on Jersey.

The Russian prisoners including Poles, Ukrainians, Baltic peoples, and other Slavs were treated worst of all. A thousand arrived in Alderney in July 1942 and were followed by another 1,800 a month later. They made up the majority of prisoners on the main Islands, and there were still about 300 there at liberation. So badly were Russians treated, that Islanders made numerous efforts to help them, and on Alderney the German Commandant even had to issue an order forbidding Wehrmacht troops from giving food to Russian prisoners. Similar warnings were given to the Islanders in November 1942 and April 1943, and they were warned of a penalty of six weeks in prison, or a fine of £3,000. The Germans issued warnings about helping escaped Russian prisoners, and the fate of Mrs Louisa Gould dying in Ravensbrück was a reminder of what might happen for committing this offence. In August 1944 the Germans had to admit there were still 13 Russians hiding on Jersey, and the efforts of those like Robert and Connie Vaynor to conceal them have already been described. Their rations were supposed to consist of half a litre (1 pint) of coffee substitute for breakfast, half a litre of cabbage soup for lunch, another half litre in the evening, and a kilo (two pounds) of bread varied very occasionally with a little butter, sausage, or vegetables. Even this diet by no means always reached the prisoners. In Alderney, there were cases of diverted supplies. Two quartermasters in the Wehrmacht were charged in June 1944, and one committed suicide while two Todt officials were also tried for the same offence. Prisoners would go to any lengths for food. When two Russians were shot, the police reported that they had been living in a cave on straw beds with mussels to eat. Death rates were considerable. On Jersey, for instance, between August 1942 and March 1943, 59 Russians died and their women and children no doubt suffered even more, although little is known about them. Ronald Mauger saw a prisoner killed at the underground tunnels for asking for another bowl of soup, and Edward Blampied caught sight of a slave hanging by his heels. On Alderney of course there were hardly any witnesses, but there is evidence about brutality from four sources: statements given to Major Pantcheff in 1945, survivors' accounts, reports given to MI9 by escapers, and List's trial record.

Pantcheff cites the death of a Pole, Antony Onuchowsky which was described by a friend from the same village. He had swollen feet. 'One day, after work when our squad was marching back to camp, he could not keep up, and fell behind. I saw the Truppführer remain with him and get to work with his truncheon. Later we lost sight of him ... The next morning after reveille when I went to the latrine Onuchowsky lay there on the other side of the barbed wire at the side of the camp.' He died on 28 September 1942. William Wernegau and Robert Prokop, who were inmates had given accounts of what they saw. Lieutenants Klebeck and Braun were active. So too were Corporal Rebs, a French army deserter, Corporal Wese, a Czech, said to have shot a German political prisoner, Rudi Busch, and Private Rometsch, a Croat, said to have killed Josef Lammel. One of the German prisoners, a member of the Gestapo sentenced for some offence, called Franz Eschke, was said to have been hanged in the kitchen. Wernegau referred to shooting and strangulation as the main methods of killing. According to an escaper's evidence, a German political prisoner was shot dead in Oliver Street, and another was killed by an Alsatian dog.

During his trial for negligence, List said he had considered the transfer of sick prisoners from Sylt unnecessary because he 'could deal with the matter on the spot'. This chilling reference raises the issue of how far Sylt was a small scale death camp; it was certainly the annex to other death camps like Neuengamme. Total extinction was a possibility before evacuation was decided upon instead. Some inmates have argued a death tunnel was made at Norderney for the purpose of killing prisoners, and statements were made about this in 1945 by Jean Joseph Bloch and Henri Uzan. Both of them claimed that Heinrich Evers held a rehearsal and, 'forced us into the tunnel which had an entrance, an exit and air vents. These were all sealed. At the entrance there was a concrete structure with a machine gun. Evers told us that we were being put into the tunnel for our own safety because the Allies had mounted a seaborne invasion of Alderney.' They were kept in this tunnel for a quarter of an hour and many became ill from asphyxia and vertigo.

The answer to the questions: how many Todt workers died, and how many Sylt prisoners died, are difficult to provide. Robin Cox made a study of 29 Island graveyards, and reached a total of 509 for all camp burials on the Islands. Of these 433 have been identified by name, and 76 are uncertain. 387 of them were on Alderney clearly showing a higher death rate there. Unfortunately, this total is not the whole story. There is evidence from survivors about individuals whose graves cannot be traced. Two Russian survivors testified to a number of names: Gorbatch, Pashko, Bojko, as being untraceable. Nor is there any trace of those like Rudi Busch and Josef Lammel shot at Sylt. There is also evidence that Alderney victims were buried elsewhere – the solitary Chinese killed by Evers ended up in Le Foulon, and Italians were buried at St Brelades in Jersey until Italy changed sides in the war.

Todt certificates were signed by sick bay staff who might be orderlies without medical knowledge, and copies of these were sent to the bauleiter, Cherbourg headquarters, and the Kommandantur. Burial was arranged by the firm of Kniffler. Mayne noticed the arrival on Jersey of coffins for this purpose, but on Alderney, besides ordinary coffins, there was found in May 1945 a coffin with a bottom trap which could be reused. Although this was found at Longy, it was the same as a ship's coffin for quick disposal at sea. The whole purpose of such burials was to conceal the evidence. Both Font and Prokop insisted bodies were thrown into the sea at Fort Clonque, a high point half a mile from Sylt. Misciewicz claimed prisoners who had died were thrown into the harbour, and speaks of a box being used over and over again. Eblagon and Prokop also said that this happened, and Font heard it happened from another Spanish prisoner. Occasionally bodies were washed up from the sea, as one was in October 1942, claimed to be that of a Russian escaper from Elizabeth Castle, but later changed to a Frenchman.

Sylt SS death certificates were no more than routine documents, made up in advance. They were supposed to be signed by the camp medical officer, but as there was none at Sylt this task was performed by a military doctor. On one occasion when the Luftwaffe doctor Köhler was called in to sign, he refused to do so because there had been no post-mortem. These certificates concealed the fact that most deaths in Sylt were due to overwork and starvation. They also concealed which prisoners had been beaten to death, strangled or shot, and for all their apparent detail were often wrong.

When the British stepped ashore in Alderney, a week after liberation, the few Islanders there claimed there had been atrocities, and George Pope referred to a thousand deaths. This figure actually entered official documents at one point as a telegram from the British Embassy in Moscow to the Foreign Office (22 May 1945) refers to British authorities who 'are investigating suggestions of Germans killing one thousand Russians and Jews on Alderney during occupation'. In fact Pope was unable to prove his case. The landing forces had already come across Longy cemetery, with its marked graves, and two other graves containing 83 and 48 bodies respectively, over one of which they erected the first memorial. An investigation was carried out by Major Sidney Cotton, Captain G.C. Kent, and Major F.F. Haddock. They visited the camps, and Kent did a careful study of the graves on 7 June 1945. Their report has vanished.

The number of graves, and the certificates, provide some check on wild assertions, but they are incomplete, perhaps not accidentally. In the case of Sylt, there is every reason to suppose that up to a third of the thousand or so prisoners died on the Island or in transit away from it. List and Klebeck speaking in 1943 saw it as a camp whose inmates should be worked to death. Within a few months of their arrival, 200 were unfit to work, and in June 1943, arrangements were made to transport them to Neuengamme. By the time they left (a month later), 50 had died. Other transports left the Island from time to time, and the master of the *Gerfriede* which used to move Alderney prisoners was instructed to make conditions unpleasant by Braun, the commandant. 280 prisoners were confined in a hold measuring 969 square feet. Some died on the voyage across. If horror stories of deliberately walling up prisoners are unproven, there was no doubt deaths due to hazardous work in building the fortifications. Workers were killed by RAF raids, and although no precise figures are given in the raid of January 1942, Ronald Mauger saw ambulances at work throughout the night, and believed there was 'heavy loss of life'.

Deaths from these various causes add 300 to the figure of just over 500 graves. It is difficult to be more precise, but the 'official' figure is too low.

For the Todt workers a grisly footnote was added in 1959. The British and German governments agreed in August that when the German dead, with the exception of those in Fort George, were removed to a mausoleum built at Mont-de-Huisnes, Todt workers, too, would go and be counted as German war dead. The French association of former camp inmates objected, but was ignored. The eight identifiable Jewish graves were excluded, three removed for private burial, and five being reburied at St Ouen north of Paris. The mausoleum at Mont-de-Huisnes was dedicated in September 1963 and next to those whose government brought them to the Channel Isles, lie those who perished there as a result of German policy.

16

The Deportation of the Islanders

On 7 February 1943 an order from the Germans arrived in Sark for the deportation of between 30 and 40 people. This was the second deportation from the small Island, but the first had involved no more than 11 people. Served with an order telling them to report at the Gaumont Cinema in St Peter Port with 'warm clothes, solid boots, some provisions, meal-dishes, drinking bowl, and if possible a blanket', people had only a few days to prepare for a journey into the heart of Nazi Europe. The first Sark contingent contained Sibyl Hathaway's American-born husband, relatives of Island officials like the Carrés, the vicar, Gilbert Phillips (removed, said Hathaway, because a pro-German person on the Island heard him criticizing Hitler too freely), Mrs Pittard (who had just returned from prison in Guernsey), Miss Duckett and Miss Page (who had managed the Dixcart Hotel where with Mrs Pittard's information the commandos had ended up), a number of elderly and single people who lived in the centre of the Island where the new strongpoint was sited, and the schoolmistress Miss Howard.

Five days later the first party left Sark. The vicar held prayers in the hall, and they set out with blankets and haversacks, 'all trying to bear up, bursting with grief inside'. It was blowing a blizzard on the day they arrived at Creux harbour where 'Before we said goodbye to our friends they agreed that as they left the little harbour they would burst into song, and Norah said the tunnel echoed with "Pack Up Your Troubles" and "There'll always be an England".' (Julia Tremayne) Two weeks later, the remainder of the Sark contingent left.

Between 26 September 1942 and 25 February 1943 about 2,200 Channel Islanders were deported to half-a-dozen camps in France, Germany and Austria. This was four per cent of the population, and came to form half the interned British population in Germany. As a result of negotiations, 337 of them were repatriated because of age or illness before the end of the war. By the time the camps were freed in April 1945, 46 Islanders had died far from home, many of them elderly people for whom such disruption clearly proved the most serious additional burden. Some Islanders broke down mentally, and had to be left behind.

Deportation began as a result of Hitler's personal anger over an unrelated matter; became an issue involving the Führer's authority when by accident it was not carried out when ordered; and was finally used partly as a police measure to punish Islanders for the commando raid and successful escapes. Cruickshank performed the service of revealing for the first time the origins of the *Führer befel* of 9 September 1942 which began deportation, and showed that deportation had been considered a year before, and that as usual the Island authorities had co-operated from the start in providing the necessary lists of people and making no protests.

In August 1941 Britain and Russia jointly occupied Persia (Iran) and deposed the pro-German Shah. There had been fears of a Nazi putsch, and some 500 Germans in the country were interned. Hitler's wish was that for every German interned ten 'British born' Channel Islanders – an ill-defined term throughout – should be interned in retaliation, and as there were approximately 6,000 'British' residents on the Islands, this seemed a neat solution. On 16 September 1941, Coutanche was told to provide the first of a number of lists of various groups of British residents and the lists were completed by 3 November. Carey on Guernsey had his lists ready seven days later. On 12 September, Hitler discussed the coming deportations saying he wanted the Islanders taken to the Pripet Marshes in Poland, and their property given to 'native-born' Islanders.

When the British government was told of German intentions via the protecting power their immediate reaction was muted indeed. It was no more than a comment that such action was a violation of the Hague Convention, illegal and inhumane. Churchill often listed Nazi 'crimes', but never referred to this particular one in the Commons. Impending deportation also broke the commandant's initial promise to respect the lives of the Islanders.

It was not until September 1942, when the protecting power suggested to the Germans that Islanders who wanted to go to England might be permitted to leave, that Hitler realized the 'English' Channel Islanders were still there. General Warlimont of OKW was asked to investigate, and his report found that, as so often happened in Nazi Germany, several authorities involved had been at cross-purposes. OKW in France had begun preparations, and located a camp near Cologne, but on checking with the Foreign Ministry they were told nothing was required, and so stopped preparations.

Warlimont's report ended with an extremely revealing passage. He stressed the military argument that there was no need for deportations. The population had been thoroughly loyal, there had been no military sabotage, and no passive resistance. German orders had been carried out quickly, and without obstruction by the Island authorities. But however successfully German policy was working this did not mean the Islanders were safe. Hitler was naturally furious as an order had not been carried out. A precise order was sent to Paris, and arrived in the Channel Islands on 15 September 1942. It was for the immediate deportation of all those without permanent residence on the Islands including those caught there by circumstance of war, and all men between 16 and 70 'who belong to the English people' together with their families.

There was a flurry of activity on the main Islands. Coutanche said he protested and the Jersey superior council considered resigning *en masse*. All that happened was that they did not issue the deportation orders themselves. Some people on Jersey had less than twelve hours to prepare for deportation on 16 September when 280 left the Island at nine in the evening. 'Should you fail to obey the order', said Knackfuss 'sentence by court martial shall be effected'. Buses were laid on from the country where knots of people gathered at village halls while those in St Helier walked to the harbour. Maugham watched people walking with their heads held high, and left the scene 'with an unaccustomed constriction in my throat, but also burning with indignation and disgust'. One man who collapsed was placed on a stretcher and carried aboard. Possibly this was J.P. Walters, aged sixty-eight, who died in the drear and rough conditions at Dorsten on 10 October. The St John Ambulance Association did their best to distribute food parcels. That evening the boat left, and those on Mount Bingham could hear patriotic songs as the ship pulled away. As the first group their worries must have been the greatest. Next day orders were issued for a second group to be ready for 18 September.

Public reaction to deportation began to gather strength, and took different forms. Apparently some girls contracted marriages with Islanders. Tragically a man and his wife at Beaumont were the first to attempt suicide, the woman dying in the attempt, and they were followed by others in the next few months. Medical exemptions were pressed to the uttermost. A few brave people volunteered to go in place of others. Three of the conscientious objectors who had come to do harvest work in 1940 went instead of a clergyman and his family. But in spite of all about 340 people were assembled at the Weighbridge on the evening of the 18th. Michael Ginns recalled how his father, an elderly, sick man, fortunately included later among those repatriated before April 1945, fainted, and was revived so he could go aboard. Two boats had arrived. The *La France* was all right, but the other was the *Robert Müller*, an unsatisfactory craft. As a result only about half those due to go left that evening and joined a convoy to St Malo at two in the morning. The rest were told to go home, and report again on the 25th. This led to further suffering where homes had been shut up, and even more disreputably, where people found their homes had already been broken into. The delays which included the ramming of a harbour crane by the reversing *La France* brought out crowds in the streets and the first public anti-German expressions of feeling.

On the 23rd came the third Jersey notice to assemble at the Weighbridge two days later, and on this occasion youngsters indulged in a small riot for which 14 people were arrested, and one man received three years imprisonment. There was a new feature of the list of deportees. It included 20 Jerseymen who had been convicted of offences by the Germans, although this group was reprieved at the last minute. This showed that the Kommandantur was starting to think deportation might be a way of removing small groups of potential troublemakers. On 29 September, although the sea was rough, two small boats with over 500 on board sailed out at twenty to nine in the evening. They only reached St Malo in the morning after many had been sea sick in rough conditions.

In spite of brave singsongs and heads held high, there can be no doubt that deportation was a terrible blow. On 15 September the order also arrived in Guernsey. Carey kept in the background, and it was Louis Guillemette who hurried to Brosch to protest, only to be told it was a Führer order, and that those required must be ready by 20 September. A form was issued in the press for all those covered by the German order to fill in, and return by the 18th. Had anyone failed to fill these in, the lists prepared by Carey the previous year would have provided an unseen check on defaulters.

As there were a few more days warning for the first Guernsey deportees, it was possible to do a little to mitigate their going. Medical exemptions could be gone into more carefully and two Guernsey doctors were allowed to be present when German doctors vetted the Island doctors' exemptions. There was time to appeal for exemptions. Essential workers were exempted, as were all employed by the Germans. Some doctors volunteered to go with the people, but Doctor William McGlashen, who had complained about the Germans taking over Island hospitals, was forced to go instead even though he was ill, and had to be included among the first batch of repatriated Islanders in September 1944. Harris says 'a few of the older people' committed suicide on Guernsey, including a couple who took poison, the woman recovering, and the man dying.

The departures were scheduled for 21 and 23 September, and involved over 800 people. They assembled at the Gaumont Cinema for a final medical, picked up their luggage, and made their way to the White Rock. Feldpolizei confiscated valuable goods including silver-framed family photographs as they went on board. Once again the *La France* and the *Robert Müller* had arrived, and the people went on board even though a gale was blowing up. In the *Müller* there was simply a dark hold with a bench round the wall, and children were terrified by their confinement. Knackfuss had just arrived on Guernsey, and told Brosch he could not use the *Müller*. The people spent the night in the boats, and were disembarked the next day.

People then returned to find looters had already been at work. A couple who had left a girl in charge found neighbours had called and told her they had been asked to remove various articles. In one house all the coal had gone; in another, the light bulbs had vanished. The people had to report again on the 24th, but weather conditions were too bad, and it was only on the 25th when the *La France* was joined by the *Minotaure* that they were finally able to embark, and set sail on Saturday 26 September arriving at St Malo at seven in the morning. The boats returned to take on the rest of the deportees on Sunday. On board too were nine residents of Sark, but small though the number were there was tragedy. Major John Skelton and his wife decided to commit suicide, and left notes with Sibyl Hathaway telling her, which she did not open, believing them to be ordinary farewell letters. The couple were found with their wrists cut on the Common after they had failed to turn up to leave. Mrs Skelton survived, and later returned to the Island. On Sunday 20 September Mrs Tremayne described how, 'The Thanksgiving Service was very saddened by a prayer being offered by the vicar for the evacuees leaving for Germany, and all the new laid eggs sent to the Festival are to be hard-boiled and given to the people as they leave the Island.'

Hitler's order had now been partially obeyed, but the Kommandantur officials were seeking ways of extending registration to include other groups. On Guernsey, Brosch required all men, single women, widows and wives of Guernseymen or any other nationality to be registered, and shortly before Christmas the Controlling Committee was ordered to provide details of convicted persons over a period of ten years. The commando raid on Sark had several unfortunate consequences. The British government had been able to publicize the deportations. It was clear the commandos had received some help. German soldiers had died, and a row broke out over the shackling of prisoners which once again brought the Islands to Hitler's attention. The same month as the deportations the first successful escape since 1940 occurred. The Kommandantur could not be seen to be slack, and the 1943 deportations were essentially a police measure to strike fear into people. During January requests similar to those already made on Guernsey were made on Jersey although there was no clear indication who would be involved this time. Mention was made of a very mixed bag: Jews, freemasons, members of friendly societies, and religious groups like Jehovah's Witnesses, Communists and other political suspects, work-shy people (who presumably had refused to work for the Germans), unemployed youths, prominent Islanders suspected of being anti-German, officials, and those involved in criminal cases like the wives and children of policemen convicted in the black market scandal.

Knackfuss said the second deportation was entirely caused by the need to remove Mrs Pittard whose name would inevitably come up in court-martial proceedings, and that this prevented her trial. This was no more than a convenient story to cover the basic fact of a severe order which would reinstate the Kommandantur in Hitler's good books.

But bureaucratic muddle prevented immediate action because of the need for careful checking, and in the end no deportations occurred in January 1943. The numbers involved shrank from a thousand to 500, and eventually only about 200 were involved including 47 from Sark. Among those in high places said to have been listed were the bailiffs and their families, the Sherwills, Leale, Symons, Falla, and Robert Hathaway. Some like Sherwill and Hathaway had to go. So too did Crawford-Morrison, organizer of the only effective military intelligence espionage. Clergymen seemed to be a particular target for the Germans, and a number were deported including James, Flint, Phillips, Atyeo, Wood and Gerhold. Those who had been friendly to the Germans did not find this worked in their favour on every occasion. A barber who said his business was much patronized by Germans, and a man who said he bottled beer for the troops, were not exempted. On the other hand a businessman who had been reprieved in 1942 was reprieved again in 1943, because 'he was used in various ways as an informer'.

On 6 February people in Jersey were told to hold themselves ready. Sixty-three were ordered to appear, but a man at Grouville committed

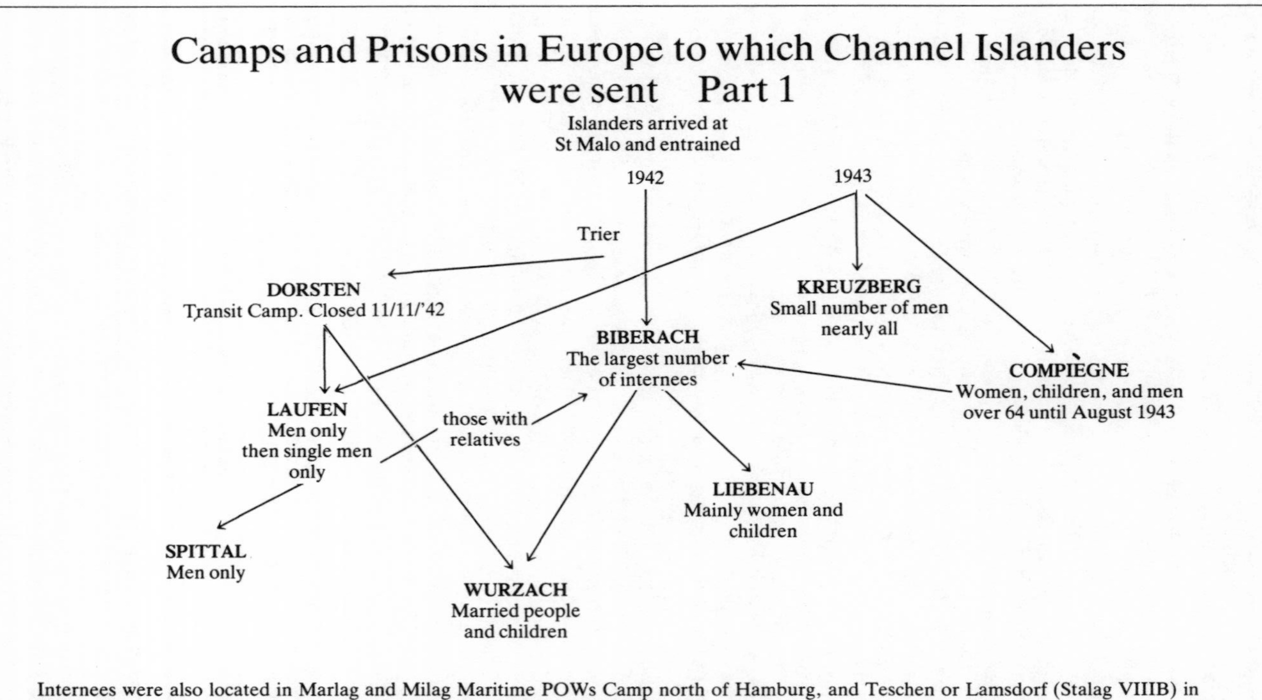
Camps and Prisons in Europe to which Channel Islanders were sent Part 1
Islanders arrived at St Malo and entrained
1942
1943
Trier
DORSTEN
Transit Camp. Closed 11/11/'42
KREUZBERG
Small number of men nearly all
BIBERACH
The largest number of internees
COMPIÈGNE
Women, children, and men over 64 until August 1943
LAUFEN
Men only then single men only
those with relatives
LIEBENAU
Mainly women and children
SPITTAL
Men only
WURZACH
Married people and children
Internees were also located in Marlag and Milag Maritime POWs Camp north of Hamburg, and Teschen or Lamsdorf (Stalag VIIIB) in Silesia. From the latter, two groups were moved on to Kreuzburg and Laufen.

suicide, and this led to delay. Postponements meant that people did not assemble at the Plaza until 12 February, sailing the next day at seven in the evening. This group were told that on landing they would be separated due to lack of accommodation so that women and children were to remain in France for a while.

Delays occurred before the last groups left on 25 February from both Islands. On Jersey it seems this second group consisted of 'undesirables' and amounted to only 27 people. Some effort was made that week to induce more to work for the Germans by threatening those that would not with deportation. The last contingent from Guernsey numbered only 13, and it was therefore the Sarkees who attracted the most attention. Two groups left: 20 on 12 February, and 24 on 25 February. On Guernsey Mrs Cortvriend went down to see them go: 'My heart ached as I saw so many whom I knew, some of them close friends, crossing the gangway. One little fellow of six held my hand until the last minute ... I learnt, some weeks later, that he had contracted asthma as a result of being housed in damp and unhealthy premises.'

On the other side of the Channel, on the wet and windswept quays of St Malo, and at the station after a ration of a loaf of bread, a German sausage, and a bowl of soup had been given out, the Islanders were seated in second class carriages to begin their journey into the Third Reich.

Where they were to go had been a matter of brisk argument between the army, the foreign ministry and the SS camp authority. There was a shortage of camp accommodation in Germany, apart from two former POW camps at Biberach and Laufen, and for this reason the first internees ended up in some cases for a time at the unpleasant Dorsten camp. Then a third camp, Wurzach for women and children, became available, and a series of moves took place which the accompanying diagram makes clear. The Reichsführer SS, Himmler, was ultimately responsible for all camp guards, but in the case of the camps in the south, effective day-to-day control was in the hands of the state police supervised from Stüttgart or Munich. Discussion of the Islanders occurred from time to time in the first three months of 1943, but at last on 8 March Knackfuss reported that as far as could be judged the evacuation was over.

The German decision was that single men should be based at Laufen, married couples, single women and children at Wurzach, and the rest at Biberach, and once that was decided on 25 October things moved swiftly, and between then and 12 November the Islanders were moved to a large extent to the appropriate camp.

Laufen was the most attractive scenically of the camps in a former palace of the archbishop of Salzburg. Inmates were treated in Salzburg general and mental hospitals with every consideration. Because Laufen was for men only it was possible to enforce clear rules, and set up the traditional committee and disciplinary tribunal elected by inmates. Frank Stroobant became the commandant, until Ambrose Sherwill arrived, and took over in June 1943. At Wurzach, the Islanders were in a castle which had been a Catholic monastery. When inmates arrived they found French POWs had left it in a disgusting mess which took a week to clean up. The camp commander Captain Ashton Hilton proved less effective, and when he fell ill in the autumn of 1944, he was replaced by his deputy, Major F.A. Ray. The women were represented on the committee by Mrs Downer, and as will be seen the atmosphere in this camp, cramped by admissions of other categories of prisoners – like Jews – was the least satisfactory of all.

No sooner were the first deportees settled than the second wave arrived, and the Germans' accommodation problem was renewed. This time the men were sent to Laufen, and a few to Kreuzburg near Breslau, and the women, children, and men over 64 to Compiègne in France. Twelve men ended up at Kreuzburg where they found a Guernsey POW, and by May 1943 some 35 Channel Islanders were listed as being in this camp. The majority left for Biberach in August 1943, and only one was still there at the end of the war. The group who went to Compiègne numbering about 130 found poor conditions for the women prisoners. Those who went there were not able to send mail, and vanished from sight for several months. In June 1943 they were moved on to Biberach and Wurzach, except for one woman who had a breakdown and was left behind. When, in August 1943, any men in Laufen with relatives were transferred to Biberach, it must have seemed that all were neatly behind barbed-wire at last.

In fact Islanders found their way to four other camps. Liebenau, seven miles north of Lake Constance was a women's camp to which about a half a dozen people like Miss Duckett and Miss Page from Sark were transferred. By March 1944 the camp had about 240 women from Britain, and a hundred from America. That year single women at Biberach were moved there by early October, and the camp became increasingly overcrowded. On liberation there were nearly 450 in the camp, including 91 families from the Channel Islands. A similar move occurred for men from Laufen who moved to Spittal, south-east of Innsbruck during October 1943. There were still 22 in the camp at liberation.

Rather more rarely, Islanders turned up in other camps which were for POWs. One at Marlag and Milag Nord, north of Hamburg, was for merchant seamen and rescued passengers, and eight Islanders are mentioned as being there. Teschen or Lamsdorf was a major Allied POW camp in Silesia containing up to 40,000 prisoners, and among them were over a hundred Channel Isles POWs. In June 1942 six men were transferred there from neighbouring Kreuzburg. It is unclear why a small number of Channel Islanders also ended up at Oranienburg.

On the Islands people waited anxiously for news, and when it came the changes of camp made it confusing. In January 1943 Julia Tremayne referred to the deportees who: 'complain of the cold and ask for food and warm clothing. This does not sound too good, poor souls, taken from their warm homes here.' Soon after the second batch of Sarkees were deported in February she heard from Miss Carter that they were 17 in one room all day, with straw beds, and she wanted her lilo sent. In another letter Mrs Tremayne was shocked to hear baths had to be taken ten people at a time, and that they had been put into barracks where there were lice.

But as the months passed, and the internees settled down in camps with their organization, and entertainments, and above all with the regular supply of Red Cross parcels, life became more tolerable. Indeed their food was better than the Islanders, and they were to be liberated first. Miss Carter sent a letter saying they were all well and contented.

Throughout their imprisonment the Islanders were under threat from a brutal regime, and they were aware of what was going on around them. Dachau lay halfway between two of the camps. Jews from Belsen arrived at Wurzach. The mental strain of internment must have been considerable. Stroobant referred to 'one or two of our number' who broke down under the strain and were sent to Schussenreid or Salzburg hospitals. At Wurzach the number of neurotic cases was increasing sharply in 1945, according to the Red Cross, and a number of such cases had to be left behind on liberation.

Red Cross reports commented unfavourably on Channel Islanders' apathy towards work. Morale also depended on camp leaders and their committees, and here the camps varied. At Wurzach Captain Hilton was described by Red Cross delegates as not suitable for his task because he 'does not act as he should and is not sufficiently severe'. During 1943 matters grew steadily worse. After sharp practice over the camp bread supply was revealed by the Island doctor, Doctor Oliver, the bread committee resigned, but Oliver was undermined, and left for another camp. An American replacement, Doctor Roscoe, soon came into conflict with Hilton, and began to create an oppposition. On 16 March, Major Fraser was given five days solitary confinement by the disciplinary tribunal. Trouble continued, and in November Roscoe, and three other men were removed from the camp by the German police. Hilton managed to get himself re-elected camp leader after this, but the wives of the men concerned became thorns in his flesh. Representatives of the protecting power and the foreign office visited the camp, but rejected demands for transfers. Hilton resigned due to poor health in the summer of 1944. Garland at Biberach, and Stroobant and Sherwill at Laufen, proved much better administrators, although Sherwill showed he had not forgotten he was a member of the Island ruling class when he permitted those of officer rank to be exempt from certain fatigues.

The internees were not POWs and there was no responsibility on them to escape, although Stroobant mentions that some did try it from Laufen only to be quickly recaptured. At the other extreme, camp inmates were subject to German propaganda. John Lingsham from Jersey chose to leave Laufen and work for Goebbels' Concordia Bureau for which he received five years in prison after the war.

Most interestingly of all, Frank Stroobant and Wynne Sayer were selected to join a party of foreigners dispatched to Smolensk to be given evidence that the Katyn Massacre had been carried out by the Russians. At Smolensk they were well looked after and photographed before being driven the fifteen miles or so to the forest a few days later. When they returned to the barracks at Smolensk there was a marvellous evening meal, and, remakably enough, 'every English-speaking German east of the Rhine' was there. One of them assured Stroobant he had been born in north London and was an Arsenal supporter. Stroobant says, 'I told him in so many words ... I had no intention of doing anything which might result in my neck being stretched after the war was over.' It is likely that this was an attempt to inviegle Stroobant into the British Frie Korps. One of them, Dennis John, was the son of a German baker in north London, and had been to Jersey.

Some internees did not complete the full period of internment. There were 46 deaths in Germany among the Islanders. At Wurzach there were 12 deaths, and they were buried in the town cemetery where a monument in Jersey stone now stands. At Laufen ten deaths were recorded, although nothing else is known about them. At Biberach there were 20 deaths ranging from a small girl of two to an old man of 74.

The other group of internees who did not serve the full term were those repatriated early. According to Cruickshank it was Britain in December 1943 which took the initiative in proposing an exchange of 600 of the Islanders, but Harris says it was the camp leaders like Stroobant and Hilton who raised the issue with the Germans, and that, as a result, in February 1944 discussion of repatriation began. The trouble was that Islanders might not have any home in Britain, and the home office thought that 'they should stand down in favour of those whose ties are here'. As a result of such quibbles no Channel Islanders were included in the first batch of 1944 repatriates. Questions were asked in parliament, and 125 were included in the second exchange, and arrived at Liverpool on 15 September 1944. A further group arrived at Liverpool on 23 March 1945.

For the rest there were to be two and a half years of camp life in Germany. At Laufen Stroobant and Sherwill ruled effectively through an advisory committee, and a tribunal elected by secret ballot to hear disciplinary cases. The camp was run smoothly with a large number of classes and entertainments, and plenty of sport. The German Kommandant Kochenberger, disliked Nazis, and got on well with the internees. He knew that Stroobant and others had managed to construct a wireless, and warned them when a Gestapo search was about to take place. Wurzach with its poor organization and disputes seems to have been a much more miserable camp. Overcrowding was made worse by the inflow of inmates from mid-1944, and by early next year people were 30 to a room. There were severe shortages at first, and in December 1942 Doughty wrote that they were living on potato peelings. Later conditions improved, only to deteriorate again when fuel ran low, and Christmas 1944–5 passed without parcels. Although medicines were in good supply, and treatment available at three local hospitals, the camp infirmary was small, and had to cope with such events as a scarlet fever outbreak, and typhoid or septicaemia caused by mosquitoes during the summer.

At Biberach, on the other hand, under Garfield Garland's leadership unsatisfactory conditions to start with were transformed into a successfully run camp by the middle of 1943. It was at Biberach that the communal bath which shocked Mrs Cortvriend was found; in fact this was one of the best facilities. Food, too, was short at first, but by early 1943 Red Cross parcels began to arrive every 12 days. The camp worked well with amateur dramatics, keep fit and educational classes.

Liberation from the camps was a moment of immense joy. Biberach was first on St George's Day, 23 April 1945. After four more weeks in the camp for interviews by intelligence officers, and the issuing of identity papers, they boarded Dakotas at an American base and flew home. At Wurzach, Preston Doughty recorded the final week in his diary. First came retreating Germans, hundreds of planes passed overhead shaking the building, and at last French tanks were in action in the next village. On Saturday 28 April, 'a tank was seen coming over the top of the hill which leads down into the village, great excitement took place at the camp, the tank had stopped, and the least sign of opposition would have been the end of many British subjects in the camp, because as the French told us afterwards all their guns were trained on this building thinking it to be a German headquarters. The French did not know we were here, so we in the camp owe our lives to the German *Volksstorm* [Home Guard], the old men of the village, who ran towards the tanks with white flags. The first tank pulled up outside the camp at 12.15, a great shout went up, and a Union Jack was flown from the balcony.' Between 2 and 9 June, the Wurzach internees were flown home.

The Americans liberated Laufen on 4 May as the 40th Armoured Division entered the area. They were flown home after some delays from Salzburg airport, and like the others went to Stanmore for a debriefing during which they were carefully questioned about any possible German brutality, and asked to describe German conduct on the Islands as well. Then, loaded with forms, they could board the boat from Weymouth and return to the Islands.

17

The Fate of the Jews on the Islands

The 450,000 members of the British Jewish community were among the luckiest of their faith during the Second World War. Listed for extermination at the infamous Wansee Conference they escaped the Holocaust.

One small group of British Jews on the Channel Islands had to face the Nazis, and their fate is the concern of this chapter. Remarkably enough, it is still unclear what happened to this tiny group. Angus Calder said, 'several were dispatched to an obscure fate on the Continent'. Norman Longmate said they were deported. 'Nothing', he said, 'seems to have been done to save them and their fate is uncertain'. Later he elaborated a little more by saying, 'some seem to have been murdered in German camps'. Others have been more misleading by suggesting no harm befell them. Frank Falla said that Louis Cohen and a couple of other Jewish businessmen left with the 1940 evacuees, and that the German search of Island records for Jews proved unsuccessful. Raymond Falla, head of the purchasing mission, actually stated there was a decision 'not to co-operate with the Germans in their anti-Jewish policy', which was the reverse of the truth. Alexander Coutanche was suitably vague saying, 'The Jews were, I think, called upon to declare themselves. Some did, some didn't ... Those who didn't weren't discovered. I've never heard they suffered in any way'. It seems he and others chose to ignore the significance of having to mark Jews with a red 'J' in the lists of various groups on the Islands they were required to compile.

The Island governments were not guilty of sending anyone to their death in the way the Vichy authorities were across the water, but they did collaborate administratively in the process by which the small number of Island Jews were first of all punished, and then deported. Early in 1939 Hitler said Europe would not find peace until the Jewish question was settled. If there was war caused, as he put it, by international Jewish finance, the result would be 'the annihilation of the Jewish race in Europe'. The small number of Island Jews, particularly those who had come from Austria in 1937–8, would have been fully aware of these dangers, and for that reason some of them at least left the Islands in June 1940.

In November 1940, A.J. Roussel, the greffier on Guernsey, received the following letter, a copy of which was sent to the Kommandantur.

'Dear Sir, I consider it my duty to inform you that I am renting the premises known as 'The Exact' 27 Commercial Arcade, Guernsey, from Mr David Rudnidsky, whom I believe is a Jew, and when last heard of was residing at 7 Winchester Road, Andover, Hants, England.' The Middleviks who conducted a clothing business in St Peter Port had been among the evacuees, and their business was handed over to the Germans. In some cases the Germans were more destructive. Egypt Farm on Jersey was ransacked because its absent owner was Jewish.

Action against Jews in the Channel Islands began in September and October 1940 at the same time as anti-Semitic laws were introduced in France. The first regulations issued on 27 September stated that any person with more than two Jewish grandparents was a Jew and that all such people together with their families must present themselves for registration. All remaining Jewish businesses were to be labelled 'Jewish Undertaking' in English, French and German, and such signs began to appear in the few shops concerned – there were only three in Jersey. Imprisonment, fines, and confiscation were the penalties for failure to comply.

The second set of orders in October stated an administrator for Jewish affairs would be appointed. This was Doctor Casper of the Kommandantur whose orders applied in both Islands, and who, according to Steckoll, communicated with the SS in Paris asking for yellow cloth stars printed in English to be sent to the Islands. Further financial provisions followed. Any legal transactions after 23 May 1940 by Jews were declared invalid.

In May 1941 came the third and final set of orders referring to the Jews, apart from the enforcement of a tighter curfew on them in June 1942. Those with two or more grandparents even married to Jews became liable to register. The administrator was to take over Jewish businesses that had been discovered, with instructions to grant allowances to the former owners only for 'absolute necessities'. There was to be no compensation. Lastly, Jews were banned from entering all kinds of public places. On Guernsey, Carey faithfully reported that two Jewish women on the Island had been warned not to enter restaurants in September 1942.

Before these measures could be properly enforced, registration was vital. Cruickshank noticed Kommandantur and other Island records dealing with police and Jewish matters had disappeared although such records had clearly been kept as surviving indexes show. In 1982, a book by Solomon Steckoll included a small fragment of the administrative correspondence of the Guernsey Controlling Committee. Although the letters are few they are extremely important. There is no reason to think they differ in tone from those destroyed and their tone is conciliatory in the extreme, even allowing for the more courtly style of official correspondence in the 1940s. Although Carey is supposed to have taken a back seat, in this matter as in others he acted directly as bailiff and governor.

In the original occupation orders it was stated the Island governments were required to register all German edicts, and this meant that they would appear under the Royal Coat of Arms after the greffier had carried out official registration. On Guernsey the first anti-Jewish measures were registered on 23 October. This gave the weight of Royal authority and Island government to a German order which, if it had been published without them would have been seen as something opposed by the Island government.

The letters show the Island authorities performed their duties willingly when it came to carrying out the laws. Sherwill wrote after the event, 'I still feel ashamed that I did not do something by way of protest to the Germans'; but whereas in other administrative matters formal protests were registered, in this case not even that was done. In October 1940, Carey replied to a request to know how the list of Jews was proceeding by saying Inspector Sculpher had prepared a report. There had been some delay caused by bad weather in getting a reply from Sark. 'I can assure you that there will be no delay, in so far as I am concerned, in furnishing you with the information you require,' said Carey. Two days later the Sark details had arrived, and he hastened to inform Brosch of this.

As a result of Carey's and Coutanche's activities the Germans once more had their lists, and it seems that 26 Jews were still on the Islands, 22 on Jersey, and four on Guernsey. There is some evidence that a Jewish woman on Sark, Annie Wranowski, was not registered, and a story given by Norman Longmate describes how another Jewish resident evaded registration by escaping down the fire escape, and hiding in her friend's house.

Although yellow stars ordered by Casper did not come, the effect of the anti-Jewish laws was to isolate the small number of Island Jews. Two of the women concerned on Guernsey were Mrs Elizobet Duquemin, and Mrs Elda Brouard. Elda Bauer as she was before her marriage had come from Italy, and Elizobet Fink from Vienna with some other girls to learn English. She had married Harry Duquemin, and they had a daughter, Janet, who was only 18 months old in February 1943. Details of their incomes were given by the police to the Germans along with those of other Jews showing that Island banks paid no attention to confidentiality. Mrs Duquemin had £80 which she was saving for her daughter's education. Mrs Brouard had more, even though she worked as a housekeeper paid 10s a week with full board. She had £250 invested in war loan and £60 deposited in Barclay's Bank. These two women were told by Carey not to enter restaurants. Mrs Brouard, Mrs Duquemin, and her daughter were deported to Biberach, and Mrs Brouard subsequently moved to Liebenau. Henry Duquemin was also deported, and it is interesting that his is the only name to appear in the published lists of deportees.

The other two Jews on Guernsey disappeared before the deportation. It seems they left for France in April 1942 and were not subsequently traced. Both of them were from Vienna and knew Mrs Duquemin. Theresia Steiner was a 26-year-old nurse at the Castel Hospital, and Auguste Spitz was a 41-year-old hospital maid. Mrs Duquemin said the two had come to see her to borrow a suitcase, and were terribly frightened.

On Jersey, two French Jews ran foul of the Germans. In October 1944,

Suzanne Malherbe and Lucille Schwab were arrested. Von Aufsess wrote that 'there are very few Jews on the Islands. The two Jewish women who have been arrested today belong to the unpleasant category.' They were sentenced to death for distributing anti-German propaganda, but subsequently reprieved and imprisoned in Jersey.

Although the lists of deportees have been carefully studied, hardly any other Jewish names can be found except in the lists of deaths. It may well be that the rest of the Island Jews were also removed at the same time to vanish in European camps. Among those listed as dying are A. Nathan at Biberach, Emanuel Solomon, Alfred Weismann and Nathan Guter in Laufen, and Raymond Gould at Wurzach. The only Jewish families which appear to be listed among the deportees are the Goulds, and the Schutzs.

This is not the complete story of the Channel Islands Jews. It sheds a little more light accounting by name for the fate of 12 or so of them. Steckoll claimed he had seen a letter from Casper to the SS in his own handwriting dated 17 June 1942 recommending the removal of the Island Jews to Dachau. But in the absence of the records, no more can be said for the time being. Senator Wilfred Krichevski, who represented the Island Jews at the time and was in Britain during the war, would have known the rest of his fellow religious, and it would have been easy enough to check how many returned. Krichevski played down their loss, and declined to support a request to the Board of Deputies of British Jews for a memorial because he could not 'see why they ought to be specifically remembered quite separately from the other foreign labour'. (Steckoll, p.110). Eventually, a privately sponsored one was erected and dedicated at a ceremony Krichevski did not attend. Even in this case there seems to be a spirit of forgetfulness abroad in strong contrast to what happened elsewhere in Europe.

18

Belsen, Buchenwald, Frankfurt, Naumburg, Neuengamme, and Ravensbrück

The War Crimes Commission assembled at the Courts of Justice in the Strand in October 1943, and a month later the Big Three Powers issued the declaration that at the end of the war those guilty of war crimes would be brought to justice either in the country where the crime was committed, or elsewhere if they were guilty of initiating more widespread policies. The first trials in the British zone were held at Lüneburg in September 1945 and resulted in the first executions of 11 Belsen commanders and guards. The Nuremberg trials themselves began in November 1945, and throughout Europe, trials and executions of Nazi war criminals and their accomplices went on for years.

But there were no such war trials in the Channel Islands. The victims of the Kommandantur were unavenged, and those responsible for breaches of international law and for prison sentences which led to the deaths of Channel Islanders were never brought to trial. The deportation of 2,000 people, acts of individual brutality and illegality all went unpunished. Although Morrison said investigations were to take place, by the time he arrived in the Islands he was able to affirm that 'there appears to be no evidence of anything which could be regarded as a war crime as far as the Germans on Jersey and Guernsey were concerned.'

The Germans on the Islands were arrested and sent to British POW camps from which they were released within three years. Although detailed statements were taken from escapers, deportees and the Islanders in 1945, the result was that the evidence was stated by the next home secretary, Chuter Ede, to be inadequate for prosecuting any Islanders or Germans. The Treachery Act of 1940, and the Trading with the Enemy Acts were not extended to the Islands, and no attempt was made to make actions like fraternizing and informing into criminal offences.

It is often said that no executions of Islanders as a result of German action took place, although a number of death sentences were passed. This is true, but it omits a group whose numbers and fate still remain uncertain: the Islanders sent to prisons on the Continent. Somewhere

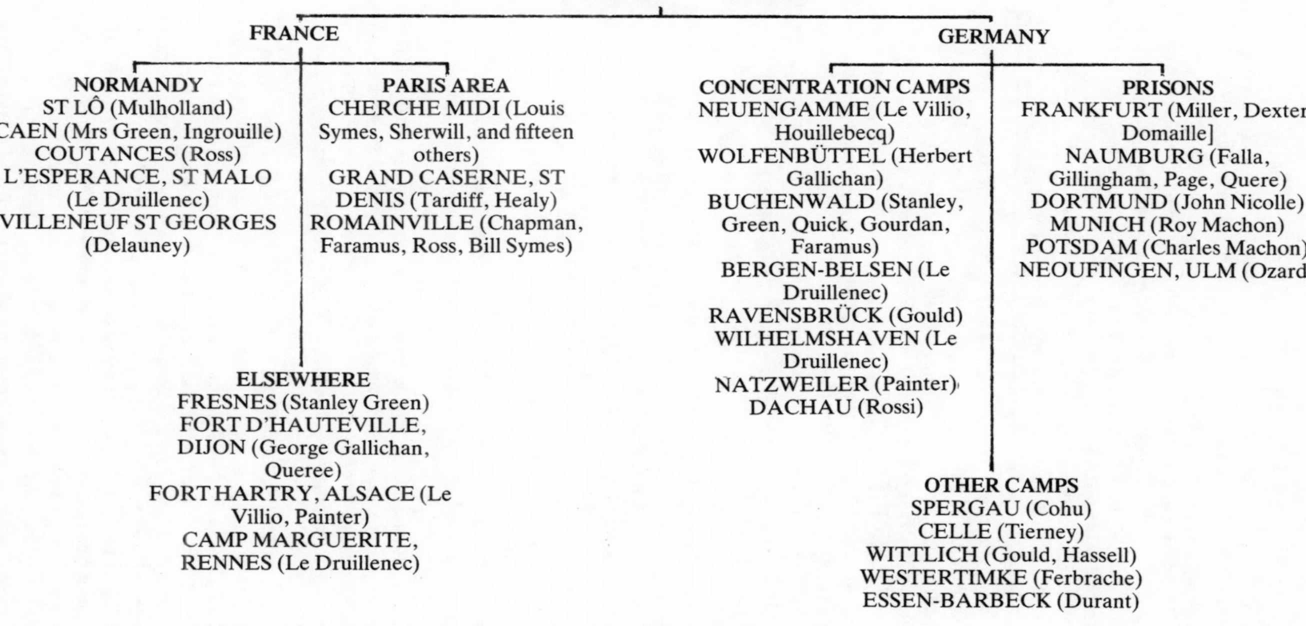
Camps and Prisons in Europe to which Channel Islanders were sent Part 2
FRANCE
NORMANDY
ST LÔ (Mulholland)
CAEN (Mrs Green, Ingrouille)
COUTANCES (Ross)
L'ESPERANCE, ST MALO (Le Druillenec)
VILLENEUF ST GEORGES (Delauney)
PARIS AREA
CHERCHE MIDI (Louis Symes, Sherwill, and fifteen others)
GRAND CASERNE, ST DENIS (Tardiff, Healy)
ROMAINVILLE (Chapman, Faramus, Ross, Bill Symes)
ELSEWHERE
FRESNES (Stanley Green)
FORT D'HAUTEVILLE, DIJON (George Gallichan, Queree)
FORT HARTRY, ALSACE (Le Villio, Painter)
CAMP MARGUERITE, RENNES (Le Druillenec)
GERMANY
CONCENTRATION CAMPS
NEUENGAMME (Le Villio, Houillebecq)
WOLFENBÜTTEL (Herbert Gallichan)
BUCHENWALD (Stanley, Green, Quick, Gourdan, Faramus)
BERGEN-BELSEN (Le Druillenec)
RAVENSBRÜCK (Gould)
WILHELMSHAVEN (Le Druillenec)
NATZWEILER (Painter)
DACHAU (Rossi)
PRISONS
FRANKFURT (Miller, Dexter, Domaille]
NAUMBURG (Falla, Gillingham, Page, Quere)
DORTMUND (John Nicolle)
MUNICH (Roy Machon)
POTSDAM (Charles Machon)
NEOUFINGEN, ULM (Ozard)
OTHER CAMPS
SPERGAU (Cohu)
CELLE (Tierney)
WITTLICH (Gould, Hassell)
WESTERTIMKE (Ferbrache)
ESSEN-BARBECK (Durant)
The names given are examples and do not constitute a complete list
The whereabouts of some prisoners like Ogier and Soyer are unknown

between 70 and 100 Islanders served sentences in Europe, and at least 20 of them died there in captivity, or shortly afterwards. This penalty was exacted not for murder or sabotage, but for acts like insulting a German or listening to the wireless.

Channel Islanders were scattered in at least 30 places in France and Germany. They found themselves in German gaols with ordinary criminals, or in French ones with captured resistance workers, SOE operatives, and RAF personnel. Stanley Green sentenced for having a wireless set at West's Cinema in St Helier which was not his, found himself at Fresnes at the same time as Wing-Commander Frederick Yeo-Thomas when he was being beaten up and taken for daily torture at the Avenue Foch. Green, like Yeo-Thomas, was destined for Buchenwald. Islanders would end in Belsen, Neuengamme, and Ravensbrück among well-known names in Germany and Romainville, Cherche Midi, and Fresnes of equal infamy in France.

On 17 April 1944, Charles Machon, ill with his ulcer, was the first of those sentenced for his part in producing *GUNS* to leave the Island. He was transferred from Potsdam Prison to Hameln-Weser Hospital where he died on 26 October 1944. The other four men concerned: Falla, Duquemin, Legg and Gillingham were sent to the Continent on 4 June just two days before D-Day. They were destined first for Frankfurt prison and remembered hearing the D-Day news at a wayside station as they travelled there. The prison contained over 800 inmates among whom, according to Falla, were 15 Island prisoners. Some were there as a result of acts of defiance, but others were there for crimes like the policemen involved in the black market affair on Guernsey. Gillingham, Legg, and Falla were confined in one cell, and Duquemin with two French prisoners. The four men were at Frankfurt for two months. Among those they met was Percy Miller, who had been informed on for listening to the radio. He became ill, and died in the infirmary there in August that year, aged 61.

In August, the four *GUNS* prisoners, together with seven other Channel Islanders, were transferred to the much grimmer prison at Naumburg south of Leipzig. Its 300 inmates were a complete cross-section of German prisoners, and a range of Allied nationalities. Falla managed to get a pencil, and wrote on tomato paper hidden in his shaving-stick the names of those who died there. They included Joseph Gillingham, George Cox, William Marsh, Frederick Page, Emile Paisnel, Sidney Ashcroft, and Clifford Querée. Falla, Duquemin, and Legg were subjected to periodic beatings, and Falla saw Legg thrown down steps so that he suffered from a permanent limp. Legg had such bad dropsy, that a bucket and a half of water was drained from him. Medical treatment was minimal because the doctor was hoarding medicines of every conceivable kind, presumably to sell on the black market. When Falla got pneumonia, the doctor refused him aspirin, and he had to cope with it by himself.

Falla admitted English prisoners were treated less harshly than others although he received a beating for climbing on the table to look out of his cell window. Among those Fallae met at Naumburg were two other Islanders. They were victims of informers being punished for listening to the radio, and had formed part of the group around Canon Clifford Cohu.

John Nicolle sentenced to two years was to die at Dortmund in 1944. Falla met the Canon himself and Joseph Tierney. They believed they were being moved on to Laufen, but in fact were in transit to other camps. Tierney died at Celle and was buried at Kaschitz. Cohu was lost sight of in the prison system. His wife heard from him in June 1944, but it was not until December 1945 that she heard from a fellow prisoner at Spergau of his fate. Ill though he was he had been compelled to work, and sleep outdoors in a tent. Dysentery had overtaken him, and he had died. Under his shirt was found a small Bible.

The women sent to the Continent were usually confined in French prisons. Caen Prison received among others Mrs Winifred Green, for her remark about Hitler and the rice pudding, and Mrs Le Norman and Mrs Kinniard convicted of displaying the V-for-Victory signs. Mrs Michael and Mrs Mulholland arrested for helping the British agents in 1940 were sent to St-Lô and placed under house arrest. But others suffered more. One woman placed in solitary confinement by the Germans became mentally disturbed and returned to the Islands after the war a broken woman. The most tragic case was the death of Louisa Gould. Together with her brother Harold Le Druillenec, and her sister, Mrs Ivy Foster, she had been sentenced for harbouring a Russian fugitive, and possession of a wireless. Harold and Louisa travelled to St-Malo together, and were then separated. By an unknown process, possibly connected with her Jewish name, Mrs Gould was sent to Ravensbrück, the women's concentration camp 50 miles north of Berlin. This camp killed at least 50,000 women, and among them were several British victims like Violette Szabo, Lilian Rolfe, and Denise Bloch shot in the back of the neck in the yard behind the crematorium. A number of English prisoners including Odette Churchill survived to give testimony when the commandant, Suhren, and the assistant commandant, Schwartzhuber, were brought to trial and hanged. Among the camp guards was a kapo or trustee from Guernsey where she had been trapped by invasion in 1940. Mrs Julie Barry admitted she had treated other prisoners brutally as part of her duties, and was able to describe the usual method of execution by a bullet in the neck although a gas chamber was built to kill 7,000 of the women, and Mrs Gould could have died in either way.

Harold Le Druillenec survived, but only just, a nightmare prison journey through no less than six European prisons after a short stay in Guernsey prison. L'Esperance, St-Malo was followed by Camp Marguerite at Rennes, and Fort Hartry at Belfort before he arrived at Neuengamme, the parent camp of Sylt. From there he moved to Wilhelmshaven, and eventually to Belsen where he became the sole British survivor. Neuengamme was responsible, like Ravensbrück, for some 50,000 deaths. There Le Druillenec found Frank le Villio, aged only 18 who was to die shortly after his release, but he did not see James Houillebecq, who died later at Neuengamme. At Wilhelmshaven, Le Druillenec worked as a welder. He was liberated on 16 April and spent nine months in various hospitals before he recovered at a convalescent home at Chelwood Gate in Sussex, and was able to return to the Island in December only to hear Louisa had not survived. The Russians honoured him for his deed in helping the Todt worker. And finally in 1966 the only British survivor of Belsen was given £2,000 compensation by the British government.

A number of Islanders spent periods of time at Buchenwald, six miles from Weimar. Stanley Green, the cinema projectionist, left Fresnes for Buchenwald in one of the SS death transports. At Buchenwald, Green was shaved and put in prison costume. They had to sleep in the open until death provided them with places in the huts. Green found William Symes, Sandeman Bill of 'The Dive'. Both men were extremely lucky because they managed to get letters out of the camp. As a result they were transferred to Laufen. Other Islanders imprisoned at Buchenwald included Paul Gourdan and J.T.W. Quick.

In 1941 Edward Chapman, an English criminal who had been released from Jersey Prison, and his black market associate Anthony Faramus, were arrested, and sent to St Denis, and then on to Romainville, an old-fashioned fort used to keep a stock of hostages for shooting in reprisal. The two men were horrified when hostages were taken away and shot after their names were read out when they were working. Chapman's account must be taken with a pinch of salt. He was a convicted criminal, and later became a double agent for Germany and Britain in order to avoid further imprisonment. He described how informers were planted among the prisoners. Chapman referred to an Italian shot dead for waving from a window. The food was sometimes reduced to boiled vegetables with worms floating in the mess. There was no fuel for the stoves, and they removed rafters to make firewood. Chapman was interviewed three times at the prison after he had expressed his wish to be a German agent, and in April 1942 he was taken away. He said goodbye to Faramus who was moved on to Buchenwald where he managed to survive.

One of the saddest of the camp stories concerns a father and son, Peter and Peter C. Painter, arrested in 1943. Betrayed by an informer for listening to a wireless, the Germans took a serious view of the matter because Mr Painter had not turned in a First World War souvenir pistol. The two of them were sent to the Cherche Midi, and eventually ended at Natzweiler concentration camp in Silesia. Nothing more was heard of the Painters until after the war when Mrs Painter received an account of their end from a French prisoner. They had to work in the bitter winter of 1944–5 for Krupps and on a canal. Peter got pneumonia and died in his father's arms. Mr Painter struggled on, but the prisoners were moved west to prevent their liberation by the advancing Russians. On the third day travelling unfed in an open truck through freezing rain and snow, Mr Painter also died.

As far as is known only one Islander ended in Dachau. Marcel Rossi and his father, Jerseymen, were interned at Kreuzburg, and transferred to Oppeln. His father last heard of him in Dachau. Among other Islanders imprisoned in German camps were the two young escapers, Maurice Gould and Peter Hassall. Gould died at Wittlich. Herbert Gallichan spent his sentence for publishing the *Bulletin of British Patriots* at Wolfenbüttel and Peter Ozard was located at Neoufingen Prison at Ulm and repatriated in June 1945. In France, Herbert's brother, George, served his shorter sentence at Dijon in Fort D'Hauteville. Clifford Queree was imprisoned there first before going on to Frankfurt and Naumburg. Cherche Midi in Paris contained 17 Islanders imprisoned in 1940. At Grande Caserne, St Denis, there were a number of British prisoners said to include eight Channel Islanders. Among those known to have been imprisoned there were A.L. Tardiff, a Guernsey policeman, and Mr P. Healy William, deported from Jersey in January 1943.

There are also a number of prisoners whose place of imprisonment is not given. Jack Soyer, sentenced for listening to the wireless, managed to escape from a French prison, joined the resistance, and was killed fighting for them. Mr Ogier and his son were deported for making insulting remarks about the Germans. Mr Ogier died in a camp somewhere in 1943. Harry St Clair Dean was deported from Guernsey in 1944, and repatriated in May 1945. Edward Peter Muels sentenced to 15 months hard labour was removed from Jersey in May 1944.

Through the summer months of 1945 those who had survived came back, and gradually news filtered through. Frank Falla who had seen the deaths at Naumburg wrote bitterly about the aftermath of these events. As far as the Islands were concerned nothing happened. There was no memorial. There were no honours in December 1945. Above all the Island governments gave no compensation, or pensions, and these had to await the settlement between Britain and Germany arrived at in June 1964. The agreement excluded all POWs, internees, and those imprisoned in ordinary prisons in France. These people were told by the Foreign Office their claims would have to await a final peace treaty with Germany. The Island authorities appointed no officials to help anyone put in their claims which had to be handled individually. It is true some of the prisoners had been convicted of genuine offences, but others were clearly innocent, and none of those who died had been convicted of capital offences.

Airey Neave noticed the British government like the Island governments would not contribute to memorials to the victims. It seems as if both governments simply wanted to forget the past. Forgotten by the authorities, Falla described how on the last Saturday in April each year he and a slowly dwindling band of camp inmates – Legg, Duquemin, Dexter, Lainé, Domaille, and Bill Symes, would meet in a hotel to toast 'Absent Friends'.

Epilogue

The Liberation Days

After a meeting on 26 March 1944 when it was decided the Channel Islands would not form part of the D-Day operation, the formation and maintenance of a task force for liberating the Islands took a back seat in military considerations. Task Force 135 was seen as a pool from which troops could be removed for other tasks such as guard duty at Sandringham over Christmas, and early in 1945 the main infantry component of the force was sent to Germany. It was replaced by the 312th Brigade.

The plan of liberation was Operation Nestegg, and was to be preceded by a reconnaissance called Operation Omelet in which advance parties would see if resistance was offered before the main force came within range of German defences. The operation had two main purposes. The first was to remove the German and Todt presence from the Islands. The second was to restore the life of the Islands to as near normal as possible, and to enquire if any action needed to be taken against collaborators, informers, and fraternizers.

When they landed, Task Force 135 found there were 26,909 German POWs to be processed and removed to camps in Britain. They brought with them the staff of two British POW camps, set up filtering centres, and then concentrated the Germans at Les Blancs Bois in Guernsey and St Peter's Barracks in Jersey. With the exception of those needed for other purposes the Germans began to leave on Sunday 13 May. Disarmament left the British force responsible for masses of military hardware including 50,000 tons of ammunition, 600 machine-guns, 400 mortars and flame-throwers, 100 anti-aircraft guns, anti-tank and field guns by the score, and more valuable materials like lorries and wireless equipment. Some was taken to the United Kingdom, but the rest was destroyed by being sunk at sea or melted down, sealed into tunnels, or sold for scrap. Even more difficult was the question of what to do with 1,623 fortifications of one kind or another. Some were retained where they had civilian uses like sea walls, electricity, and water supplies; others like bunkers and railways were destroyed where they blocked communications, and as much camouflage and wooden superstructure as possible was demolished. Scrap merchants moved in to destroy the larger guns. Here serious mistakes were made in deciding what to preserve and what to destroy even though, as early as September 1945, the new lieutenant-governor of Guernsey was writing to the war office to suggest, that the Island authorities might be agreeable to having some of the interesting gun emplacements, control towers etc., left intact for publicity purposes and as historical relics to be shown to tourists.

By far the most important element in disarmament was the removal of 177,925 mines located fortunately in 305 marked mine-fields. Two field companies of Royal Engineers accompanied the task force; 259 for Jersey and 618 for Guernsey, Alderney and Sark, and they were assisted by 3,200 German POWs, at least seven of whom were killed.

Task Force 135 was commanded by Brigadier Alfred Snow of the Royal Artillery and he had under his command about six thousand men. It was accompanied by Civil Affairs Unit 20 commanded by Colonel H.R. Power whose unpleasant task was to investigate possible crimes or treachery during the occupation, and whose more congenial role was to preside over the operation to restore normal life. This ninety day task was successfully performed. The first requirement was to double the dietary level to 2,750 calories a day and 500 tons of food were brought ashore. Clothing rations equivalent to 15 months issue in Britain were made available and free gifts of chocolate, cigarettes and tobacco were made.

Islanders watched as the Germans left their billets for the POW encampments, and inevitably looting had begun. Some of it was entirely justified as Islanders reclaimed their furniture or cars; much of the rest was inevitable after years of suffering. It was particularly galling to see vast stores of German equipment laid out in special compounds, and there was much theft of motor vehicle parts. Later there were auctions of German goods organized by the ministry of supply at which all manner of items were picked up, not least barbed-wire for agricultural purposes. John Boucheré described how he went into St Helier where: 'Small groups of ill-clad citizens, equipped with hessian shopping bags, wandered about opening cupboards, turning out drawers, gathering up folding chairs, and unscrewing lamps and other electrical fittings in the hotels.'

A postal unit restored postal and telephone services on 18 June. Special medical packs were brought over for the hospitals. The currency which by liberation consisted entirely of Reichsmarks was restored. On board the ships in strong boxes was a million pounds for the banks. The exchange rate was fixed at 2s 1½d to the Reichsmark, and people had to exchange at this rate by 20 June. The stability of the Island government's finances was secured by giving Jersey £3,750,000 and Guernsey £3,250,000 to discharge debts incurred as a result of lack of tax revenue, and the costs of occupation, although Sark and Alderney received no such grants.

A third task awaiting the liberating forces was to deal with those in camps on the Islands. There were the Allied POWs among whom the Americans were the first to leave on 11 May after a liberation concert in aid of the Red Cross. The Todt Organization withdrew on 14 May, and the task of dealing with some 900 remaining displaced persons began. Spanish prisoners could not be returned to Franco's Spain, and came to Britain. The rest of the miscellany of nationalities left on 7 July for Granville with two exceptions. The French Africans were immensely popular in Jersey which they left on 15 June with other French citizens for Cherbourg.

The Russians received separate treatment. Their ROA troops together with Italian troops in the Wehrmacht were evacuated on 14 May, but the Todt POWs kitted out in British battledress with a special flash were gathered at Camp Ursula in Guernsey. They were visited by Major V. Gruzdiev, one of the NKVD officers allowed under the Yalta Agreement and other agreements made by the British government, to visit 'Russian' prisoners and arrange their return. There were 273 Russians, 19 Poles and one Estonian classified as 'Russian', and they were despatched to a camp at Newlands Corner, near Guildford whence they travelled to the Soviet Zone of Germany, via Dover and Ostend. On arrival at Lüneburg in the British sector, the Russians placed 140 repatriates under arrest. As part of the 32,295 Russians returned to Stalin directly from Britain, the fate of some at least of this party can well be imagined.

The week before liberation was a strange one. Through wireless broadcasts the Islanders knew Hitler's Germany was falling apart, but days passed, and nothing happened. On 4 May Mrs Tremayne said 'as it gets to the end the feeling of relief is so great', but three days later she was still waiting. 'We are all strung up and terribly excited and the glad hour comes nearer, we are certainly the last to be relieved, but, oh the joy, just to think it can really be happening.'

Hüffmeier and Wulf seemed determined not to surrender. Work on military installations continued, and Sinel noticed that guards were placed as usual. Even though military discipline and health were breaking down, Hüffmeier told soldiers they must hold out because they would be brutally treated if they surrendered. Von Aufsess noticed a proclamation on 5 May stating the German authorities 'have the power' to enforce law and order and banning all demonstrations and meetings. The Island authorities agreed with this, and Coutanche issued a statement on 6 May on Hüffmeier's orders saying, 'I appeal to you all to maintain your calm and dignity in the days through which we are now passing'.

The SS *Vega* arrived for the last time, and Coutanche said he was discussing with the Red Cross ways of improving supplies. Requisitions continued and Hathaway received demands for cattle and wood to be sent from Sark which she ignored. Hüffmeier's fanaticism went further than the Islanders knew. On Sunday 6 May he rejected a request for unconditional surrender, and planned to launch a second attack on Granville that day which had to be directly stopped by the *ersatzführer* Admiral Dönitz. According to Ramsey, the last military execution on Jersey took place on Tuesday 8 May, the day when it was clear that liberation was really to take place.

It was in Julia Tremayne's diary 'A never to be forgotten day' when the press appeared uncensored, and wireless restrictions were lifted in time for loudspeakers to be put up to hear a broadcast by Churchill on VE Day. It was the day the blackout and curfew came to an end. Molly Finigan described how, 'Mum told us to get the flags out, ready to fly them across the street. With a radio getting an airing at long last, neighbours and the family got together in the street to listen to our dear Winston Churchill giving his famous speech.'

As Islanders gathered at their wirelesses the crowds cheered and waved their flags. Churchill said: 'Hostilities will end officially at one minute after midnight tonight, but in the interests of saving lives the "cease fire" began yesterday to be sounded all along the front, and our dear Channel Islands are also to be freed today.' The cheering grew louder, and in the Royal Square, St Helier, Coutanche spoke from the court house to tell them the Germans had informed him a 'commission' was on its way, and, to even greater cheering, that the Royal Navy was approaching the Islands. He reminded them the King was to speak at nine that evening. A school holiday was announced.

But Churchill was wrong. The Islands were not quite free. The Task Force Operation Omelet group had sailed from Plymouth at ten that morning, Brigadier Snow in HMS *Bulldog*, accompanied by HMS *Beagle*. The ships carried two small parties each with two officers and 20 men who were to go ashore to test the situation. At midday the British met Hüffmeier's representative four miles south of Les Hanois lightship as a minesweeping trawler approached HMS *Bulldog* bearing Lieutenant-Commander Arnim Zimmerman. Hüffmeier had only empowered him to negotiate an armistice, and Snow had to make it clear there could only be unconditional surrender. Zimmerman had the audacity to warn Snow his ships could still be fired upon.

It was a futile postponing of the inevitable. The ships put to sea for a time, but at midnight returned to the rendezvous point when, out of the darkness, came an armed German trawler from which put out a white-painted cutter rowed by eight men. In the stern sat Zimmerman accompanied this time by Major Siegfried Heine, looking every inch the arrogant German. Talks began which lasted two hours, during which it was pointed out that Hüffmeier could not meet every condition because he had, for example, begun to destroy papers some time ago. However, the surrender was agreed, and 'At 7 a.m. a table was placed on the little quarterdeck. Brigadier Snow took his place at one side of it and the other members of his staff grouped around him. The German general was summoned, and hesitating, almost tottering – he is a man in late middle age – he came to the table. Eight times he signed his name on copies for Britain, Russia and America. The Brigadier signed and that was the end ... The time was 7.14 a.m.'

So on the same day that Bornholm Fortress surrendered to the Russians in the Baltic, and the Germans holding out in L'Orient, St Nazaire, and La Rochelle gave up the Channel Islands were liberated, among the last places to be freed, for there was only Dunkirk to surrender on 11 May, and Crete on 12 May.

At 7.45 on Wednesday 9 May, Lieutenant E.G. Stoneman and Colonel H.R. Power with 20 men of the Royal Artillery, bayonets fixed, landed at St Peter Port to be greeted by a sergeant and a policeman, the Island rulers being still in bed. 'There behind the dock gates was a seething, cheering, crying mob of men, women and children. Over them the church bells of St Peter Port were clanging tumultuously ... Then the crowd broke through the dock gates. In one second those gunners were marching like Guardsmen; in the next they were torn from the ranks, kissed, hugged, cheered ... Somehow the soldiers reformed. Two girls with great Union Jacks led them into town.' When they reached the court house, Carey and others had arrived with Leale still in his dressing-gown. Stoneham was kissed on the steps, and Power's hat was knocked off. 'One could hear a sob from the crowd, then rising to a great volume of sound they sang "God Save the King". They then stopped, looked up again and cheered – that to us seemed the real moment of the liberation of Guernsey.'

The strength of emotion released is some indication of the sense of oppression five years of German rule had brought. Molly Finigan roamed the streets all day with the milling crowds. A sailor gave her an orange, and she flung her arms round him in gratitude.

Power rang up Coutanche in Jersey to tell him to be ready to go with General Wulf to HMS *Beagle* to which Brigadier Snow had transferred for the military surrender. It proved difficult to locate Wulf, but by twelve he and two of his staff were ready. Coutanche was annoyed at the presence of three Germans and said he would take Duret Aubin and Cecil Harrison as well. On board, the Jersey party were welcomed by Rear Admiral C.G. Stuart in command of the British naval forces, and by Colonel W.V.A. Robinson. They went below to enjoy gins, have their Island tobacco replaced by the real thing, and enjoy a wash with tablets of soap. Coutanche was able to enquire about his son, Midshipman John Coutanche, and it was a wonderful birthday message for him to receive news that he was safe, and applying for leave. Wulf proved obstinate at first, but Snow spoke sharply to him, and the surrender was signed. On 12 May Hüffmeier, Wulf, von Aufsess and other German officers embarked on HMS *Faulknor* for Plymouth before being sent to POW camps from which the last of them was released in 1948.

Meanwhile excitement was building up in St Helier as HMS *Beagle* rounded Noirmont Point and anchored beneath Elizabeth Castle. The honour of being first ashore that afternoon went to the Royal Navy when Lieutenants Milne and Macdonald with four seamen came ashore, 'amidst roar after roar of delirious cheering'. It was now safe for the rest of the fleet to approach the Islands, and that evening parties of 200 soldiers landed on Guernsey from HMS *Campion* and on Jersey from HMS *Cosby*. Their first task was to disarm the Germans who were told to surrender in half-mile zones radiating from the centre of the town bringing their arms to the Arsenal at St Lawrence in Jersey. Boucheré and some of the local lads had got on quite well with the anti-aircraft battery at Greenfarm, Maufant, and had played cards with the blue clad Luftwaffe men. 'Within a few hours our Flak Company had assembled on the paths which connected the huts. At the command "*In gleischritt marsch*" the gunners marched out of our lives, and into Jersey history leaving the gunsite still and quiet.'

Amidst the rejoicing Colonel Power sounded a few sombre notes. The police force had lost considerable credit in the eyes of the public, he said, and 'needs assistance from the military at the moment'. He referred to an incident on 11 May when a woman 'cornered like a mad beast, dishevelled, torn and bleeding', was threatened by a crowd calling out, 'Throw her into the harbour', and had to be rescued by troops. Power's civil affairs unit received information from the Jersey Loyalists, and the

Guernsey Liberation Society about quislings over which, in the Woods' words, 'a bland legalist blanket' was quickly drawn down. Power noticed, too, that war had led to discontent with the pre-war system of government, some radicals wanting constitutional change finding support among those angry at the war time conduct of the Island governments. On 4 June Power wrote to the war office: 'there is a danger that discontent of the Islanders with their pre-war system of government which differs considerably from the method of government in the United Kingdom, may be so increased after the return of Islanders now evacuated to this country as to lead to internal disturbance.'

It was necessary to establish military rule and then to resume the old method of government as quickly as possible. It was on 12 May that Brigadier Snow landed at St Peter Port at 10.45 in the morning to receive Hüffmeier's formal surrender, and then in front of Elizabeth College at 2.00 p.m. to announce the formation of the military government. Snow then crossed to Jersey and the ceremony was repeated at the Royal Court where he read out a proclamation from George VI making clear that they would 'resume as soon as possible your accustomed system of government'.

Military government continued until 25 August when the former system of government was restored with the appointment of lieutenant-governors. On Jersey, Lieutenant-General Sir Edward Grasett proved a popular choice and remained for ten years while Guernsey had as its new governor Lieutenant-General Sir Philip Neame, who had spent most of the war in POW camps after capture by the Italians in April 1941. When reform had to be considered, therefore, it was the old governing class that put forward the initial proposals late in the year. A home office committee chaired by Chuter Ede, the home secretary, discussed them, and limited reforms of voting and membership of the states and appeals in the courts were introduced in 1947. A second committee considered Alderney where the position of 'Judge' was abolished, and the Island given two seats in the Guernsey States in 1948.

Sark had watched while these events took place, and various naval craft passed her shores. As soon as Hathaway heard of VE Day in Europe, she ran up the Union Jack and Stars and Stripes and lit a bonfire, and for ten days was in effective control of the Germans on the Island. The Island Commandant refused to answer calls from Guernsey, and so towards evening on 10 May a naval tug took Colonel Allen, two other officers, and 20 men from St Peter Port to Creux Harbour. They were escorted to the German headquarters at Le Manoir and after much knocking on the door, the commandant emerged, and went next door to Rosebud Cottage to sign the instrument of surrender. The Germans left on 17 May taking with them their motorized vehicles.

On 11 May at 3.45 the main bulk of the task force consisting of 57 ships set out from Plymouth, and arrived off the Islands, Rear-Admiral Stuart being responsible for Guernsey and Commander L.A. Freeman for Jersey. The fleet was escorted by a number of British, Canadian and American destroyers, and one Polish vessel. It was preceded by seven mine-sweepers, but most fascinating of all to the Islanders were the ten

Landing Ship (Tank) vessels and the Dukws which were amphibious. The LST disgorged at St Aubin's Bay, Jersey and L'Ancresse, Guernsey with long awaited stores, and then took back POWs and materials which the military had decided should go to England. Mrs Cortvriend described the scene at unloading. 'The manoeuvering of an American LST through the entrance of the inner harbour seemed miraculous to us, and we watched with wonder as its bows suddenly swung open to disgorge motor lorries laden with food, bicycles, motor-trucks and military equipment of every description. A steel track was laid over the mud and the vehicles were instantly driven across it to the road.'

Maugham rejoiced that privation was over at last, and the day after the LSTs arrived, Julia Tremayne made the last entry in her diary:: 'I go into church every day and hold a little service to myself and thank God for all His goodness to me.'

Alderney was left alone for a week giving Schwalm ample time to burn or drown any incriminating evidence. On 16 May, Brigadier Snow and Rear-Admiral Stuart approached the Island to land at Braye Harbour where they were met by Schwalm, and a group of Islanders and Russian prisoners. Frank Oselton gave them glasses of milk, and George Pope accused the Germans of killing a thousand people pointing at them as killers. It was a claim he was unable to substantiate. A German medical officer told Snow that Todt and SS records had been removed, and Schwalm would obviously have destroyed his the previous week.

Within a short time Snow initiated an enquiry by military intelligence led by Major Sidney Cotton. During May and June detailed interrogation of the remaining Germans, Islanders, and inmates was carried out, and the committee looked for 'material witnesses who had drifted further afield'. The final report and the evidence for this investigation was missing in 1982 when Steckoll investigated the matter, and he was told that need for storage space had led to their destruction. Evidence collected by the committee was offered to the Russians on Jersey who were holding their own investigation, no trace of which has been found.

From 22 May to 23 August 1945 the possibility of war crimes trials for events on Alderney was under consideration. The foreign office officials concerned were anxious to carry out every last detail of the agreements with Russia to return all Russians in British hands to Stalin. Patrick Dean wrote, that 'if victims were solely Russian, the Germans should be handed over to the Soviet government since their victims were Soviet citizens.'

The war office knew, as a result of interrogations, and from the miscellany of races on the Island in May 1945, that there were Jews and other groups in the Alderney camps. Dean said on 30 June 'I think it would cover our action, if we now proceeded to try the staff of the concentration camps [*sic*] in Alderney by Special Military Court, provided, however, that the victims of these guards were not solely Russians.'

On 11 July, Brigadier Henry Shapcott, the deputy judge advocate-general was approached by the foreign office saying the treasury solicitors needed to be very clear that groups other than Russians were involved.

Shapcott was asked specifically if Russians were mistreated in the concentration camp, and 'whether there were other nationalities than Russian among the victims'. His reply to Patrick Dean a few days later was highly confusing. After stating Russians were also mistreated in Todt camps, he replied to the second question, 'none other than possibly Germans', although he also admitted French Jews were in the camp for a time, adding in a subsequent letter 'that no atrocities were committed against the French Jews'. Either Shapcott had not bothered to enquire, or failed to pick up a telephone to speak to Major Cotton, because if he had he would have been told that the prisoners included French Jews, and that they were mistreated. The foreign office was surprised, and one of their officials said he had thought it more likely 'the German guards would be accused of war crimes against persons of various nationalities', but before long they contacted Sir Thomas Barnes, the treasury solicitor, stating, 'we have now learned from them that all the victims of the alleged war crimes were Russians who worked for the Todt organisation, or were prisoners in a concentration camp on the Island.' Under these circumstances, the foreign office preferred to hand over any accused Germans to the Russians. Barnes replied 'I therefore assume that there is nothing further for me to do', and the matter was dropped during the next month. No Germans were in fact handed over to the Russians.

Clearing up Alderney was one of the most difficult tasks facing the military government. After most of the Germans were removed in five LSTs on 20 May some 500 remained, and until some preliminary mine-clearance had been achieved worked without British troops. A German crew was also left in the Casquets lighthouse for a time. Judge French and Snow, made a preliminary visit after a week to assess the damage, and teams of WVS personnel were brought in to clean up the properties. Early in December some preliminary parties arrived, and on 15 December the first of the Islanders returned. Eventually 685 of the pre-war citizenry returned to the barren and broken-down Island.

Unfortunately Judge French, due as much to his former Indian service as to an ulcer, was unable to provide any leadership. Quarrels broke out when attempts were made to restore property to its rightful owners. Communal farming was tried, and proved a failure, and once the military left, relations between French and the people deteriorated until the home office had to retire him.

Naturally a feeling of tremendous elation followed years of repression as people gave themselves over to public ceremonies, and making allied troops welcome. From the mainland came visitors, but not Churchill. On 15 May, the home office party arrived led by Herbert Morrison accompanied by Lord Munster, Sir Frank Newman, and Charles Markbreiter whose voice Sherwill had heard on the telephone the evening when St Peter Port was raided. Morrison was received by those responsible for affairs during the occupation who lost no time in letting him know their side of the story. Coutanche described the scene in his house after the nine o'clock news when, 'we went on sitting round the table for several hours while they asked questions and I did my best to answer them. Eventually we got up and went to bed, I suppose at around two o'clock in the morning.'

Although they visited some damaged houses before Morrison went on to Guernsey, it is clear his impressions were superficial. The only result was that home office officials were seconded to the Islands to help reorganize administration. Morrison reported to the cabinet, and in August his successor, Chuter Ede, reported to the Commons using material that Morrison had gathered in less than 48 hours.

24 May was Empire Day, and another excuse for patriotic display. On 7 June came King George VI and Queen Elizabeth, an unusual royal visit in which the King was cheered by Russian prisoners and met French North Africans.

Behind the scenes of merrymaking, however, Island life was resuming its old ways. Black market operations were clearly illegal under existing law, but no prosecutions were brought, because of the ramifications concerning the recipients of black market goods that any trial would have revealed. Excess profits taxes were introduced in the Islands of 60 per cent in Jersey and 80 per cent in Guernsey on profits above standard profits. Businessmen were soon buying up property for building and the holiday trade when the Islands opened for business again in 1947.

The army did its best to dispose of German armaments. Ammunition was dumped offshore in the Hurd Deep while unstable material was exploded on the west coast of Jersey behind the escarpment. Some guns were left: others were thrown over the cliffs at Les Landes where the occupation claimed its last victim in 1977 when a weapons enthusiast disappeared over the cliffs. Other material was sealed into the tunnels although it was impossible to remove it all. As for the military supplies and confiscated civilian goods, some attempt was made to restore the latter to the rightful owners, and public auctions disposed of a good deal.

Some fortifications were blown up or earthed over. Roads, public amenities – particularly beaches – and agricultural land were cleared of anti-landing devices. But the big guns contained much valuable metal and before long businessmen from England arrived. One of the most famous was George Dawson who paid £25,000 for the iron on Guernsey, and he was followed by others down to 1953. On Jersey, the attitude of the government was that such relics of war needed to be cleared, and there was no thought of preservation. On Guernsey, Lieutenant-General Neame continued to urge the war office to preserve some items, but nothing was done. Jersey kept its collection of German weapons secret for 22 years, and it was not until the tunnels had claimed lives among their explorers that they were opened up, and their artefacts used to form museums. Molly Finigan and her sister Joyce ran guest-houses among the hundreds that sprouted up, many with their occupation stories, or features like Mrs Winifrid Green's piece of crochet work done in Caen prison. The first museum actually opened in 1946, but it was in the 1960s that the boom started with museums and guided tours of fortifications and underground works.

There are few places in Western Europe where it is easier to see what German occupation was like. Yet for all this physical evidence, the truth about what happened to ordinary people in the Channel Islands remains something of a mystery. Missing documents and the passage of time make it unlikely that the full extent of either Island bravery or treachery will ever be revealed. I have tried to build round the details of German and Island administration, and the operations of the Wehrmacht and Organization Todt, a picture of what these prosaic regulations and orders entailed day by day for Islanders, troops, and prisoners.

German documents can be supplemented by evidence like von Aufsess' diary, and Island documents by personal recollections. Both official documents and personal recollections need to be treated with caution, but they form part of a common picture. Evidence, almost without exception, shows they were a terrible five years. Similarly, evidence of camp inmates, supplemented by records like List's 1943 trial, strongly supports the view that the camps, particularly Norderney and Sylt, were atrocious places of starvation, violence, disease and death. There was less violence and suffering than in some places, but this was brought about by a greater degree of co-operation than prevailed elsewhere. This led to a moderate occupation for the rulers, and the richer black marketeers, for the women who slept with Germans, and informers.

But for the majority of Islanders, German occupation from early in 1941 was purgatory, as anti-Jewish laws, and the proposal for mass deportation showed. The rattle of gunfire shooting Todt workers, escapers, and Germans was heard on the Islands, death sentences were passed, and thousands fined or imprisoned. The German legal system condemned nearly a hundred to life in the camps of Fortress Europe. Claims about a 'moderate occupation' of the Islands were the product of the Island rulers' views who had received privileged treatment themselves, and of a joint determination by the rulers and the British government to hide collaboration in high places, shaming indeed in 1945 in the only British territory to fall under Nazi rule.

This tale of a moderate occupation denied the opponents of the Island governments the opportunity to protest, or change the form of government, and conferred on the Island rulers (and of course Whitehall) the mantle of having pursued the wisest and most subtle of policies which in Morrison's words obtained, 'the best possible treatment from the Germans commensurate with the avoidance of any semblance of collaboration.'

Honours were showered on the Island rulers including Carey, Sherwill, Coutanche, and Leale, with CBEs for Leale and Edgar Dorey, and OBEs for Touzel Bree, R.H. Johns, and H.E. Marquand. Guillemette got an MBE. Some of these were richly earned; others were ill deserved. Sherwill's broadcast on Radio Bremen, and his remarks about escapers and resisters should have disqualified him, while Carey had set his hand to orders like the anti-Semitic regulations, and the offer of cash to informers. Such men would not have been decorated in neighbouring France. Apart from a few exceptions like McKinstry, and Bertram, none of the names in this book were mentioned in the honours list in December 1945. Nor did any receive compensation. Nor did any of them even have their names carved upon a memorial. Those who helped Allied servicemen, aided escapers, upheld morale by making wirelesses, or producing news-sheets, gave assistance to Todt workers, showed defiance and stood up to the bullying and greedy occupiers, languished in gaol, died shot on the beaches trying to escape or drowning off the coast, and died in faraway camps often alone for trivial offences, were one and all quickly part of an army of Unknown Warriors.

In May 1946 the Victory Parade took place in London in which representatives from all over the Empire marched in pouring rain to celebrate victory. Molly's sister Joyce was overjoyed that she was to be one of the school children to go to London, and to receive a Liberation Day medal. Among those also invited was Frank Stroobant whose experiences of occupation had taken him to prison, and to a deportation camp. He realized as they marched through London, that the Channel Islanders were the only group unidentified by either flag or placard. They marched anonymously on Victory Parade Day as so many of them had suffered anonymously in the years of German occupation.

Appendix

An Estimate of the Totals of Dead in the Channel Islands War Theatre

This table of figures is incomplete in two ways. Some of the figures given are approximate. Some figures still cannot be given. However, an estimate helps to illustrate the numerous ways in which death came to the occupying forces, their prisoners, and the Islanders both in the Islands and elsewhere, and is further evidence that this was a tough occupation that took its toll in life.

Deaths in the German Occupation Forces

The overall total of German graves was 568.

455 were removed in 1961 and 113 remain at Fort George.

Kriegsmarine	102
Wehrmacht	457
Luftwaffe	3

The number of Luftwaffe dead was higher than this: several crashed in the sea. *CIOR* lists 24 dead.

Merchant seamen	4
Feldpolizei	unknown
SS and camp guards	unknown

Examples of causes of death

Executions by courts martial

Alderney	2	April 1945
Jersey	5	

It was said that the only convicted military rapist was executed, and death sentences were passed on looters and thieves.

Suicides

Alderney	7	1 in 1942, 5 in 1943, 1 in 1944

These included Doctor Köhler and Lieutenant Frank.

Jersey	8

It was said that some troops either killed themselves or died from self-inflicted wounds to avoid Russian service or at the surrender.

Killed in action		
Sark	3	Oswald, Essinger, Bleyer (In British raid).
Alderney	2	Bombardment by HMS *Rodney*
Granville raid	1	
Accidents		
Palace Hotel explosion	9	March 1945
Hemlock Poisoning	11	January 1945
Stepping on mines, Sark		Major Johann
Hinkel and two soldiers	3	
By mines after liberation	7	
Fights between troops	2	
Drowned		
Major-General Christiani and 7 others		November 1942
Captain Parsenow		mid 1943

Murder

Doctor August Goebel was said to have been murdered by his batman in April 1942 on Sark. The batman committed suicide, and it was later revealed a soldier had killed the doctor for refusing him a medical certificate.

Deaths in Allied forces or of Allied nationals

Islanders serving in United Kingdom forces	
Guernsey	221
Alderney	18
Sark	1
Jersey	unknown
Military casualties	
Raid on Sark (Bellamy, Dignac)	2
Raid on Jersey (Ayton)	1
Naval casualties	unknown
Included loss of HMS *Charybis*, and HMS *Limbourne* on the night of 23/24 October 1943	504

41 were buried on the Islands.

There were between five and seven naval engagements in the waters near the Islands.

Air casualties	unknown
Included:	
British air crew	10
American air crew	2
Canadian air crew	1
Belgian air crew	1

Some aircraft were lost at sea with no survivors.

Crew of Lancaster bomber who were not rescued off Alderney in June 1944 on German orders. 6

Deaths in Allied POW camps on Islands unknown

Americans Graves removed 11

French Escaper François Scornet Executed 17.3.41

Other French escapers captured on the Island were returned to France and some subsequently died.

Deaths of civilians

The number of deaths as a result of bad medical conditions, prolonged malnutrition, and mental breakdown cannot be calculated. Death rates rose during the Occupation for such groups as diabetics and the elderly.

Air raid casualties

Raid 28.6.40 44

Other raids are said to have killed 93 people, but it is not clear how many of these were Islanders, Todt workers or Germans.

Air raid casualties among evacuees unknown

Deaths of deportees 45

It is impossible to distinguish natural causes from deaths directly resulting from deportation conditions.

Suicides

At the start of the occupation 3

Louis Symes, Cherche Midi, December 1940 1

Major John Skelton, September 1942 1

Suicides at Beaumont and Grouville in September 1942 and February 1943 in Jersey 3

There were said to be suicides also in Guernsey as a result of deportation.

It is impossible to calculate how many other suicides were brought about by occupation like that of Clifford Holloway who killed himself soon after liberation having lost his son and his wife.

Accidents of war unknown

Nanette Carré, aged 4, killed by mine in October 1944.

Boy killed by collapsed shelter looking for fuel, February 1945.

Two fishermen killed by mines, June 1943 4

Murders unknown

Man killed by drunken German, New Year's Day 1942, aged 42.

Mr Jehan killed by looting soldiers, 25.8.44.

A number of people were said to have been killed for their Red Cross food parcels. 2

Shot by Germans unknown

Woman on beach, October 1944 (only mentioned by von Aufsess).

Douglas Le Marchand, 11.10.44. 2

Drowned trying to escape unknown

Known cases in Jersey:

Dennis Audrain, 2.5.42.

Ronald and Madelaine Bisson, André Gorval, Roy Luciennes, 12.11.44.

Bernard and John Larbarlastier, 28.11.44. 7

Deaths in European camps and prisons, or before returning to the islands

The final figure is not known, but stands at 20.

Apart from Symes suicide, and the death of Jack Soyer fighting with the Resistance (29.7.44) after escaping the present list is:

Maurice Gould, Louisa Gould, Peter Painter and his son Peter, John Nicolle, Ogier, Gillingham, Machon, Miller, Tierney, Cohu, Houillébecq, Ingrouille, Marsh, Paisnel, Ashcroft, Queree, Le Villio.

Deaths of Todt workers, Sylt Camp inmates, and prisoners of the Germans

The total of identified graves was 509.

Of these 387 were on Alderney. 433 contained named persons.

It is clear this is an under-estimate:

Other burials

Buried where they were working, e.g. St Ouen's Bay

Buried at sea, e.g. thrown from Fort Clonque on Alderney

Buried at site of accidents, e.g. 9 behind a rock-fall at St Lawrence, Jersey

Within the official burial grounds there are circumstances to suggest there were more bodies than graves identified:

Named Todt workers known to be buried there cannot be identified

Some were buried unofficially, e.g. at Westmount Strangers Cemetery in 1941

Shot by Germans unknown

Franzeph Losch, Fort George, 16.6.43

Wilhelm or Willy Ebert, summer 1943, St Anne

2 men hiding in cave on Alderney (Pantcheff, p.16)

Execution was by shooting, hanging, strangling with wire, and beating to death. Pantcheff, pp.14, 69, 71, and Steckoll, pp.31, 34, 78, 80 and 94 give examples of deaths.

Killed in Allied air raids on harbours and air fields unknown

Drowned unknown

Bodies were recovered from the sea, e.g. 14.10.42 on Jersey said to be an escaper.

Minotaure, sunk 7.7.44 *c*.200

Four Frenchmen drowned, and buried at Westmount, 11.2.42

Accidents unknown

4 French Algerians died eating hemlock, and 2 as a result of a gas explosion on Jersey.

17 killed by an explosion, and 5 by rock falls in building tunnels–buried in cemeteries.

Illness unknown

There were said to be 39 deaths in the typhus outbreak on Guernsey.

List said most of the 50 prisoners who died in the first few months of 1943 at Sylt were tubercular or ill in some other way.

It is impossible to know how many deaths were due to exposure, hard work, and starvation, the main causes of Todt deaths.

Leaving the Islands unknown

Transport conditions were deliberately made bad:

About 8–10 died on *Xaver Dorsch* transport, January 1943 from Braye to Cherbourg.

8 died on trains in a transport of June 1943 to Neuengamme.

2 killed at Sollstedt in transit, summer 1944.

Killed trying to escape unknown

Escape was only possible in transports leaving the Islands to cross Europe to other camps.

Kortemark at least 35

Near Toul 17

The known graves clearly only provide a basis for any final count of Todt dead. There are too many unknowns, e.g. *Xaver Dorsch* went aground with loss of life outside Braye Harbour. There are no details of executions in punishment lagers on the two main islands. It is unclear if bodies disposed of in the sea were dead already, or actual killings, and it is clear dead workers were sometimes left where they fell. The random figures given above add about a hundred to probable deaths plus two hundred on the *Minotaure* making *c*.300. Added to the 509 graves this brings the total appreciably closer to the rough total of a thousand mentioned in May 1945.

Source Notes

Short titles are used throughout: for the full titles of works see the bibliography.

Chapter 1

Cruickshank gives a clear account of events in 1940, pp. 11–79. See also Wood, pp. 1–53, and Cortvriend, pp. 1–80. Maugham, pp. 13–32 adds some Jersey details. Hathaway and Coutanche describe their first meetings with the Germans, Sherwill's is in Wood, 39–40. See also Falla, p. 18. Hitler's view of the Islands is in Trevor-Roper, p. 584. Quotations on the air raid are in Wood, p. 30 and Falla, pp. 14–15, and on Guernsey at evacuation in Durand, p. 14. The letters on the Channel crossing are in Cortvriend, pp. 29–30, and *CIOR*, 1975, pp. 8–12. The surrender demand is in Wood, pp. 45–6, and the occupation orders on pp. 41–2. Further Guernsey orders are in Cortvriend, pp. 63–4 and 68–70. For those on Jersey, see Maugham, pp. 27–8.

Chapter 2

Cruickshank, pp. 231–7 and Steckoll, pp. 65–9, deal with plans for major attacks on the Islands. For Churchill references see Churchill, pp. II, 566, 572. For the commandos see Churchill, pp. II, 147, 214, 217–19, 412–13, and Messenger, pp. 25–35. For the raids on the Islands see Cruickshank, pp. 81–102, and Ramsey, pp. 129–40. For the effects see Wood, pp. 53–64, 86–96, and Cortvriend, pp. 99–111. For the letters see Cortvriend, pp. 102–5. For the SSRF see Messenger, pp. 153–63. For the later raids see Cruickshank, pp. 238–45, Ramsey, pp. 141–67, Wood, pp. 138–45. For the Sark raid see Tremayne, pp. 101–10, 159–62. The German documents are presented by Richard Mayne in *CIOR*, 1979. For the posting of death penalty notices see Wood, p. 113, and Tremayne, pp. 48, 55. For the French on the Islands, see Hathaway, pp. 121–2, Falla, p. 83, and von Aufsess, pp. 61, 87. For Scornet, see Ramsey, pp. 216–19, and Toms, pp. 32–4. For air losses in the region see John Goodwin's article in *CIOR*, 1974, and for shipping losses, *CIOR*, 1973. For Allied escapers, see Falla, pp. 80–3, Ramsey, pp. 82, 121, and

Wood, p. 206. For warfare in the area, see Cruickshank, pp. 101–2, 245–8, Falla, pp. 70–1, Ramsey, pp. 208–9, and Steckoll, pp. 92–3. For air war see Tremayne, pp. 23, 26–7, 34, 54, 56, 60, 64, 81, 82, 85, 127, 145, 167, 170, 172, 174–5, 176–7, 179, 180–1.

Chapter 3

Cruickshank, pp. 164–205, 259–86, gives the outline of military developments on the Islands. See also Toms, pp. 53–77. Ramsey and Partridge give excellent detail on the technical aspect of the fortifications. *CIOR* 1981 gives the various fortification orders: see part pp. 6, 15, 20, 25, 26, and 28. For the tunnels see Tremayne, pp. 166, 178, 180, Pantcheff, p. 46, and Ramsey, pp. 36–8, 976–9. For the impact of the soldiers, see Tremayne, pp. 31, 37, 42, 44, 45, 49, 53, 56, 64, 86, 90, 93, 99, 109, 111, 122, 128, 147, 149, 165, 168–9, 173, 179–80. See also Bihet, pp. 25, 28, 30, 46. For looting, see Cortvriend, pp. 86, 218, Cruickshank, pp. 172–4, 282, and chapter 12 below; reckless driving, Cruickshank, pp. 126–7; rape, Wood, p. 70; brothels, Cruickshank, pp. 170–2, Pantcheff, p. 59, and chapter 8 below; drunkenness, Cruickshank, p. 169, Tremayne, p. 55, Bihet, p. 45, discuss fear of Russian service by Germans, Owen, pp. 45 and 53 for the two Chapman quotations. For military violence towards civilians see Falla, pp. 60–3, 155, Harris, pp. 159, 161, Cortvriend, p. 277, Tremayne, p. 59, Owen, p. 47, Wood, pp. 115–18, 204–05.

Chapter 4

Cruickshank has very little to say about the last year. Cruickshank, pp. 256–7 for the Granville Raid, and *CIOR*, 1975 article by Dennis Holmes for the Cèzembre action. See below Chapter 10 for political discontent in the Wehrmacht in the last year, and the sufferings of the soldiers in Chapter 14. For the orders issued, see Mayne (1981), p. 53, Wood, pp. 192, 211, and von Aufsess, p. 190. For the intention to take hostages, see Wood, p. 217, and von Aufsess, p. 5. For provocation of civilians by Nazis, see von Aufsess, pp. 140–1, 166. Von Schmettow's strong reply is in Cortvriend, pp. 294–8. So is her report of a conversation with a Nazi officer, pp. 320–1. For Hüffmeier's speeches, see Maugham, pp. 139–40, and von Aufsess, pp. 174–5. There is a brief article on Schmettow in *CIOR*, 1972. The conduct of the Island officials is in Wood, pp. 65–6, and 103, Coutanche, pp. 27–8, and Hathaway, pp. 120, 130–1, 134, 138, 159. Von Aufsess described his contacts and meals with Duret Aubin and Coutanche.

Chapter 5

Cruickshank discusses collaboration and passive co-operation on p. 157, Michel, pp. 38–9 outlines the shades of meaning in the word. For Coutanche see his own memoirs, and Longmate (1975), pp. 168, 199, 216–17. For Carey's use of language see Steckoll, pp. 130ff., quoting some of the few surviving documents. For Island government see Cruickshank, pp. 108–10. For Jersey see Coutanche's own account in *Bulletin of the Société Jersiaise* (1965), pp. 33–53, and for Guernsey, Kenneth Tough's article in *CIOR*, 1978, pp. 45–56. For the purchasing commission, see Cortvriend, pp. 95–6, Wood, pp. 79–80, and Cruickshank, pp. 125. For the MI9 report see Steckoll, p. 117, and for the atmosphere generated by collaboration, Cortvriend, p. 204. Von Aufsess is invaluable. See part pp. 20, 22, 32, 34, 42, 65, 86, 102. I cannot agree with either Morrison's (Steckoll, p. 67) or Cruickshank's view (p. 329) praising the conduct of the Island governments.

Chapter 6

Destruction of documents, loss after the war, and some retentions by HM Government prevent an accurate assessment of collaboration. The MI9 report is in Steckoll, pp. 117–18. For courts and prisons see Cruickshank, pp. 6–7, 114–15, Chapman, pp. 35–47, Tremayne, pp. 98, 170, 176. For German security forces see Cruickshank, pp. 106, 111–12, 119. For the Feldpolizei (not Gestapo) see Cruickshank, p. 306, Falla, pp. 142–3, Steckoll, p. 119. I have altered Gestapo to Feldpolizei or Feldgendarmerie where appropriate. For the black market, see Maugham, p. 110, Bihet, p. 43, Owen, pp. 52, 55, Falla, pp. 63–4, von Aufsess, pp. 43, 62, 65, Stroobant, pp. 52–6, and Cortvriend, pp. 226–8. For penalties, see Maugham, pp. 78–9, Marr, pp. 183–4, and for Mr Baird, Tremayne, p. 81. For fishing controls see Cruickshank, pp. 121–3, Tremayne, pp. 92, 150–1, *CIOR*, 1978, and for house searches see Bihet, p. 43, Tremayne, p. 88, and Cortvriend, pp. 316–17.

Chapter 7

The introductionory letters are taken from a photograph in Ramsey, p. 235. Cortvriend, p. 204 and Hathaway, p. 148, refer to informers. See Longmate (1973), p. 517, and (1975), p. 219. Carey's orders are in Cortvriend, pp. 202, 205. The Hungarian case is in Cruickshank, pp. 154–5. The Irish are discussed in Cruickshank, p. 131, Falla, p. 101, and Steckoll, pp. 63, 117. See also *CIOR*, 1985, p. 34. Cruickshank, pp. 129–32, examines the labour question. For details see Cortvriend, pp. 92–3, 177–84. Tremayne, pp. 22, 40, 82, 85, 177, refer to labour matters. Leale's view is in Wood, pp. 99–100, and von Aufsess' comment in his diary, p. 124. Cortvriend, pp. 178, 271, for numbers involved. For Alderney see Pantcheff, pp. 42, 51–2, and 59–60. For Matthew's Party see

CIOR, 1974. The escape of two workers is in *CIOR*, 1978. Toms, pp. 137–45 has pictures of Alderney workers, and Steckoll, pp. 112–13 raises the issue of their failure in the end to give testimony on German conduct.

Chapter 8

Ginger Lou was one of Lewis's patients (pp. 70–3). For MI9 comments, see Steckoll, pp. 117–20. For Boots see Wood, pp. 68, 71. Tremayne's views are on pp. 31, 44, 49, 64, 90, 99, 111, 145, 156, 186, and Cortvriend, p. 147 mentions the baby advertisements. Von Aufsess discusses relations with women in the period mainly after D-Day on pp. 13–14, 20, 23–4, 31, 35, 133, 142, 150, 153, 162, 179–80. For officials and Island women, see Falla, pp. 25–6, Steckoll, p. 119, Cruickshank, p. 154, and Pantcheff, p. 59. For brothels, see Ramsey, pp. 39, 244, Pantcheff, p. 59. For illegitimacy, see Wood, p. 246, Hathaway, p. 148. For venereal disease, see Steckoll, p. 120, Falla, pp. 89–90, and Cruickshank, p. 172. For abortions see Steckoll, p. 119.

Chapter 9

For differing views on the value of resistance see the articles by Alan Milward and M.R.D. Foot in Hawes and White, pp. 186–221. Longmate (1973), p. 513 for unfavourable view, and Cruickshank, pp. 156–7 for view that resistance was pointless and virtually impossible. Cortvriend, p. 81 discusses collaboration and resistance. For resistance involving intelligence-gathering see Wood, pp. 129–30, 147, 193–5, 207–9, *CIOR*, 1978, pp. 15–16. Marr, p. 181, for Symes; Wood, pp. 187–8 for Houillebecq; Wood, p. 130 for Cook; and for the five teenagers, *CIOR*, 1975, p. 24, and Wood, p. 209. For control of information, see Cortvriend, pp. 158–60, Wood, p. 68, and Falla, p. 32. For newspapers, see Falla, pp. 46–50, and Wood, p. 69. For German papers, see Toms, p. 79, Falla, p. 42 and Tremayne, pp. 94, 147, 164. For the wireless ban, see Cortvriend, pp. 228–9, Falla, p. 95, Wood, pp. 151–5, Harris, p. 162, Hathaway, p. 129, and Tremayne, pp. 39, 40, 59, 91. For wireless resisters, see Maugham, pp. 57–8, Falla, pp. 97, 115, 123–6, p. 162, and Wood, pp. 151–5. For equipment, see Cortvriend, p. 270, Wood, p. 209, and Longmate (1973), pp. 516–17. For news-sheets, see Wood, pp. 134, 177, Marr, p. 183, Tremayne, p. 182, Longmate (1973), pp. 218, 220, and Falla, pp. 99–112.

Chapter 10

For the limited amount of sabotage, see Falla, pp. 56–70, Cortvriend, pp. 201–2, 205, Longmate (1973), p. 514, Wood, pp. 74, 111–12, and Harris, p. 162. For German sabotage, see Maugham, pp. 136–7, Ramsey, p. 242, and von Aufsess, pp. 140–1. For demonstrations, see Falla, pp. 70–1, Stroobant, pp. 58–9, Wood, p. 137, Harris, pp. 15–16 quoting Sinel, Tremayne, p. 176, Longmate (1973), pp. 221–2. For attempts to enforce order, see Cruickshank, p. 284, von Aufsess, p. 187, and Maugham, p. 60. For political troubles among troops, see Tremayne, pp. 179–80, 198, 199, 201, 202, von Aufsess, pp. 166, 168, 176, 179, and Wood, pp. 217–19.

Chapter 11

The basic sources for information on escapers are two articles in *CIOR* by David Kreckeler in 1978, and Richard Mayne, in 1975. The Woods have useful information in Chapters 35 and 39. Sherwill's views are in Wood, p. 83, and Cortvriend, p. 106. Von Aufsess' comment is on p. 50 of his diary. For help to Russians, see Cruickshank, p. 161, Longmate (1973), p. 218, Wood, pp. 153–4, 173–4, Falla, pp. 157–8, and Richard Mayne's fine article in *CIOR*, 1972. For later Russian interest, see Ramsey, p. 212, and Harris p. 163. For more about the Russians, see below chapter 15. Escapes from Alderney or in transit away from it are dealt with in Steckoll, pp. 72–4, 82–3, 100–2, 168–71. For Ebert, see Pantcheff, p. 35. For the Bertrams, see Ramsey, p. 82, Wood, pp. 185–8, 205–6, 209, 236.

Chapter 12

Island banking in the occupation is dealt with in Wadsworth. Morrison's views are in Steckoll, pp. 58, 60, 62. Hathaway's account of financial matters is on pp. 173, 176, 178. There are sketches of financial affairs in Wood, pp. 101–2, Maugham, pp. 30–1, Cruickshank, pp. 128–9, 314, and Cortvriend, pp. 97, 184–6. Economic disruption is dealt with in Cruickshank, pp. 117–18, Wood, p. 78, Cortvriend, p. 91ff., 136, 168, 175, 187, 190ff. For requisitioning, see Maugham, pp. 20, 25, 27, 35, 42–3, 50, 54–5, Cortvriend, pp. 167–78, 172–4 (including Leale's and Müller's letters), 187, Cruickshank, pp. 118, 125, 172–3, Longmate, (1973), p. 518, Wood, pp. 52–3, 100, 158–9, and Tremayne, pp. 27, 43, 55, 56, 92, 118–19, 164. For eggs, see Tremayne, pp. 32, 47, 49, 56, 86. For billeting see Maugham, pp. 43–4, 45–6, 60, Bihet, p. 49, Cortvriend, p. 211ff. (includes documents), and Tremayne, pp. 33, 54, 60, 64, 83–4, 101. For destruction of property, see *CIOR*, 1975 article by Frederick Martin on Guernsey church property, Cortvriend, pp. 212–14, and Tremayne, pp. 30, 39, 55, 60, 61–2, 81, 82, 87, 88, 103–4, 106, 147.

Chapter 13

Tremayne, Maugham, and Cortvriend are used in this and the next chapter for the Islands of Sark, Jersey and Guernsey supplemented by Bihet, Sinel and von Aufsess. See also *CIOR*, 1975, Margaret Bird's article 'News From the Kitchen Front'. For bad conditions between 1941 and 1944, see Tremayne, pp. 47, 48, 49, 53, 54, 56, 63, 84, 86, 90, 112, 156,

161, 165, 166, and for Christmas 1943, Cortvriend, p. 259. For rationing and food reductions, see Tremayne, pp. 42, 44, 47, 122, 153, 171, Maugham, pp. 80–1, 104–31, and Cortvriend, pp. 132–6, 170, 241, 297. For other ways of getting food, see Bihet, pp. 39, 47, Cortvriend, p. 141, Hathaway, pp. 163–5, and for improvisations see Toms, p. 120, Cortvriend, pp. 136–8, Tremayne, pp. 48, 54, Bihet, p. 33, Maugham, pp. 88, 98, and Wood, p. 156. For other goods, see Longmate (1973), p. 519, Tremayne, pp. 51, 119, 126, Maugham, pp. 102, 107. For clothes and shoes, see Tremayne, pp. 42, 44, 46, 80, 107, 113, 155, 158, 167, and Maugham, pp. 102–7. For gas and electricity, see Tremayne, pp. 30, 57, 158, 164, Maugham, pp. 112, 124. For health and hospitals, see Cortvriend, pp. 120–30, and pp. 284–6 (giving contemporary doctors' reports), Tremayne, pp. 44, 46, 59, 96, 118–19, 123, 152, 156–7, 167, 169, Bihet, p. 37, and Cruickshank, pp. 136–7.

Chapter 14

For the everyday sufferings of the Islanders, see Tremayne, Maugham, Cortvriend, and Bihet. See also Wood, pp. 200–1. For the fuel crisis, see Maugham, pp. 124, 130, von Aufsess, pp. 51, 119, Tremayne, p. 200, and Hathaway, p. 169, and for the water crisis, see Cortvriend, p. 317, and Wood, p. 197. Lack of British concern about the Islands is noticed in Tremayne, pp. 117, 146, 166, and Maugham, p. 116. For Churchill's policies in 1944, see Cruickshank, pp. 263–4, 267–70, 287–8. I deal with the actual liberation operation in the epilogue, 163–74. For the German army in the last year, see Cruickshank, pp. 278–80, Tremayne, pp. 171, 179, 182, 191, 194, 196, 199, Maugham, p. 130, Cortvriend, pp. 277, 313, 323, Bihet, pp. 58–9, and von Aufsess, p. 72, 117, 122, 162. See also above chapter 4 for the decision to hold out and starve the Islanders, and also chapter 10 for discontent in the Wehrmacht. For SS *Vega* see Bihet, pp. 58–66, Tremayne, pp. 193–4, 196, 202, Cortvriend, pp. 277, 306–8, 313, Maugham, pp. 120–22, Coutanche, pp. 40–1, and Hathaway, pp. 167–8. *CIOR*, 1974, pp. 21–2, gives details of the five voyages, their times, and contents of the ship.

Chapter 15

Cruickshank gives a basic administrative account on pp. 200–5. Pantcheff, pp. 5–21, 27–39, and 64–76, for an excellent account of Alderney. Steckoll's account is not always accurate, but it does have the merit of interviews with inmates: the evidence of Eblagon, Font, Herzka, Prokop, Beernaert, Wernegau, and Misiewicz which Steckoll supplies is convincing; details of the List hearing in Berlin in 1943 on pp. 166–71 reveals the true nature of the Sylt Camp regime. Accounts of Todt workers on Guernsey and Jersey are given by Ronald Mauger and Richard Mayne in *CIOR*, 1969 and 1972. For Losch, see Falla, pp. 83–4, and for the guard at Les Vauxlebets, Wood, p. 126. For the fortifications see chapter 3 above. See also *CIOR*, 1979, A.C. Bishop and E. Launert, *A Wehrmacht Geologist in Jersey 1941–44*, and *CIOR*, 1978, Michael Ginns, *Wartime Quarries in Jersey*. Cruickshank, p. 203, for over all numbers of Todt workers. See also *CIOR*, 1985, p. 30, showing nearly 900 still there in May 1945. Margaret Ginns, French North African POWs, *CIOR*, 1985 is excellent on this subject. For the graves see Ramsey, pp. 206–25, drawing on work by Robin Cox. For allegations of deaths followed by non-burial in a recognized cemetery, see Ramsey, p. 78 (Ho 8), p. 190 (St Ouen's Bay), Steckoll, p. 99 (Fort Clonque), and in the sea in general, Steckoll, p. 49.

Chapter 16

Cruickshank, pp. 215–26, gives an administrative account, and details of the 1941 origins of deportation. Longmate (1975) pp. 191–5, is as usual perceptive and thorough. Wood, pp. 135–8, 146–50 deals with this atrocity sympathetically. See Cortvriend, pp. 231–40, and Tremayne, pp. 99–101, 117–19, for the misery of those who watched the deportation. For Coutanche's reaction see p. 31, and for the British government's reaction, Harris, p. 169. Harris gives a comprehensive account of the deportations, although the lists given do not include all those deported as no such list was ever compiled. Deaths are on pp. 210–11. He uses Preston Doughty's unpublished diary for Wurzach Camp. Harris, p. 39 for a map of the camps. Stroobant, part, pp. 72–113, and 141–62 is useful for Laufen. For Denis John who may have met Stroobant at Smolensk see West, pp. 165–7.

Chapter 17

For this and the next chapter information is very limited. Cruickshank, pp. 113–14, and Maugham, pp. 37–8 for anti-Semitic laws. Longmate (1975), pp. 198–200 includes the story of the escaped Jews. For the intended fate of British Jews, see Longmate (1975), pp. 196, 200–6, Wheatley, pp. 122–24, and Noakes and Pridham, 1130. Harris, pp. 198, 204, 210–11, for Jewish names among deportees, though not all Jews deported are listed (e.g. Mrs Duquemin and her daughter Janet). Steckoll, pp. 120–44, who draws on Guernsey records found in the Holocaust Archive at Jerusalem is central to the chapter as this seems to be the only evidence to survive.

Chapter 18

Details of some of the treatment of British concentration camp inmates are in Cookridge, part, pp. 382–9, Lord Russell, part, pp. 163–225. Bruce Marshall, pp. 132–62, for Fresnes, and 179–211 for Buchenwald. Minney, pp. 169–86 for Ravensbrück, including mention of the woman camp guard from Guernsey, Julie Barry. Attention was drawn to the Island camp inmates by Richard Mayne in *CIOR* 1974, *Forgotten Islanders*. Harris, pp. 156–66 gives excellent coverage and the best list so far. It was still growing when he made it in 1980. Falla, pp. 112–136, deals with Frankfurt and Naumburg, and Owen, pp. 55–65, with Romainville. The Woods, pp. 151–5, 171–6, give useful details. Cruickshank does not deal with Islanders sent to Continental prisons. Slowness in providing compensation, and meanness in distributing it is dealt with in Falla, pp. 163–7, and mentioned in Neave, pp. 317–18.

Epilogue

Cruickshank, pp. 296–302, deals prosaically with liberation. Michael Ginns, *Operation Nest Egg and Task Force 135*, *CIOR*, 1985, is excellent. It reveals much more than Cruickshank. Norman Longmate (1977), pp. 116–26 deals with liberation and quotes the war correspondent with the task force. Tremayne, pp. 202–3, Cortvriend, pp. 326–7, Bihet, pp. 67–71, and Maugham, pp. 141–3 can rejoice at last. Coutanche, pp. 45–56, and Hathaway, pp. 169–7 describe events in official circles. John Bouchère (1975) reminds us not all was law-abiding rejoicing that week. Ramsey, pp. 168–92, has a useful post-war survey of events. For the issues of the failure to punish war criminals or reward war heroes and heroines see Falla, pp. 156–68, Wood, pp. 234–7, Steckoll, pp. 41–57. The occupation honours are in Wood, pp. 244–5. Missing documents are discussed in Cruickshank, p. 332 and Steckoll, p. 39.

Bibliography

1 General works

Churchill, Winston S., *The Second World War, Vol. II* (Cassell, 1949), selected references

Cookridge, E.H., *Inside SOE: The Story of Special Operations in Western Europe 1940–45* (Arthur Barker, 1966)

Dank, Milton, *The French Against the French: Collaboration and Resistance* (Cassell, 1974)

Foot, M.R.D., *Resistance: European Resistance to Nazism 1940–45* (Eyre Methuen, 1976)

——, *SOE: The Special Operation Executive 1940–45* (BBC, 1984)

Foot, M.R.D. and Langley, J.M., *MI9: The British Secret Service that fostered Escape and Evasion 1939–1945* (Bodley Head, 1979)

Grasset, Bernard, (Michel, Henri, (trans.)), *The Shadow War, Resistance in Europe, 1939–1945* (André Deutsch, 1972)

Hansen, Holger Hørsholt, *Triumph in Disaster: Denmark's Fight Against Germany* (HMSO, 1945)

Hawes, Stephen and White, Ralph (eds), *Resistance in Europe 1939–45* (Allen Lane, 1975)

Littlejohn, David, *The Patriotic Traitors: A History of Collaboration in German Occupied Europe 1940–45* (Heinemann, 1972)

——, *Foreign Legions of the Third Reich, Vol. 2* (includes the British Free Corps) (San José, California, 1981)

Neave, Airey, *Saturday at MI9* (Hodder & Stoughton, 1969)

Noakes, J. and Pridham, G., *Nazism 1919–1945* (University of Exeter Publications, 1988)

Petrow, Richard, *The Bitter Years: The Invasion and Occupation of Denmark and Norway, April 1940–May 1945* (Hodder & Stoughton, 1975)

Rings, Werner, *Life with the Enemy: Collaboration and Resistance in Hitler's Europe* (New York, 1982)

Russell of Liverpool, Lord, *The Scourge of the Swastika* (chapter 4) (Cassell, 1954)

Seth, Ronald, *Jackals of the Reich: The Story of the British Free Corps* (New English Library, 1972)

Thomas, Nigel and Abbott, Peter, *Partisan Warfare, 1940–45*, (1985)

Trevor-Roper, H.R. (ed.) *Hitler's Table Talk* (Weidenfeld & Nicolson, 1973)

West, Rebecca, *The Meaning of Treason* (Macmillan, 1949)
Wheatley, Ronald, *Operation Sea Lion* (Oxford, Clarendon Press, 1958)

2 Works on the occupation of the Channel Islands

Bulletin of the Société Jersiaise
Channel Island Occupation Review (*CIOR*)
Appleyard, J.E., *Major John G. Appleyard* (Blandford Press, 1947)
von Aufsess, see Nowlan, Kathleen, J.
Banks, A.L. and Magee, H.E., *Effects of Enemy Occupation on the State of Health and Nutrition in the Channel Isles* (Bulletin of the Ministry of Health, September 1945)
Bihet (nee Finigan), Molly, *A Child's War* (Guernsey Press, 1985)
Boucheré, John, *The Day Peace Broke Out* (*CIOR*, 1975)
—— *A Boy at War* (*CIOR*, 1979)
Cortvriend, V.V., *Isolated Island, A History and Personal Reminiscences of the German Occupation of Guernsey, June 1940–May 1945* (Guernsey Star and Gazette, 1947)
Coutanche, see Pocock, H.R.S.
Coysh, Victor, *Swastika over Guernsey* (Guernsey Press, 1955)
Cruickshank, Charles, *The German Occupation of the Channel Islands*, (Oxford University Press for Imperial War Museum, 1979)
Durand, Ralph, Guernsey under German Rule (Guernsey, 1946)
Falla, Frank, *The Silent War* (New English Library, 1967)
Franks, Xan (ed)., *War on Sark: The Secret Letters of Julia Tremayne* (Webb and Bower, 1981)
Ginns, Margaret, *French North African POWs in Jersey* (*CIOR*, 1985)
Ginns, Michael, *Commando Raid on Sark, A German Report* (*CIOR*, 1979)
—— (ed.), (Kreker, Hans (trans.)), *Verstarkung der Kanalinseln, 1941, Hitler's Fortification Orders* (Archive Channel Isles Occupation Society, 1981)
—— *Operation Nest Egg and Task Force 135*, (*CIOR*, 1985)
Goodwin, John, *Channel Islands Air Losses* (*CIOR*, 1974)
Hansard, Vols. 410, May 1945, and 430, November 1946
Harris, Roger E., *Islanders Deported, Part 1* (Channel Islands Specialists Society, 1980)
Hathaway, Sibyl, *Dame of Sark, An Autobiography* (Heinemann, 1961)
Herzka, A., *Slave Labour in Alderney 1940–45* (*CIOR*, 1970)
Kreckeler, David, *Escapes from Guernsey and Alderney during the Occupation* (*CIOR*, 1978)
Lassen, Suzanne, *Anders Lassen, V.C.* (Frederick Muller, 1965)
Leale, Sir John, *Five Years of German Occupation*
Le Sauteur, P., *Jersey under the Swastika* (Streamline Publications, 1968)
Lewis, John, *A Doctor's Occupation* (New English Library, 1983)
Longmate, Norman, *How We Lived Then* (Appendix 1) (Arrow, 1973)
——, *If Britain Had Fallen* (BBC Arrow, 1975)
——, *When We Won the War* (Hutchinson, 1977)

Marr, L. James, *A History of the Bailliwick of Guernsey* (Phillimore, 1982)
Marshall, M., *Hitler Invaded Sark* (Paramount-Lithoprint, 1963)
Mauger, R., *Slaves and the Organization Todt in Guernsey* (*CIOR*, 1969)
——, *Islander's Escape from the German Police* (*CIOR*, 1970)
Maugham, R.C.F., *Jersey under the Jackboot* (New English Library, 1968)
Mayne, Richard, *The Builders of Fortress Jersey* (*CIOR*, 1972)
——, *Forgotten Islanders* (*CIOR*, 1974)
——, *People who Escaped from Jersey* (*CIOR*, 1975)
——, *Channel Islands Occupied* (Jarrold, 1981)
Messenger, Charles, *The Commandos 1940–46* (William Kimber, 1985)
Mollet, Ralph, *Jersey under the Swastika* (Hyperion Press, 1945)
Nowlan, Kathleen J. (ed. and trans.) *The von Aufsess Occupation Diary* (Phillimore, 1985)
Owen, Frank, *The Eddie Chapman Story* (Allan Wingate, 1953)
Packe, M. St. J. and Dreyfus, M., *The Alderney Story 1939–1949* (Alderney, 1971)
Pantcheff, T.X.H., *Alderney, Fortress Island, The Germans in Alderney* (Phillimore, 1981)
Partridge, C.W., *Hitler's Atlantic Wall* (D.I. Publication, 1976)
Pocock, H.R.S. (recorder and ed.), *The Memoirs of Lord Coutanche, A Jerseyman Looks Back* (Phillimore, 1975)
Ramsey, Winston, G., *The War in the Channel Islands, Then and Now* (After the Battle, 1981)
Renouf, W., *Occupation Story 1939–1945 (CIOR, 1972)*
Sinel, L.P., The German Occupation of Jersey, A Complete Diary of Events June 1940–June 1945 (Jersey Evening Post, 1945)
Steckoll, Solomon, H., *The Alderney Death Camp* (Granada, 1982)
Stroobant, Frank, *One Man's War* (Guernsey Press, 1967)
Toms, Carel, *Hitler's Fortress Islands* (New English Library, 1967)
Tough, Kenneth, *The States of Guernsey* (*CIOR*, 1978)
Tremayne, Julia, see Franks, Xan
Wadsworth, John, *Counter Defensive* (1967)
Wood, Alan and Mary, *Islands in Danger, The Story of the German Occupation of the Channel Islands 1940–45* (Evans Brothers, 1955)
Wyatt, H., *Jersey in Jail* (Ernest Huelin, 1945)

Index